SOLDIER
OF THE
CHURCH

THE LIFE OF IGNATIUS LOYOLA

by

LUDWIG MARCUSE

Translated from the German and edited by
CHRISTOPHER LAZARE

SIMON AND SCHUSTER
NEW YORK · 1939

Table of Contents

BOOK I

Isabella   3

Juana   12

Germana   18

The Wounded Hero of Pampeluna   25

Victory in Loyola Castle   32

Work Is Degrading   41

Íñigo's Lady, Queen of Heaven   49

Íñigo Does Battle with Íñigo   56

Venetian Spring   65

Diplomatic Notes Between a Good Big Fighter and
   a Good Little One   80

Picnic at the Holy Sepulcher   85

No Use for Heroes   93

The Teacher and the Women   103

Conformity Is Good in the Eyes of God   112

End of the World   116

Dinner with the Inquisitor   122

The Capettes of Montaigu   129

War in Dog Street   139

Pierre and Francisco   147

A King Cannot Do as He Pleases   155

Paradise in Babylon   164

Heretics to the Flames   169

v

CONTENTS

BOOK II

Pope and Emperor   177
The Prodigal Son   191
Rosy View of Venice   200
Somber View of Venice   209
Courtesans and Ascetics   221
Audience in Frascati   227
A General Is Drafted   237
Between Ireland and Japan   250
The Agent in the Far East   271
Purge in Portugal   303
The Final Ordeal   321

BOOK I

Isabella

QUEEN ISABELLA lay down to die in Medina del Campo. The year 1504 had been a frightful one. On Good Friday an earthquake spread horror and misery from Castile clear down to Morocco. In Seville houses, fortifications, cathedrals collapsed. The crops failed. Plague incubated in the famished population. Autumn brought endless floods, pouring from inky heavens. Late planting rotted.

She was ready to die. For thirty years she had guided the unwieldy empire with steady hand. Her limbs swelled beyond recognizable proportions, her skin stretched taut over her bloated body. Fever parched her with unquenchable thirst. In every church of the country prayers rose to heaven. Long processions filed through the cities in pious testimonial, anxious exhortation. "Do not grieve for me," she said. "Do not waste time in idle prayers for my recovery." All her life Her Catholic Majesty had prepared for the end. Why postpone it?

She could have wished to be spared for the sake of the country and of the dynasty. Her province of Castile would pass, at her death, as would the whole great empire at the death of her husband, to the mad Infanta, the love-crazed Juana.

Queen Isabella had seen the heirs apparent, and their heirs, taken one by one, long before their time.

3

In 1490 her eldest daughter, the Princess Isabella, married Alonso, heir to the throne of Portugal. The Portuguese court spent six months preparing the festivities accompanying the betrothal. A month of revelry honored the love of the young couple and the harmonious alliance of the two neighboring nations. Tourneying lists on the banks of the Guadalquivir were hung with cloth of silk and gold. Shaded by canopies and tapestries embroidered with the arms of the ancient houses of Castile, the Infanta sat enthroned in a circle of seventy noble maidens and one hundred youthful hidalgos. The wedding took place on November 22, 1490. On June 22, 1491, the bridegroom was killed by a fall from his horse.

In 1497 Queen Isabella's only son, the gifted and spiritual Juan, welcomed his intended bride, Archduchess Margaret, daughter of the Holy Roman Emperor. Landing in Santander after a stormy voyage, the seventeen-year-old girl plighted troth to the young prince before the Patriarch of Alexandria. The Archbishop of Toledo performed the final wedding ceremony at Burgos in April. Pomp, carnival, and spectacular displays of knighthood and soldiery celebrated the nuptials of the Spanish Crown Prince and the daughter of the Hapsburgs. In September the twenty-year-old Juan, sickly from birth, fell ill of fever at Salamanca. The physicians advised a brief separation from his temperamental young wife. Queen Isabella insisted, "What God hath joined together let no man put asunder." On October 1, 1497, her adored son, "her angel," passed away. The

4

walls and gates of the city were draped with black.
Places of business closed for forty days. The court
mourned in sackcloth instead of the customary white
serge.

Juan's posthumous daughter was born dead.

Just as Juan fell ill, the younger Isabella consented
to marry Manuel ("the Great," "the Fortunate"), who
had become King of Portugal in 1495. True daughter of
her mother, she demanded of her husband, as a wedding
gift, the expulsion of the Spanish-Jewish emigrants. The
royal couple spent Easter at Guadalupe, installed themselves ceremoniously at Toledo in June, and reviewed
the Corpus Christi procession at Saragossa. In August
1498, in the archepiscopal palace of Toledo, the younger
Isabella died an hour after giving birth to a son. At the
age of one hour Don Miguel inherited the thrones of
Spain and of the united Iberian kingdoms. He was carried through the city in the arms of his nurse, escorted
by grandees. This last and least hope of Queen Isabella
lived only two years.

Poor demented Juana, the only possible successor,
had "embarked on the stormy sea of matrimony" in
grimly literal truth when she sailed to join her Flemish
bridegroom, the last of August, 1496. Isabella fitted out
a hundred and ten ships for the bride in the harbors of
Guipúzcoa and Biscay. The sixteen-year-old girl, melancholy and without charm, always jealous of her sisters, always rebellious against maternal guidance, left
her parents' home without sorrow. Six weeks later, after

a tempestuous voyage and heavy losses, with many dead and ill on board, the bridal fleet anchored in the harbor of Middelburg. Juana suffered torments of yearning for the handsome Philip. He did not come to meet her. He had written her tenderly, just two months before, "I would I might leave all behind and fly to you on wings." She had dared and suffered hardship and he had remained with his father, the Holy Roman Emperor, in the Tirol. He did not take his dynastic marriage too seriously. Juana did.

The dying Isabella contemplated the conduct of Juana not as a sad memory but as a distressing problem. Vague, incredible rumors about her daughter had come from the distant court and when Isabella sent the Subprior of Santa Cruz to investigate, she learned the hideous truth. No one could have expected the handsome Philip to devote his life to the extravagant demands of an unbalanced spouse. His mother-in-law would hardly have concerned herself with his extramarital indulgences if they had not been part of a political flirtation with France, Spain's hereditary enemy. As if deliberately to humiliate the house of Castile, Philip treated Juana's Spanish retinue abominably. Her servants, Isabella's subjects, actually went hungry at the Flemish court. Juana did not even resent the outrageous prevarications with which her husband's privy councilors evaded all complaints. She did not care what happened to her Spanish subjects if only she could gaze at the magnificent long curls of her handsome Philip. The sentimental lunatic! Because she could not bear a few weeks of separation from her contemptuous husband she refused to set foot in the country which soon she must govern.

Juana did not revisit Spain until 1502, when the handsome Philip accompanied her. Isabella sent trains of mules to forward their baggage from Bayonne, as Flemish carts were useless in the Pyrenees. The future rulers received vociferous popular welcomes and splendid official greetings in Burgos, Valladolid, Medina del Campo. Isabella, to whom ceremony represented a vital part of religion, dwelt luxuriously on these recollections of pageantry. A magnificently arrayed multitude went forth to welcome the young couple into Toledo. First came the king's falconers in green tunics with ash-gray sleeves, then the royal choir, then the alcalde with his legal aides and many burghers in scarlet robes and doublets of cramoisy silk. A half mile in front of Toledo, Ferdinand himself appeared with a retinue of six thousand dignitaries, at his right the ambassador of France and at his left the ambassador of Venice. Under a canopy embroidered with the arms of Spain and the Netherlands the father and his daughter and son-in-law paraded into the festive city. Archbishop Ximenes and his canons awaited them in the vestibule of the cathedral beneath a cross of gold and precious stones, as the organ tolled *Te Deum*, while Isabella sat on the royal throne in the great palace surrounded by the ladies of honor in stiff solemnity. Suddenly the music ceased. The gorgeous colors blurred. A courier had brought the news that Arthur, Prince of Wales, husband of the youngest Infanta Catalina (Catherine of Aragon), was dead.

After the pomp of Toledo, handsome Philip returned to his own dominions. Juana opposed the separation vehemently, but she was pregnant and could not travel. The moment she had borne a child she insisted on hastening after her beloved husband. Isabella, realizing the circumstances fully, tried to restrain her. But Spain meant nothing to Juana. She made frantic efforts to hasten the equipment of the fleet which would take her to Flanders. Then Philip wrote that he had secured her safe conduct through France. In the middle of the night, wearing only a shift, she darted out of her bedroom as if to go to her husband on foot. The Bishop of Burgos and the Governor hastened after her, beseeching the fugitive to come home, but she turned her back on them and ordered the watch to open the gates. They were forced to keep her under lock and key. She threatened to hang her jailer the day she should ascend her mother's throne. Isabella finally gave her the grudging permission to depart. Juana made a public display of violent hate, before a great crowd of burghers and peasants.

After eighteen months the crazed wife finally joined her handsome Philip. He had not spent the time in anxious yearning. Frantic with jealousy she slapped Philip's mistress in the presence of all the ambassadors, then snipped off the siren's long fair hair. Philip cursed "vilely and foully" and vowed never to see his wife again.

Poor Juana. Poor Isabella. She had no alternative. Isabella, as Queen, was supposed to embellish the social structure of which she formed the apex, not to overturn it. Her will and testament designated as sole heir the helpless Juana, enamored and betrayed, who could not even control her own actions.

To the devout Christian Queen the will represented a means of continuing her earthly rule from the beyond. It reflected perfectly the impulses determining her existence. Isabella's life consisted of certainties and regulations which kept melancholy and doubt completely under control. Through grief and frustration her mind remained calm and clear, and her will balanced all accounts, heavenly and earthly, dynastic and charitable. She directed her executors to pay every debt within a year, out of the revenues and the liquidated goods and chattels of the Kingdom of Granada, then, from specified sums, to dower girls without means, to purchase the admittance of poor virgins to cloisters, to provide for twenty thousand masses in the churches of her realm, to ransom two hundred prisoners from the infidels, to distribute alms in the cathedral of Toledo and the church of the Virgin at Guadalupe. The Apostolic See had contributed, from the Crusade fund, to the conquest of Granada, and the Spanish monarchs had used some of the money for other purposes. This recollection weighed heavily on the dying woman's conscience. Three

9

days before her death she added a codicil that the total amount used unrightfully must be repaid within a year. Under this provision, Queen Isabella made her last signature in irregular, scarcely legible characters.

Isabella's will had none of the complacence of the purse-proud testator, none of those pompous expressions supposed to be called forth by the majesty of death but frequently betraying poverty of intelligence and meanness of spirit. The style did not differ from the many statements she made on occasions of lesser magnitude. She had sat with her legal councilors, Friday after Friday, in judgment in the Alcazar of Seville, insisting scrupulously on the execution of decisions without discrimination for rank and privilege. Once again she admonished the grandees of her country not to hinder the people of their districts and domains from seeking justice in the royal court of law. She exhorted her heirs to rule benevolently and justly, above all to make reparation for the injustice perpetrated on the inhabitants of the islands of Christopher Columbus. Although practical statesmen had tried to keep the Queen from knowing about the Christian plundering in the unconverted lands, she had an idea of the conditions under which the gospel of exploitation was beaten into the savages. She imparted to the will a last message for her beloved husband, with whom she had been perfectly happy ever since she had learned to pension off pretty ladies of honor and put virtuous matrons in their places. To Ferdinand she entrusted her jewels. They would twinkle at him after Isabella's eyes closed, assuring him that she who once had worn these precious stones could no longer say to him, "I wait for you."

With a coarse monk's habit as her shroud she went to her rest at Santa Isabella, the Franciscan cloister of the Alhambra. The body was not embalmed. She had more faith in divine magic than in the visible evidence that all things transitory turn to dust. The burial vault, humble and unostentatious, bore only a simple inscription. As she had specified, the money saved by this unpretentious interment went to the poor. She had appointed as executors, among others, her father confessor, the Cardinal Ximenes, and her Lord High Treasurer, Don Juan Velásquez de Cuellar, a powerful grandee who ruled wide domains, august officials, and a vast retinue of highborn squires and pages.

One of the pages had been christened Íñigo. Of his many proud Basque surnames the last was De Loyola.

Juana

ISABELLA had lain in the Franciscan crypt not quite two years. Rumor circulated that French troops threatened the border. The handsome Philip, with his lovesick wife, stopped at Burgos on the way to Vitoria. He intended to consign her to a madhouse. On the eleventh morning of his stay he felt extremely ill. He had caught cold playing pelota, to which he was passionately addicted. He spent the day hunting. His fever rose. A Burgos doctor, a famous physician from Milan, and Dr. Yangas, physician in ordinary to the Archbishop of Toledo, held a consultation. Yangas advised bleeding. The other two disagreed. A few days later the handsome Philip, an ambitious but carefree citizen of the world, son and heir of Maximilian the German ruler of the Holy Roman Empire, son-in-law and heir of Ferdinand the Catholic and the late Isabella, died at the age of twenty-eight.

According to Flemish custom, the body was draped with robes of state and seated on a throne in a hall of the palace open to the public. Then two surgeons removed the entrails and, after administering preservative, wound cloths around them and placed them in a lead box to lie beside the embalmed body. The handsome Philip was laid to rest in the neighboring cloister of Miraflores. On the Sunday after the funeral, the Flemish retinue

12

of the departed, led by Cardinal Ximenes, appeared before the widow. Her husband's will had specified that she must grant them the money to return home. Juana, who gave audience behind a grated window, refused. She had more important business—she must pray for her dead husband. The next day several grandees, the members of the royal council, and the highest authorities of Burgos called on her. The Cardinal was admitted. He asked the Queen for her signature to the edict summoning the Cortes. Juana refused. The Cardinal insisted. Juana wanted him to wait till her father returned from Naples. The Cardinal urged her to sign a letter entreating Ferdinand to come as quickly as possible. Her fingers could not hold the pen. She stammered that she did not wish to inconvenience her father. She must. The regency had to begin at once.

Oblivious to the needs of the kingdom, Isabella's heiress sat in a cell-like cubicle in the palace of Burgos, her sharp chin propped on her thin long hand, her eyes blank, her little mouth shut tight as if she feared that it might let out a secret, her mind and body paralyzed by the grief which she could not understand. She felt constricted, oppressed by a weight which did not permit her to sigh, sob, scream, complain, accuse. Yet her grief had its secret, subterranean words, which poisoned life as life had poisoned Juana. Spain, the world, did not exist since she could not have Philip. She was unconsolable, irreconcilable. She did not reject efforts to bring her slight alleviation. She admitted the singers who had come from Flanders with Philip, but she made violent resistance to anything resembling an attempt to inveigle her into resuming the life prescribed by royal etiquette without him.

Suddenly she started up. A flood of energy broke loose. Suspicion aroused her. Philip's countrymen would take him home to Flanders. They would steal the heart which belonged to her. At Allhallowmas the Bishop of Burgos must open the coffin. The prelate objected. It was impious to disturb the dead less than six months after burial. Juana would not yield. The Papal nuncio, the ambassadors of Maximilian and Ferdinand, four bishops, examined the body. They swore to its identity. Dry-eyed, expressionless, she ran her cold hand over the shapeless mass. She had no sensations except oppression and constriction. Her grief found no outlet.

The dead man's child would soon come into the world. Suddenly she gave the unexpected order to remove the handsome Philip to Granada, where Mother Isabella reposed. One December night, accompanied by the bishops of Jaén, Málaga, and Mondoñedo, the widow Juana journeyed with her mute husband across Cavia toward Torquemada. A coach drawn by four Frisian horses bore the gold and silk draped coffin over rough roads to a cathedral for temporary safe-keeping. Juana had it guarded. No one, especially no one of her own sex, might come close to the handsome Philip. She would possess him dead as she had never possessed him living.

She had the burial service held for him morning and

evening as if he had just died. Two Carthusians had watched over the coffin since the departure from Burgos. They convinced the widow that she must never part from the dead. They commended the daily rites as a means of winning death's victim back to life. One of them assured the eager Juana that he had read of a king who was resurrected fourteen years after his dying day. The intransigent Juana had found her salvation, a certainty which nullified the world of others. Her sense of oppression and constriction did not leave her: she came to enjoy it. If he returned to life in the flesh, with all his youthful beauty, she must remain where she could meet him at once. She would not put him away in Granada.

Soon afterward her daughter was born. Then plague broke out. Juana refused to leave. It would not be convenient to travel with her beloved. Not until one of her chamber ladies and eight persons belonging to the retinue of the Bishop of Málaga had died did she decide to move on. That stormy night, a violent wind whipped the torches. Their fitful light flickered over the coffin, over the pale face of the mad widow, over the armor of the knights and the cassocks of the monks. A cloister stood by the roadside. She decided to halt and give herself the pleasure of looking at him. She learned that the cloister was a nunnery. She would not go there. She must protect the handsome Philip from women. The cortege halted in the open field. She had the coffin opened. Tiny lights danced about the waxen hollows of her withered face. Feverishly she appeased her yearning eyes. She saw the handsome Philip rise from the mass of decay. The wind extinguished the lights. The royal retinue stood silent in the pitch darkness, around the mad lady. A prelate tried to persuade her to go on to the seat of the royal council. She replied, "It is not seemly for widows to traverse splendid cities and great domains."

King Ferdinand had returned from Naples. His Armada had anchored in the harbor of Valencia. After sunset, Juana, with her dead husband, her household, and the Cardinal, set forth to meet the king at Tortoles. She would travel only by night. Asked if she was ashamed to go about with a coffin in the daytime, she replied haughtily, "Widows, robbed of the sun of their lives, must not expose themselves to public gaze in the light of day." She hated the sun because the handsome Philip could see it no more. Perhaps fear of ridicule dictated her nocturnal marches. Certainly they expressed her defiance of life. Father and daughter met ceremoniously but affectionately. Juana knelt and would have kissed his hand. Ferdinand, who had heard many dark tales on the way from Valencia, mastered indescribable emotions as he took his daughter in his arms.

He tried in vain to release her from the hypnotic daze of grief. She had sanctified it. They soon reached an agreement about the regency. The queen assented to every proposal. To only one request, demand, order, she made unwavering resistance. She had a rendezvous with her beloved. She would not part from him.

Juana looked as if she were determined to overtake

16

her coffined lover in the process of decomposition. Her
hair became a snarl of discolored shades, her face a
ruin of wrinkles and seams and mold-gray welts. At
night she slept on the bare floor in a soiled, rumpled
dress. She thought it a lie and a betrayal to feel smooth,
fresh cloth which had known sunlight and air.

Her father managed to restore a vestige of common
decency. Some care for her person restrained her a little.
Again she had her hair combed and her nails trimmed.
Again she slept in a bed and wore clean clothing. Henry
VIII courted the young widow, who, after all, was Queen
of Castile, heiress of Ferdinand of Aragon. The Briton,
never averse to taking a chance, declared that she could
find no better husband than himself. What if she were
a little off? He would soon bring her to her senses.

The dead man's wife sat in her palace at Tordesillas
and looked with unchanging gaze at the cloister of Santa
Clara. There lay the coffin which held her handsome
Philip. Now she had him entirely for herself. From her
window she could watch vigilantly over his sleep. Surely
one day, as she looked at Santa Clara, the coffin would
open and Philip would stride toward her in the grace of
his youth.

The mad Juana believed that her husband would re-
appear in the flesh before the Last Judgment. Her sane
subjects did not doubt that Jesus Christ, more than fifteen hundred years before, had risen two days after
His death.

The little page Íñigo pitied the Queen, but never
thought of questioning his teachers.

Germana

WHEN Isabella went to her Christian rest she left her jewels to her adored husband in the hope of making him forget the gulf between life and death. Ferdinand, however, did not resemble his daughter Juana in the least. He made no vows to the dead. He clung to the world of the living. For him, the jewels had no such meaning as Isabella intended. Ten months after the death of the queen he married the giddy young niece of Louis XII. His subjects were disgusted. The Duke of Najera called the Count of Cifuentes "no true Castilian" for acting as intermediary in promoting the shameful alliance. Isabella had not deserved so ill of him that he should help provide an unworthy successor.

The personal effects of the French princess, thirty shiploads of gowns, hats, shoes, linen, perfumes, and cosmetics, arrived at the port of Valencia. The Archbishop of Saragossa, an illegitimate son of her future husband, welcomed her at the Spanish-French frontier. Ferdinand, never troubled by squeamish delicacy of feeling, received her in Duena, where, thirty years before, he had sworn lifelong fidelity to Isabella. Ferdinand was now fifty-three, his bride was eighteen. Like Isabella thirty years before, she had blue eyes and chestnut hair. Slender, pretty, she looked exquisite in white

18

satin. The French called her Germaine, the Spanish, Germana.

At the magnificent processional entry of the handsome Philip and the mad Juana into Toledo their majesties Ferdinand and Isabella had worn woolens so modest that a disappointed chronicler did not deign to describe them. The frugal Ferdinand had the habit of boasting, with genuine pride, that his doublet was "of wonderful material, it had outlasted three pairs of sleeves." Isabella's cardinal wore the once splendid robe, stained and threadbare, as if it were the poor cassock of the humblest monk. By natural reaction a period of extravagance followed. Under the plain-living Isabella the country had entered the world in want, had developed to respectable poverty, and grown great. Germana, brought up at the prodigal court of her royal uncle, enjoyed with perfect unconcern what Isabella had accumulated. Meals cost ten times as much as before. The pampered young queen demanded regular deliveries of the choicest fish and fowl from Seville to the summer residence, Arevalo. The royal cooks despaired. The dishes which appealed to refined Parisian taste were not described in the Castilian Court Cook Book of Roberto de Nola, sometime chef to *el serenisimo señor Rey Don Hernando de Nápoles*. Even under the temperate Isabella, of course, not all the Castilians had eaten and drunk only to the glory of God, but never had they gorged and guzzled as now. Guests not accustomed to

19

dining on a vast scale often overindulged to the point of death.

The loyal subjects of Isabella changed their ways completely, as subjects must, in their loyalty to the new regime. The wife of the grandee Don Juan Velásquez de Cuellar, Governor of Arevalo, had faithfully disdained feminine adornment, avoided coquetry, praised God, and listened to hymns. Now, just as faithfully, she enjoyed delicious culinary novelties and gay French madrigals. Doña Maria was beautiful and clever, a great lady, an admirable wife, a good mother, a perfect imitation and constant attendant of her mistress, first of the austere Isabella who loved God, then of the indulgent Germaine who liked her wine. Doña Maria and Queen Germana became intimate friends.

The boy Íñigo was one of the pages in the household of Don Juan Velásquez de Cuellar, Governor of the fortresses of Arevalo and Madrigal and Lord High Treasurer of their Catholic Majesties. Íñigo knelt to hand the new queen the golden dishes and the gem-encrusted Burgundian court goblets. When the queen left the table he preceded her with the taper or followed her bearing her cloak. He was not very big, but lithe and sinewy. He had a broad, high forehead and aquiline nose, sharp features, and olive complexion. The white ruff added a note of formal distinction to the juvenile face. Íñigo wore silk stockings, buckled shoes, and the rather girlish uniform of the page. His velvet doublet with slashed sleeves displayed gorgeous linings and the dagger at his side was a decoration but a real weapon, too. He had entered the household at the age of seven on the invitation of Doña Maria, a relative of his mother. In Arevalo he learned court deportment, essential to an Oñaz y Loyola. The less important knowledge of reading, writing, and the catechism he got from the Dominicans resident nearby. He recited to them in the castle library, which contained very few books but vaunted impressive arrays of arms and armor, panoplies of the former governors. The future apostle now lived only "to the greater glory" of the illustrious and munificent feudal lord whom the deceased Isabella had esteemed especially and named her executor. Íñigo existed for the purpose of parading with his comrades when the house of Cuellar gave a demonstration of its magnificence, or when the powerful noble rode to court in stately cavalcade to add his splendor to that of his superior.

As a servant of servants Íñigo had only indirect, remote experience of the masters, but even at his distance all the vicissitudes of court affected him. The pages of Arevalo certainly did not regret the relaxation of discipline after the death of the strict Isabella. Íñigo de Loyola was thirteen when the Queen went to rest in the Franciscan crypt. The great drama of death in the royal house had been enacted on the far horizon of his youthful world. Even farther away glimmered the shadowy figure of the ghostly Juana. Isabella's successor, the beautiful and gay Germana, was the center of his existence. When the page Íñigo became knight of Loyola he chose the enchanting Frenchwoman for his lady. Her colors were red, yellow, red. When she leaned from the velvet-hung balcony and tossed a rose or even a lace kerchief into the young knight's course, he saluted her proudly. He must not forget to doff his helm when he met her. According to the breviary of chivalrous love such an offense would have signified that he loved her madly.

He did. He loved as his hero Amadis, natural son of King Perion of Gaul, adored Oriana, daughter of King Lisuarte of Great Britain. Amadis, idol of pages and knights, of court ladies and unrescued princesses, was his model. At fifteen "the Knight of the Green Sword" fared forth into the perilous world of romance, strove ever triumphantly with magicians, giants, and dwarfs, to the renown of the Lady Oriana, whom at last he won as his prize. Should not Don Íñigo de Oñaz y Loyola, following Amadis, attain to the heights where his king's wife sat enthroned in gracious majesty? He dreamed of Germana many hours when his fantasy caught him up out of Arevalo into the future. At less poetic moments the vigorous and not unsophisticated youngster pursued ladies who did not make him wait so long as Amadis had to wait for Oriana. He found precedents and directions for unromantic adventures, too, in the bible of knights. Brother Galaor was the gay Lothario, the perfect foil to Amadis whom not even the sweet Briolanja could make unmindful of true love. Íñigo, jaunty, audacious, often followed the example of Brother Galaor.

The Governor of Arevalo belonged to the party which

tried to keep the Hapsburgs from succeeding to the throne of Spain. If the elderly Ferdinand managed to have an heir by the young Germana, Charles, the son of Juana and the handsome Philip, would not inherit. The opponents of the Hapsburgs thought they must help nature a bit. Germana and her friend Doña Maria brewed a mighty love potion to rejuvenate the aging man. The elixir had only the effect of making Ferdinand keener on shooting stags with the crossbow. Weather which would have daunted a younger sportsman could not keep him from the hunt. Courtiers whispered and snickered about the failure of the magic. They also commented on the jealous surveillance to which the vivacious queen was subjected. Isabella had waited in the Franciscan crypt twelve years when Ferdinand caught cold on the way from Madrid to Seville. Soon he joined her, after a separation which he had found not unpleasant.

This time the nobles of Arevalo could not change allegiance so readily. The love potion to prevent the Hapsburg succession had proved too loyal. The Hapsburg Charles became King of Spain. Despite well-documented agreements, valid for generations, Don Juan de Cuellar was ordered to give up his fortresses. He refused, defiantly. He recalled what his ancestors of old had always chanted to the king in paying homage: "Each of us is as great as you, and all of us together are many times greater." He would not yield. He assembled his relatives, friends, tenants, strengthened his fortifications, and sent for more artillery. Cardinal Ximenes, regent of Spain in Charles' absence and a friend of the rebel, tried vainly to mediate. Royal troops besieged the fortress of Arevalo. Blood flowed on both sides. The Governor had to capitulate. He had chosen the wrong time to prove himself the worthy scion of haughty ancestors.

When the opponents of the Hapsburgs fell, their servants fell, and the servants of the servants. There was too little room in the world, and the new lords needed space for their own retinues. By the stern law of incalculable circumstance, Ferdinand's impotence cost the lusty young Íñigo de Loyola all his chances of a high place at the Spanish court. The wife of the dispossessed governor gave him two horses from her stable and five hundred ducats to make his start in life.

The Wounded Hero of Pampeluna

AT THE age of twenty-five the knight of Loyola became
an officer in the bodyguard of Don Antonio Manrique,
Duke of Najera, recently appointed viceroy over the
northeastern outpost of Spain, the province of Navarre.
The master of Najera was one of the most powerful vassals of the royal master Charles. The Duke could raise
an important army among his tenants, seven hundred
horsemen and three thousand infantry whom he equipped
and maintained at his own expense. The knight of Loyola
had not come down in the world by entering the service
of such a retainer.

The fate of the subject depended not only on his own
masters but on his neighbors' masters as well. When the
young Basque officer came to the buffer state of Navarre,
which Spain and France tossed back and forth for centuries, taking, losing, recapturing it, sometimes making
it autonomous, the seventeen-year-old Charles had been
King of Spain for a year. He had never met his young
rival the French ruler. Their natures were as antagonistic as their interests. Francis, heir presumptive, not
heir apparent, of Louis XII, knew the amenities rather
than the burdens of royal succession. Spoiled by his
mother Louise and his sister Marguerite, delighted with

what the world offered him, he led a gay life. At fifteen he assaulted an attractive chambermaid of the palace. At nineteen he climbed into the window of a young matron while the husband, a worthy barrister, slept peacefully in the next room. When Louis married the young sister of Henry VIII, the ever enamored prince just managed to avoid an indiscretion which would have given Louis an heir and thus have kept himself from the throne. Francis loved servant girls, bourgeoises, and ladies of the highest nobility with equal ardor. He would not be deprived of their presence. "A court without ladies," he said, "is a year without springtime, or a springtime without roses." So he gave spring and roses to a court which recognized woman only as a lecherous episode or as a super in spectacular ceremonies. Francis made pleasure a fine art. He used his prerogatives royally, unrestrained by etiquette. Having a very serious appointment with Henry VIII, he rode to Henry's dwelling at an indecently early hour. The King of France wakened his British colleague with a lusty poke in the ribs. "I wish," said Francis, beaming at the astounded Englishman, "that Your Majesty may have no other servant than myself this morning." Francis was a capricious regent, not a proper sovereign. He took without hypocrisy what his predecessors had accumulated. In the first days of his reign he issued the edict that obligations of government must not keep him from the joys of the chase.

Charles had grown up under the strict tutelage of an aunt, in the staid atmosphere of the conservative, autocratic Burgundian court, far from the country which he must rule though he could not speak its language. He was taciturn, delicate, covetous, not sure of himself, an old man in his teens. Slow to understand, he spoke and moved deliberately. His motto was *nondum*, "Not yet." He had reddish hair, melancholy eyes, and a vast protruding jaw. He inherited much of the earnestness of his grandmother Isabella and not a little of his mother Juana's obdurate hostility to fact. Charles was the antithesis of the sparkling Francis, and his most dangerous European rival. Many realms burdened the stooped shoulders of this pale youngster. From his father he received seventeen Dutch provinces and Franche-Comté; from his grandfather and grandmother—Ferdinand and Isabella—Naples, Sicily, Sardinia, the Iberian peninsula excluding Portugal, the entire New World, undisputed as yet; from his grandfather Maximilian the German possessions of the Hapsburgs and the expectancy of the elective imperial crown.

The hereditary enemies France and Spain—and what neighbors are not hereditary enemies?—never had so many points of friction as at the time when Charles became ruler. He rubbed against France in the Pyrenees as King of Spain, and on the east as Duke of Burgundy. As heir of the Hapsburgs he had to compete with French influence in upper Italy. The diplomats long tried to apply the panacea of that century and intertwine the interests of the two houses by marriages. Charles had first been betrothed to Claude de France, daughter of Louis XII.

She married Francis. Before he was seventeen Charles plighted himself to wait for her daughter Louise, not quite a year old. When this fiancée died at the age of three, the nineteen-year-old monarch was betrothed to Louise's younger sister Charlotte. The betrothals did not prevent the conflict. Preliminary skirmishes occurred on the terrain in which the Basque, Loyola, served the viceroy of Navarre as officer of the guard.

The tiny country on the Bay of Biscay remained loyal to its old king whom the Spaniards exiled five years before Loyola's arrival. The ex-king of Navarre did not reconcile himself to his fate but tried his luck again. The Spaniards beat his army at the Pass of Roncesvalles, razed his fortresses, and set up a viceroy—Loyola's chief. Rebellion kept smoldering throughout the conquered province. France had an interest in the independence of the border country. When Charles ascended the throne of Spain he pledged himself to indemnify the king without a country. Then, for many years an absentee, he neglected this obligation and countless others. Spain seethed with discontent. Nobles and municipalities rebelled. Francis wrote to the ex-king of Navarre, "Dear cousin, you have an excellent opportunity to win back your realm. Expect all the aid I can give you." He put Gascon troops at his dear cousin's disposal.

The knight of Loyola was serving his fourth year as an officer on this trouble spot when mobilization for Louis's Navarrese adventure began at Bordeaux and Toulouse. The enemy spent the winter preparing for the campaign. France's agents made contact with the revolutionary Spanish burghers. In the spring, when the French army advanced, the civilian population of Spain became quiet enough, but the border was virtually undefended. Besides a few undermanned garrisons Loyola's chief had at his disposal only two hundred and fifty infantry and thirty squads of mounted lancers, four men to a squad. Against this pitiful band the enemy brought twelve thousand infantry, eight hundred squads of mounted lancers, and twenty-nine cannon. There was no resistance. The fortresses surrendered. The citizens drove out the Castilian authorities and hailed the old ruler with rejoicing.

On May 19, the vanguard of the French army arrived in Pampeluna. The inhabitants tore down the Spanish insignia and plundered the abandoned palace. The council could not hand over the keys fast enough. The little garrison had to shut itself up in the fortress. It had not enough cannon, munitions, supplies. The French marshal ordered the commandant to yield. Don Francisco de Herrera refused. The French generalissimo proclaimed himself viceroy of Navarre. He invited Herrera to a parley. Don Francisco took three officers with him. Íñigo de Loyola was the youngest.

Almost five years now he had been drilling on the bleak rock plateau in front of the city gates; day in, day out, rasping the same commands; day in, day out, supervising the desperate efforts of the Basque peasant lads to become machines. It was a long time since he had sported gallant plumes and golden chains; ages since he had lifted an opponent out of the saddle with an adroit thrust of the blunted lance. No Germana inspired him here. He was now thirty. So life meant a daily grind with refractory automatons. He could remember a few trivial diversions, this last year. He had stood ready to dash out over the old seven-arched bridge at the head of his company to quell an insurrection in the city of Najera. The cowardly civilians backed down. He had led the troops into the submissive city to protect the inhabitants against looting. That was not the glory of Amadis, but the routine work of a humble policeman. The viceroy, struck by Íñigo's ability to handle men, had sent him on a mission. The young officer mediated successfully between quarrelsome parties of nobles in Guipúzcoa, his home province. That was not the glory of Amadis, either, but the apprentice task of a career diplomat. There seemed to be no jobs for heroes. The Amadis of Pampeluna was just a petty garrison officer who drew his sword when harmless muleteers pressed him close to the wall on the narrow streets of the little city.

The French generalissimo might have spared himself the trouble of explaining the military situation. A civilian could have understood it perfectly. The Spanish commandant had not much to say. He could not hold the fortress. The only concession he obtained was freedom for his garrison on evacuation. The young officer Íñigo de Loyola stood by in silence during the long haggling. The outcome was easy to foresee, because one side had everything and the other nothing. Suddenly he realized that the situation demanded a hero. He underwent a transformation. Fate had made him a giant. The Amadis of Loyola would ride against the mighty one unarmed. He took the center of the stage. Heroic words came to him ready-made. They had been sung to him in the cradle. His fiery unreason inflamed his hearers. Íñigo was wild with delight. At last he could burst out of monotony in a blaze of glory. "Rather sure death than shameful betrayal!" He could hardly have worried about betraying Charles—Emperor by the grace of Fugger—who had put an end to the delightful days in Arevalo. Charles, opening his first Reichstag at Worms, in far-off Germany, certainly had no idea of Íñigo's existence, and probably knew nothing about the viceroy or the war. Íñigo had learned, however, and very well, that there is only one betrayal for the soldier, rational thinking, refusal to sacrifice blindly to the idol Obedience. No one present committed that treason. The Spaniards, aroused by the young enthusiast, were ready to do and die.

The Spanish commandant gave the order to fire the cannon at the recreant city. The officer De Loyola made confession to a comrade in arms. The French opened a cannonade which lasted six hours. In a breach of the riddled fortress, before the attack by storm began, the Amadis of Loyola was hit by a cannon ball. It shattered the bone of the right leg above the knee and lacerated the calf of the left.

31

Victory in Loyola Castle

THE bust of Saint Ignatius in the Roman Chiesa del Gesù portrays an earnest knight in his latter twenties. The military mustache curves downward. A narrow semi-circular patch of close-cropped hair extends below the edge of the high forehead. The dominant feature of the stern oval face is the long high-bridged nose with broad tip and wide nostrils. The knight has his right hand on his mailed breast in the attitude of taking an oath. The left hand touches a lance negligently, or perhaps awkwardly as if hampered by the cumbersome iron sleeve. He means what he says. One understands and believes the firebrand of Pampeluna.

The young officer lay helpless, wounded critically, when the enemy took the bastion by storm. The French commander, personally, made sure that the hero received all available surgical aid, then, after two weeks of nursing, had him carried on a stretcher across the Pass of Alsasua to Loyola Castle, not far away. Jolted up and down steep grades, over paths which often disappeared among boulders, he suffered agony every moment of the journey. Yet he must have welcomed the picturesque mountain scenery of his native province after the Pampeluna mesa and the unlimited stretches of desolate gray knolls, treeless plains, dusty fields, and barren heath around Arevalo. As gently as possible the bearers handed the sufferer along over the weird precipitous country of his ancestors. Rock walls, pierced by black entrances into unknown horror, overhung at threatening angles. From death-still valleys where the sun never shone, the miniature procession emerged, blinking, before bright vistas of fields and pastures where tawny cattle grazed. Again the stretcher would pass in and out through tangled defiles of chestnut, oak, and beech. Bare white cottages peeped through the foliage. Thatched huts gray with age poised dizzily over a rocky abyss. Tiny carts, lightly laden, tottered up the difficult path, their wobbling high wheels creaking painfully. The oxen, their necks protected by thick sheepskins with big red tassels, strained against the yoke. Blond, blue-eyed, sharp-faced Basques with knobby foreheads, gesticulated and jabbered and plied the goad incessantly.

The stretcher bearers made their way to the center of the country, a warm and fertile bowl surrounded by high mountains. Loyola Castle stood on a hill on the right bank of the narrow river Urola. The ground story, of rough stone, formed half the building, massive, square, a grim old fortress dating back many centuries to the heroic age when the lords of such castles were kings. The upper half, two smaller stories which had been added since the beginning of the modern era, perched somewhat frivolously on the mighty monument of the past. The brutal giant body had the head of a courtier. The graceful brick superstructure, with its convenient

33

windows and purely decorative turrets, presented the appearance of a comfortable dwelling, luxurious for the period. The true character of the ancient stronghold was brought vividly to mind by the family escutcheon. This high relief, carved in the rough stone over the narrow Gothic portal, showed two wolves rearing on their hind legs, looking, with greedily outstretched tongues, into a kettle suspended by a long chain. The stretcher passed beneath the sign of the Two Wolves. The younger son of the house of Oñaz y Loyola was carried to the top story and put to bed under a silk canopy with silver fringes.

Íñigo's brother Martin, the head of the family, called the local surgeons. They tapped, pressed, kneaded, conferred, and reported that their Pampeluna colleagues had bungled the operation, or perhaps jolting had caused the fractures to knit very badly. At any rate the bone must be broken again. As a soldier, brave by profession, the patient clenched his fists and made no outcry. When he recovered, the right leg was too short. An ugly hump bulged out under the knee. The doctors declared that the pain of having the excrescence sawed off would make his previous sufferings agreeable by comparison. The bonebreakers could not daunt the hero of Pampeluna, the ex-page of Arevalo. He preferred infinitely the agony of some minutes, hours, days, to a lifetime without feminine admiration. He submitted to the saw with the composure of an Indian at the torture stake. A machine which was supposed to stretch the shortened leg several inches administered the final excruciation, without result.

Again Don Íñigo had lost his prospects of advancement. He battled vainly for his military career in undergoing the surgical atrocities of his time. Clamped motionless by the primitive orthopedic harness he clung to the past and to a future which had vanished just as irrevocably. The gleaming armor had become a part of him. Its removal tore his soul. He could not reconcile himself to a life without glory. He indulged in painful reminiscence of chivalrous achievement, troubadour love. Emancipated from the wincing flesh and the gruesome strait jacket, an ideal knight swaggered amorously, displaying handsome legs to the best strategic advantage. With the compelling eloquence of enamored youth and the adroitness of the hidalgo schooled in the intricacies of Castilian gallantry he treated the Queen to a bombardment of courtly raillery and elaborate declaration. Then, complacently conscious of plumed hat, jaunty curls, tight-fitting trunk hose, and shapely knee boots, the blood surging hot through his veins, he rode in the ring, now drawing up his legs, now thrusting them out, as the fine art of elegant horsemanship required. Plumes, gloves, signets rained down on him. Suddenly an agonizing twinge of the splinted bone consigned Amadis and Germana to the lengthening shadows of twilight in the still Urola valley.

A cannon ball had knocked him out of Paradise. The exile did not remember exacting trivialities, tedious bar-

rack duty, the years when he thought himself doomed
to remain a drill sergeant forever. Catastrophe brightened the drabness which it had destroyed. Bored, helpless, mangled, weltering in self-pity over brilliant,
frustrated hopes, he longed for *Amadis of Gaul*, the text-
book of love and glory, which had inspired and guided
his happy youth. Unfortunately the castle library contained exactly five huge pious volumes. *The Flower of
the Saints* packed all the holy legends into one crush-
ing tome. *The Life of Christ* by Ludolf of Saxony, a four-
teenth century Carthusian, required four tremendous
folios. Don Íñigo de Loyola was certainly no heathen.
He had gone to church regularly. He knew how many
genuflections a Christian knight must accord the King
of Heaven on any occasion. After trying his hand at
some amorous madrigals in the style popular at court
he had composed a hymn to the apostle Peter, patron
saint of knights. He had shunned blasphemy and proved
himself magnanimous to his enemies. Yet he swallowed
hard before the craving for reading matter of any kind
compelled him to struggle with these edifying tons of
atonement and castigation.

The holy biography began, "None shall lay him a
foundation, as the apostle saith, but that which hath been
laid down for him, which is Jesus Christ." With nothing
to do but lie motionless in a cast a knight could think
about the most unlikely things, the meaning of a sacred
text, for instance. Was Jesus the only foundation on
which to build one's life? Don Íñigo de Loyola could

not agree with that contradiction of his experience. If he had not been related to the Cuellars and Manriques he would never have become acquainted with Queen Germana. The French commander, after taking the fortress of Pampeluna by storm, would never have had a nameless prisoner of war treated, nursed, and carried home. Saxon Ludolf was mistaken. A knight's career stood firm on the foundation of good birth and the prestige and social connections which his family had won for him. On this basis the knight then built his own monument, using valor as material. Jesus Christ, blessed be His name, certainly had a right to sovereign devotion. He was the supreme patron saint, but not by any means the basis of existence.

Íñigo read on without interest. "Come unto me all ye who labor, sore pressed by the burden of your sins." He had never "labored, sore pressed." He rejoiced in revenge, seduction, adulation. The offer to rid him of infirmities did not appeal to Don Íñigo de Loyola. "Let the sinner who hath faith most prudently beware lest he fall into any such state that he place his trust in his own merits." If he did not have to rely on his own merits and could not expect the prizes of the hero and the victor, his whole life meant nothing. He might as well have been baseborn.

"It shall skill you nothing if ye read and not imitate." The author monk asked a great deal. Politely but peremptorily he challenged the reader to become a Savior. Ludolf of Saxony presumed on his betters in this world and the next. Pious hermits might sit at the feet of Christ and ponder His word, but the knight who adored Queen Germana had other things to think about. Or could a hopeless cripple still call himself a knight?

In the other book he read the wonderful tale of King Latus and the miller's daughter Pia, whose illicit union produced Pontius Pilate. Íñigo remembered the origin of Amadis, a waif set adrift on the sea in a basket. Saint Dominic, a Spaniard like Íñigo, volunteered to sell himself as a slave that a mother might have the money to ransom her captured son. Such a sacrifice would not ill become a knight. Dominic possessed an enviable power. When he gave himself up to prayer, his face turned toward heaven, his hands clasped over his head, all physical difficulties fell away from him. He scored splendid triumphs over the unwilling flesh. Francis of Assisi could tame wild beasts with a word, a wordless nod, without knight's armor, without handsome legs, without a feminine audience. Dominic and Francis won no royal ladies to wife, but they did perform heroic deeds. Emperors and princes bowed down before them as before Caesar and Alexander. He glowed with enthusiasm for God's hidalgos, whom he had just discovered.

Thus was Don Íñigo de Loyola converted. He underwent no fundamental change of motive or desire. An insurmountable barrier had checked the knight in midcareer. A detour presented itself, a new path to the old goal. Following Dominic and Francis, he could perform heroic deeds of will, though crippled, unfit for military service. As subject and retainer of the grandee, the emperor, and the Christ, he, Loyola, could march on to glory, despite the French cannon ball. The soldier looked about for exploits on the new terrain. He could fight a battle against rebellious instincts, cut down Pride with the gleaming weapon of prayer and set free the Princess Humility. The forces of good must assail the evil realm of human desire. Victory was certain, under General Christ and His saintly staff. Francis had earned citations in this army, Dominic had won promotion. The knight of Loyola, too, would make his name renowned. His model, Amadis, rescuer of the distressed, assumed the features, the equipment of the Redeemer.

God's recruit won the first, the decisive victory on the sickbed at Loyola Castle. The inert and useless flesh yielded to the mighty will which compelled the convalescent to conquer the earth. He was handicapped not by the feeble, disfigured leg, but by the spiritual exhaustion following a riot of disordered imagination. The future dictator decreed: "Those mental images which disquiet me come from the devil, and must begone. God sends me those which give me ease. Therefore I cherish them." He had found the perfect criterion. If the ambitious cripple thought of tournaments and the alluring gaze of women, his heart warmed, his outlook brightened, at first, but very soon he remembered bitterly that he would never cut a dashing figure again. Such thoughts, originally ingratiating, were evil. His past belonged to

Satan. In God's hierarchy the maimed were counted the equals of the physically fit. The idea of a pilgrimage to Jerusalem, or of a life such as Dominic had led, did not set him aflame at once but left behind a soothing tranquillity. The angels had sent it. This attitude determined his life course. He benefited mightily from the simplication which allied him with his fate.

Heaven sealed the pact by granting him a vision. The Virgin appeared to him with the Child in her arms. He contemplated with disgust the vanities of Arevalo and Pampeluna.

Íñigo's mighty will forced him to harmonious reconciliation with himself. Under his new master he followed his old profession.

Could he find no other?

Work Is Degrading

THE future general entered the army of Jesus Christ as a limping private in August, 1520. At approximately the same date his compatriot, only slightly older than he, Hernan Cortez of Medellin, Estremadura, conquered Mexico, the warlike empire of the Aztecs. With five hundred and fifty musketeers, sixteen mounted lancers, two hundred Indians, and fourteen cannon he landed on the east coast of Central America. Burning his ships, he ascended the mountains and looked upon marvels more wondrous than any which had ever met the gaze of fabled knight-errant, even of Amadis.

Hernan Cortez fought his way into a land of enchantment where eternal fidelity, knightly address, and virginal beauty meant very little. The mighty military empire of the Aztecs had developed agriculture and mining, pottery and weaving, painting and gold-working. The architecture and sculpture of the Mayas equaled the best of Europe. The gods fed on "the jewel of man." Priests, painted black, clad in tanned human skin, tore open the victim's breast and offered the heart to the gods, then distributed the flesh, baked into loaves, among the worshipers. Immense pyramids supported the sacrificial bowls of basalt. Blood poured down the hundred steps of Teocalli. Mounds of skulls glorified the divinity whose

41

high priestess called herself "collector of women's heads." At market stalls the devout could buy children to offer on the altars, like candles in Christendom. Hernan Cortez was not asked if he had remained faithful to his first love. The Aztecs had long expected that the bearded Toltec god Quetzalcoatl, the banished deity of the people whom they had conquered, would avenge himself by sending monsters out of the eastern sea. They recognized the iron men whose instruments hurled death with thunder. The Aztecs tried to propitiate the avengers of Quetzalcoatl by throwing them slaves to eat.

The ex-knight of Loyola, at a loss for a life purpose, might have thought of sailing after Christopher Columbus across the western sea. He would have found adventures marvelous as any in *Amadis of Gaul*. But Íñigo was an aristocrat. His ancestors had never dreamed of voyages westward over the unknown ocean. Their sea was the Mediterranean. For a thousand years, those who sought adventure had fared to the Holy Land, the center of a flat earth. Íñigo inherited a tradition. He went the natural way, that of his fathers. Cortez, appearing suddenly before the lagoon city Tenuchtitlan and taking the Emperor Montezuma prisoner by an audacious surprise attack, quelling a mutiny of the Spaniards with great bloodshed, had conquered, reconquered Mexico. At the same time the Portuguese Magellan sailed through a rocky, icebound strait, a maze of canals and creeks, into an unknown ocean which he christened *Mar Pacifico* because it received him in peace. Their contemporary,

Íñigo de Loyola, just as ambitious, audacious, energetic, went on daydreaming of Amadis and Oriana, of Arevalo and his royal lady, of Saint Dominic and the Promised Land. He would conquer not the future but the past.

The world opened wide in those years. The Spanish Empire reached from the Netherlands, from Naples, Sicily, and Sardinia, to the Indian Ocean, to the Ladrones, and the Moluccas. Thrown off his track, Íñigo was free to take any of a thousand paths, but the psychology of his caste prevented him from seeing them. For instance, did it ever occur to him, during those days and nights of brooding, to earn his living in a less heroic way?

A farmer could have his choice of vast fertile domains which lay idle. He enjoyed special privileges created by the imperial government as inducements to settlers. The arms industry at Segovia, the silk-weaving mills of Toledo, Granada, and Valencia paid good wages. Barcelona had begun to compete with Venice in the production of glass. The banks of Medina del Campo had an important influence on world exchange. He knew nothing about these matters. The American trade yielded a fair enough profit, two to three hundred per cent. Perhaps a Loyola did not know what per cent was. Even if he learned, it would never win him Oriana-Germana and the renown of Amadis-Dominic. As an imperial officer he must have heard that the cities haggled constantly over the crown taxes. No doubt he felt infinite contempt for the covetous tradesmen. The rebellion of the city

bourgeoisie had necessitated the withdrawal of the
guards of Navarre when the French attacked the frontier. Thus civilian insurgents had caused the defeat at
Pampeluna. Decidedly Íñigo de Loyola would never run
a cloth shop in Barcelona or a jewelry business in Seville.

The limitation of vision which kept him from considering the possibility of becoming a farmer or artisan
or tradesman was by no means peculiar to him. Three
hundred thousand hidalgos accepted as part of their creed
the teaching that a useful occupation disgraced a gentleman. In addition to these nonproducers, a hundred
and eighty thousand monks and sixty thousand nuns
lived only to the glory of God. Two million Jews and
Moors, Maranos and Moriscos, had borne the entire economic burden. Then the Spanish lords, whose blue blood
was liberally reinforced with Arabian, Berber, Negroid
strains, if not with Jewish, like that of Ferdinand the
Catholic, got the idea that a country did not need agriculture and industry so long as its inhabitants could
prove purely Gothic descent. The streams of gold pouring into the old state's coffers from the New World built
churches and cloisters. Grandees vied with the crown
in establishing chapter houses, endowing them with important capital and valuable real estate. A spiritual
career yielded high profits. The cloister, a dependency
of the castle, a proper refuge for an impoverished noble,
appealed naturally to Don Íñigo. The factory did not
exist in his world.

WORK IS DEGRADING

The ruling class set the fashion and the humbler followed. The bourgeois adopted the code that work debases, whereas consumption without production signifies superiority. Every well-to-do merchant tried to establish a primogeniture which would assure his sons hidalgo dignity and aristocratic uselessness. A Spaniard would not till the soil if he could go to war or to "India." Those who had to work and keep the more decorative members of society alive were indemnified by a hundred and two holidays a year, on which they could feel almost like masters.

Rich in natural resources, Spain had known genuine prosperity of agriculture and animal husbandry, mining, industry, and commerce under the Carthaginians, the Romans, the Arabs. At the time of Ferdinand and Isabella the empire glittered with barren splendor. Fabulous treasures were extorted from the baptized and unbaptized savages. "God dung," as the Aztecs called gold, did not fertilize the country. The precious metals which poured in from America had only unfavorable influence on trade. The economic dogma of the time forbade the export of gold and silver. Accumulating, they depressed the value of the currency and raised prices so that home industry could not compete with foreign in spite of high tariffs. Each year a million six hundred thousand gold dollars' worth of wool went to Flanders, France, and Italy, to be made into cloth and sent back. On all the battlefields of Europe Spaniards defended the possessions of their masters. Conquistadors plundered the

Maya culture of the Aztecs, the gold land of the Incas, the spice islands of the Moluccas. Ships of five hundred tons came up the Guadalquivir to clear their cargoes at the Torre del Oro. Yet Castile, heart of the world empire, wasted away.

During the sixty years when the fiefdom of Isabella and of Charles became the mightiest power in the world its population declined from eight to four and a half millions. Burgos, the capital of Old Castile, had seven thousand five hundred inhabitants. One of the busiest cities of the monarchy, Medina del Campo, had dwindled to twenty thousand. There was a saying that it would be a miracle to see a woman not begging in Madrid and a cavalier without a tinge of the merchant in Seville. The Andalusian metropolis, "queen of the ocean," port of departure and return for the ships that sailed to America, had less than forty thousand inhabitants. Means of communication had virtually ceased to exist. Roads were deplorable, bridges ruined, rivers choked with sand. Arabian aqueducts stood useless. Only the expelled Moors knew how to maintain them. Self-consuming Spain exported skill and enterprise.

Íñigo had a servant carry him to the window of his sickroom. The tall oak, the stable, the windmill, awakened recollections of boyhood. He looked fondly at the familiar landscape, apple orchards, meadows, mills, forges. The ancestral castle of Oñaz stood in a little valley, invisible from where he reclined. On the eastern horizon was the city Azpeitia. There a kinsman had bap-

ized him, thirty years before, in the old church San
Sebastián de Soreasu, where Loyolas had officiated from
time immemorial. His family owned residential and business property in Azpeitia, the church square, the only
cloister of the city, and a tithe from the cathedral.
Íñigo's gaze wandered over a wide area to the west. The
mines of Aranaz and Iberruola, at the mouth of the little
river Urola, near Zumaya, paid his family two thousand
maravedis a year. The treasure of the clan lay spread
out before his eyes, castles and city property, mines and
mills, pastures and timber, workers and peasants. A
look at the lower story of the castle reminded him of
haughty ancestors who had encountered the kings of
Castile on equal terms. True, the masters of this mighty
blockhouse finally had to bow, but majesty itself felt
respect for so much possession. When summoning their
subjects to exact an oath of allegiance or a grant of
money, Ferdinand and Isabella honored only twenty-
four families, among them the clan with Two Wolves
in its escutcheon, with special invitations. These reflections did not bring joy. As a younger son, Íñigo was one
of the disinherited. Shadows fell over the Loyola riches.
His gaze turned upward for signs of promise. His heart
expanded and warmed with love for his new master.
"How dark is earth to me," he thought, "when I look
at heaven."

In spring a wounded knight had been carried home.
That winter an apprentice saint illuminated gospel stories and pious texts for his own edification. Lovingly he

ruled the parchment. Devoutly he inscribed the elabo
rate characters: the words of the Lord in red, those o
the Virgin in blue, those of the lesser holy personage
in other colors. He had a servant inquire about the
rules of the Carthusian order. Should Íñigo de Loyola
naturally without revealing his aristocratic identity
enter the Carthusian monastery of Seville? Or shoul
he wander as a penitent from place to place? He had no
decided yet. First he would go to Palestine. There Go
would make known what He intended.

Why to the Holy Land? Ludolf of Saxony had written
"Let us lament the sloth of Christendom in our day
which seeth so many lofty examples of yore yet dot
not hasten to wrest from the paynim the soil whic
Christ made holy with His blood." This lament was no
a hundred and fifty years old, and still the spirit o
militant Christianity slumbered. For more than two hun
dred years, since the last stronghold of the Crusader
had fallen into Arab hands, only messengers of peac
had gone to Jerusalem. The conquistadors went west.

The youngest Crusader, his mighty will directe
toward the past, would reconnoiter the unredeemed prov
ince in the guise of the peaceful pilgrim, a general with
out an army, a Don Quixote destined to become a laugh
ingstock and a dictator.

Íñigo's Lady, Queen of Heaven

IN EARLY spring, not quite a year after the battle of Pampeluna, the converted cripple recovered his strength. His altered attitude had made itself felt throughout the castle. When he announced his intention of visiting the Duke of Najera, Don Martin suspected that the journey would not end at Navarrete. With righteous authority the chief of the Loyolas admonished the younger man not to disappoint the high hopes which he had given the family as a spirited page and a distinguished officer. "You must not step out of line, Íñigo. Our ancestors conquered and ruled. Beltram and Juan Perez fell in Italy. Fernando went to death subduing a strange far country. You lost a brother in battle against the Turks. You bear our name as they did. Do not forget the Two Wolves emblazoned on your escutcheon."

Accompanied by two servants, Íñigo left the house of his fathers for a purpose which he did not disclose. His brother Pedro, chaplain of Azpeitia, went with him a short distance. In the sanctuary of the Blessed Virgin of Aranzazu the brothers devoted a whole night to prayer. The former disciple of Amadis and Galaor took the oath of chastity. He scourged himself night after night. At Navarrete he visited the Duke in whose serv-

ice he had been crippled. He collected the pay due him
and settled his old bills. The small balance he donated
for the repair of a dilapidated Madonna.

He sent the servants back. Exchanging his horse for
a mule, he rode alone from the Basque mountains down
into Catalonia, to the first station of his long pilgrimage
the Benedictine cloister at the summit of Montserrat
On the way he had some words with a Moor, a Christian
like himself, and yet his enemy. They argued about
the Virgin. The dispute took a dangerous turn. How
could a Moor, though baptized, appreciate the charms
of Íñigo's new Lady, the Queen of Heaven? The ex
knight loved Mary with the same aspiration and ardor
which Germana had aroused. The converted Moor be
lieved in the immaculate conception, as the regulations
required, but supposed that the Mother of God could
not have remained a virgin after the miraculous event
He took leave of Íñigo politely. The romantic pilgrim
fumed with indignation. His Lady not pure? Comparable
to other women? In Pampeluna he had drawn his sword
instantly when even the most inoffensive muleteer jostled
him. The firebrand was not entirely quenched. Íñigo
put the case before God by a method which he had
learned from Amadis. He gave his mount free rein. If
at the crossroads it chose the way which the Moor had
taken, the blasphemer must die. Íñigo's mule did not
follow the Moor into the side road but kept to the
highway. The half-heathen was saved, perhaps by the
renounced Allah, perhaps by the merciful Virgin Mary,

perhaps by a slight pressure of the militant Christian's knee, wiser than his head at the moment. But probably the practical quadruped simply preferred the highway to a rougher bypath.

Shortly before reaching his first goal the pilgrim had a cassock made, of prickly, coarse sackcloth. He intended to leave his worldly habiliments at the monastery and set forth as a holy itinerant. The garb would conceal his feet, the left properly unshod, the right, which still swelled painfully, protected by a bast slipper. With the rope which would later serve as a girdle he tied the cassock to the saddle beside a gourd and a beggar's scrip containing bread. Carrying *The Flower of the Saints*, he rode up haunted Montserrat.

In pagan antiquity a temple of Venus stood at the tip of that sublime and horrible, that sacred and demon-infested crag. When driven from Olympus the fallen deities held spectral court there, an infernal Arevalo. Drawn by the song of a nightingale, a Christian maiden scaled the rocky height. The obscene phantoms, dancing around a ruined altar, vanished before the chaste presence. In purple splendor Saint Michael leaned out of the clouds and smote the sullied peak till it glittered as at the dawn of creation. The rapt maiden sank to her knees. The nightingale praised God on high. One night, centuries later, shepherds saw a light over Montserrat. Choral psalmody streamed from every crevasse. Gundemar, Bishop of Manresa, visited the singing mountain. In a cave he found the statue of the Virgin which

51

Saint Luke fashioned and Saint Peter brought to Spain. Gundemar would have carried the image down to his city but its feet clung fast to the rock. On this holy spot the church of Mary was built. Centuries later, triumphant Mohammedans ascended to the sanctuary of the Virgin. The Benedictine sisters who lived in Gundemar's church cut off their noses and lips to repel the lust of the conquerors. While a Moorish prince sat enthroned on Montserrat, believer and unbeliever could hear faint chimes and hymns within the mountain at Ave Maria. Ferdinand and Isabella thanked the Virgin of Montserrat for her aid when their knights completed the conquest of the Spanish Moorish empire, the year Íñigo de Loyola was born.

Fresh groves, little oases of life among the bleak gorges, marked the numerous caves where hermits dwelt. These latter Saint Anthonys had so tamed the mountain birds that old and young sought food and caresses from them. On stormy nights hosts of demons assailed the holy refuges. A legion of devils tried to uproot a huge rock and hurl it down upon the Virgin's sanctuary. Outscreaming the winds of the tempest the evil cohorts tugged amain. With all the strength of their lungs the kneeling hermits chanted a prayer which seemed but a whisper in that infernal uproar. The summit swayed. The rock toppled. Angel bands flying to the rescue tossed a silver chain around the destructive mass, deflected it, guided it far from the threatened sanctuary, and let it fall, harmless, into a chasm.

ÍÑIGO'S LADY, QUEEN OF HEAVEN

The pilgrim rode over the storied ground, among the aged, long-bearded hermits who fondled birds by day and battled demons at night, to one of the proudest palaces of his Lady.

The Montserrat cloister, garrisoned by a hundred and forty Benedictines, Spanish and French, Italian, German, Flemish, received a hundred and fifty thousand visitors yearly, of all classes and nationalities. Perhaps the difficult ascent increased rather than lessened the popularity of the shrine. This flourishing center of piety offered many secluded places. As Saint Bernard said, Jesus Christ, the bridegroom of the soul, is a shy lover and does not like to visit His bride in the presence of the crowd. Íñigo secured a tiny, quiet cell and awaited the bridal visit to his soul. The deceased abbot of Montserrat, Garcia de Cisneros, in *The School of the Spiritual Life* had written, "The conscience is a mirror. Keep it unclouded, that when God gazeth into it He may see, pure and clear, the reflection of none other than Himself." Íñigo scoured resolutely. He wrote his confession "as a knight shamed before the King and His court for having outraged the most gracious and beneficent Master."

For three days Father Xanones went over the past with him. Íñigo remembered, for instance, robbing an orchard with other roistering blades of Arevalo, some seven years before. An innocent man was prosecuted and fined six ducats. The insolent youngsters laughed heartily at the miscarriage of justice and made not

53

the slightest effort to avert it. Íñigo had sinned against the Church, too. One Shrove Tuesday he and his brother the chaplain played an appalling prank on the worthy burghers and dames of Azpeitia. When the Corregidor of Guipúzcoa called the jokers to account, they appealed to the ecclesiastical court, Íñigo having received the first tonsure as a child. Influential fathers thus assured their sons of light penalties for future escapades. "Could you have exhibited a tonsure at least as big as a papal seal four months before committing that infamous action? Did you wear ecclesiastical or secular clothing? Conduct yourself as a servant of God or as a scapegrace above the law? Thus, Don Íñigo de Loyola, men make Our Father's house a den of thieves."

He would leave Montserrat on Annunciation Day. The eve of that festival he gave his knightly raiment to a beggar, secretly. He heard, but did not heed, a whisper deep within him, "Would it not be better to retain the robes of your rank?" Such thoughts would never influence him again, but for a long time yet they continued to annoy him. Wearing the coarse cassock girt by a rope, holding the long pilgrim staff, Íñigo de Loyola prayed all night in the chapel of the Virgin, like Amadis and Galahad. He sacrificed sword, lance, and shield on the altar of his Lady. He concentrated, as Garcia de Cisneros counseled, "with the love of a bride." He raised his hands like Aaron. He bowed the knee like Solomon. He prostrated himself like Christ on the Mount of Olives. Like Mary he sat at the feet of the Lord. He stretched out his arms like one crucified. Like the publican he lowered his gaze. Then he raised his eyes to heaven like the Apostle at the Ascension.

Thus he kept the vigil the long, cold March night. He thought of his master Jesus, of the heavenly empire and its grandees, of Amadis keeping similar vigil at the castle of King Lisuarte, and of the heroic deeds he would perform for the Virgin with his new weapons.

A ship awaited him in Barcelona harbor.

Íñigo Does Battle with Íñigo

To REACH the Holy Sepulcher he must make his way from Montserrat to the harbor of Barcelona, by sea to Gaeta, from Rome over land to Venice, by Venetian pilgrim ship along the Istrian and Dalmatian coast, past the islands of Crete, Rhodes, and Cyprus to Jaffa, through Turkish territory to Jerusalem. Long, perilous, and difficult as this journey was—and all adverse elements, storm and illness and hostile human beings united against the pilgrim—the first stage, apparently the shortest and safest, proved the longest and most dangerous. He spent almost a year traversing the few miles between Montserrat and neighboring Barcelona. In this his hardest year he fought monsters such as not Amadis, not Cortez, ever encountered.

He would travel as the poorest of pilgrims, avoiding the direct road to the city, because he did not wish to meet people he knew. He left his mule at the monastery. Clad in the coarse, ugly robe, leaning on his staff, and dragging his right leg, which still hurt, he had hobbled along about a mile when he was overtaken and stopped by servants from the cloister. The beggar to whom he had given his knightly raiment on the holy eve spent in vigil had sported the finery, by no means beggarly, and had been arrested for stealing it. Loyola testified to the prisoner's innocence and wept the first tears of his pilgrimage. He had not known before that a poor man wearing good clothes could upset the balance of the world. At the Hermitage of the Apostles, where the road turned off toward Manresa, he found a company of pilgrims returning from Montserrat. Without raising his eyes he approached one of the women and asked if she could direct him to any hospice nearby, where he might find lodging for a few days. The young and attractive widow, Doña Inez Pascual, kept a busy shop in Cotton Weavers' Street, Barcelona. Shrewdly she appraised the limping penitent. The humbled gallant fluttered her pious and susceptible heart. She offered him her horse. He would accept nothing but a letter of recommendation which she wrote to the mother superior of the Hospice Santa Luzia in Manresa. On reaching the little city that evening the prosperous lady found a good meal awaiting her. She sent a bowl of broth and a chicken to the poor man she had met by the way.

Plague broke out in Barcelona. The harbor closed, under quarantine. The pilgrim, who had intended to remain at Manresa only a few days and make some entries in his spiritual diary, would have to postpone his voyage indefinitely. At the Hospice Santa Luzia, which ministered to all the sick and poor of the surrounding territory, Christ's apprentice experienced the first tortures of his new career. The ex-courtier had to breathe the stench of foul diseases. He tossed and writhed, trying in vain to sleep on straw. His vocation required that he love his suffering and increase it. Devoutly he attended patients whose squalor nauseated him. Zealously he mingled with beggars and tried to overlook their appalling uncouthness. They persecuted and scorned him because, like the widow Pascual, they immediately saw through the penitential guise and recognized the fine gentleman. Was he a simpleton or a sharper? Only a fool or a knave would come to them voluntarily. He tried to win their confidence. He ate with them, from their foul dishes. He let his hair and beard go unkempt and his nails untrimmed. The street boys ran after him, jeering, stoning him as a clown. Once the eyes of a beautiful young queen had delighted to linger on this man.

Íñigo disciplined himself cruelly to tame "the old animal" for the tasks of God. The officer with Two Wolves in his escutcheon had been taught "not only to conquer but to crush the enemy." Ferociously he punished that part of himself which had played pranks in Azpeitia, enjoyed the gayeties of Arevalo, and rattled the saber in Pampeluna. Christ demanded of an aide, he told himself, what a great Christian king would require of a volunteer. Such a king would say, "It is my will to subjugate the unbelievers. Whoever wishes to march with me must be satisfied with the sort of food and drink and clothing I allow myself. Like me, he must strive by day and lie awake by night. Later he may share the glory of victory proportionately as he

58

has shared the hardships." The stranded pilgrim considered what the volunteer must reply to so magnanimous and condescending a king. The candidate for saintly knighthood swore to the Lord who had been crowned with thorns for the salvation of humanity, "I will undergo Thy sufferings that I may share Thy joys." He spent seven hours a day on his knees in prayer. Once a day he ate bread that he had begged. One cup of water must suffice his thirst. When exhausted he lay on the floor or the ground. Íñigo denied his body even the solace of sleep, arousing himself in the middle of the night to praise God. He wore an iron chain under his rough robe next to the skin. Three times a day he whipped himself till the blood came. He wished to bring a worthy sacrifice to Christ, his king, and prove his qualifications as lieutenant to the heavenly commander.

Perhaps too he was angry because the flesh could not dissemble its opposition. "Conquer thyself!" he repeated. The scion of the Loyolas, passionate, vindictive, eager in holy dissipation as in secular, knew how to grip an adversary. Also he had studied the practices of the grimmest ascetics. Ammonius seared himself with a red hot iron until scars covered him from head to foot. Benedict of Nursia rolled in thorn hedges. Marcarius sat naked on an anthill. Evagrius Ponticus stood in a well a whole winter night. Íñigo de Loyola could not have displayed more aggressiveness at the head of his company than in his penitential cubicle. He exhausted himself relentlessly. Saint Anthony had said,

59

"When I am weak I am strong." Íñigo, worn out, exulted.

Like any monk, soldier, scholar, artist, any one who ever bore the rigor of a law, Íñigo experienced the temptation to desert when the fight became too hard. He dallied with the thought of relinquishing his new responsibilities. "How do you expect to endure this all your life?" asked the Loyola which wished to back down. The dominant Loyola raged as the opposition survived. He fought a frightful punitive campaign, a war of extermination. He gloated when he denied the rebellious faction an hour of sleep, a bite of bread, a swallow of water. Unfortunately the victim, suffering, twitching, nervous, formed an essential part of the aggressor. The hero wavered. Suspicious doubts, bewildering visions clouded the triumph. In broad daylight he saw "a thing with many glittering snake eyes."

Suddenly he would have to battle anew for a sector which he thought he had subdued long ago. Father Xanones of Montserrat had given him absolution for the confessed sins of the page, the knight, and the officer. Had he remembered every sin? He sifted his conscience finer and finer, discovering a thousand new accusations of the past. A learned theologian who preached in the parish church that Lent heard his confession and dissected it with him. The more he confessed the more he found to confess. The more conscientious he became the more trouble he had with his conscience. The more he meditated the more he was bewildered. Harassed and beaten, he longed to escape in death.

The rebellious nature of a Loyola was a tough adversary, even for a Loyola. It clamored for power. Denied, it slashed at the tyrant will. He wished to be independent of hunger and thirst, of sleep and mood, of vanity and self-righteousness. The momentary illusion of having won such independence made him vain and self-righteous indeed. He chafed at the difference between himself and Francis, who roved the earth in Eden serenity. The cassocked knight lost his temper. He had battled with extraordinary valor. Peace of mind belonged to him, as his due. His lordly ancestors had never hesitated to make the king feel their power. The incensed hidalgo decided to bring his heavenly sovereign to terms by a hunger strike. He recalled precedent in the book of saints' legends which he had read on his sick bed. Egyptian monks fasted until their prayers were answered. Thus Íñigo would hold out for tranquillity. Continuing his expiatory practices, he went without food and drink for a week. Heaven was not impressed. His father confessor enabled him to relinquish the role of Prometheus by threatening to withdraw absolution. For a while he felt great relief. When rested he renewed the conflict. Only Loyola could bring peace to Loyola.

Sainthood did not come so easily as he had supposed under the canopy at the castle. Lying in the strait-jacket, however, he had discovered the formula by which to tell whether his thoughts were good or evil. He applied it now and was saved. What saddened and weakened him came from the devil and must be driven out. Importunate and intrusive scruples of conscience distressed and fatigued him. He must cure himself of these as of an illness. Thus he checked backsliding. So simple is life for a dictator.

Before the gates of Manresa lay the lovely valley of the little river Cardoner. A path cut into a rocky hillside formed the Balcony of Saint Paul, leading to the church and priory of the same name. Wandering there, Íñigo discovered a dark little cave concealed by thorny brush. In this seclusion he beheld the resplendent figures of heaven, not with his physical eyes but with his spiritual ones, as he stated expressly. He had won profoundest peace by conquest of fear. He even had to forbid himself to contemplate death because he found too much comfort in it. Íñigo could now show others the way to salvation. His experiences in the mazes of despair, with the contradictions which he had reconciled, he catalogued under the exhaustive title, "Spiritual exercises to conquer oneself and regulate one's life, and to avoid coming to a determination through any inordinate affection."

By the time he made peace with himself he had depleted his bodily forces. He was a skeleton. He fainted in the middle of the road and was carried to the Hospice Santa Luzia. Eight days he lay lethargic, his heart beating faintly, his temperature far below normal. When he rallied, he immediately resumed his expiatory practices. He had learned to spare the soul, but he still overestimated the body, its resistance broken now. He suffered from recurrent fainting fits. A pious citizen took care of the penitent. Prominent ladies thronged around the bed. The whole town marveled at the strange pilgrim. The ladies whispered that he had renounced great wealth. Legend wove its first fine threads around him. Adulation provoked ridicule. The man in the cassock was a comic figure. The gossips of Manresa mouthed as a choice morsel the presence of the elegant ladies at the bedside of the humble *caballero*.

He lost ten months before the gates of Barcelona.

He slept again. He had his hair cut and his nails trimmed. He no longer wore clothing of the coarsest material. At the request of his friends he put on a warm coat in cold weather. He covered his head. He had visions, friendly ones now, which comforted him. He saw no images, but vivid spots which he identified fancifully. He saw whiteness burst from radiant light. This meant the creation of the world. He saw a kind of luminosity, not large, not small. That symbolized the humanity of Christ. He saw another whiteness, again without shape, and called it the Virgin Mary. The characters of sacred history appeared to him, never as bodies, only as light effects: Jesus Christ as a great round golden radiance like the sun, the Holy Trinity as a radiant sphere a little larger, the Godhead as violent lightning. Íñigo was more expounder than seer, more terminologist than fantasist. He got his explanations from the same source that yielded Don Quixote the names of his knights and princesses.

When he closed his eyes, Íñigo, like everybody else, saw circles, spheres, radiations, flashing white spots. Modern science gives these everyday phenomena the name photism. Íñigo lived in a world to which the optic nerve was more occult than Satan and the Virgin Mary. Mechanical irritations of a muscle received lofty names because nature had supernatural meaning. He still ate no meat. One morning on waking he saw a prime roast as plainly as if with his physical eyes. Imagination has thus mocked thousands trying to violate desire. The miracle on this occasion was the famished pilgrim's interpretation of the apparition: "God wants me to eat meat." As an ancient monk said: "Blessed simplicity, which leaves the way of difficult investigations and marches forward on the smooth and safe path of God's commandments."

The pilgrim had had illuminating experiences. He felt the necessity of communicating them. If he prepared a speech he expressed himself clumsily, but he found steady inspiration in the give and take of dialogue. He visited and invited visits, as opportunities for saying what he had to say. He would not spend his life as a nameless hermit in a rock cave of Montserrat. He would teach what he had learned.

Before he could become a teacher he wandered ten years through many countries, heroically overcoming great personal handicaps and mighty opposition.

Barcelona harbor opened. He embarked on the second stage of the long journey.

Venetian Spring

BECAUSE of plague epidemics in all the territory surrounding Venice, the chief public health officials, Sier Nicolo Trevixan and Sier Marco Barbarigo, asked the Senate to forbid the Ascension Day festivities. Give up the most lucrative business of the year? The Senate rejected the safety measure by a vote of ninety-five to fifty-five. The Signoria proclaimed in Chioggia and other neighboring towns, even those known to be infected, the usual invitations and inducements to attend. Visitors might bring death, but they would certainly spend money.

Determined to preserve the public health, despite the ruling by the highest authority, the sanitation officers required thorough inspection of all who entered the city. The representative of the Duke of Ferrara, traveling incognito, was subjected to many indignities at the gates. Yet the dourest policeman, hunting down the most elusive invader, could not spoil the Venetian Maytime. The lagoon city glittered in the spring sunshine. Booths and shops, exultant advertisements of the joy of life, displayed marvels of wool and wood, of metal and glass, of silk and sugar. The sightseers, from all countries, gaped with awe at the glassware of Murano, the Venetian confections; the decorative wax candles which contributed largely to the pomp of every religious ceremony from Russia to Spain; the stuffed bolsters of Venetian silk which went to the Turkish harems; the bone lace which was just discarding the monotonous old arabesque motif and assuming the exquisite traceries characteristic of an exuberant epoch.

Of all the masterpieces of cunning workmanship the most magnificent fabrication was the city itself. The Campanile of Saint Mark looked down on ancient belfries, leaning towers, high-arched wooden bridges, huge weather-beaten tenements, narrow water thoroughfares congested with craft of all kinds. In the Grand Canal ships lay side by side, their masts forming a forest which continually floated apart and together again. The square in front of San Giacometto on the Rialto, the financial center of the world, hummed with polyphonic murmur. Slender, blond gentlemen walked at easy, meditative pace discussing business in measured tones. This open-air exchange had a golden frame of porticoes in which money-changers and goldsmith-bankers sat at tables, above them a long row of pretentious shops.

Conspicuous in all the festive processions, in all the crowds gathered before the luxurious displays, were bearded men wearing brown cassocks and capes, their broad-brimmed hats trimmed with cockleshells. They walked with great dignity, and each of them wielded his long pilgrim staff self-consciously, exhibiting the badge he wore over his heart, the fivefold cross—a great crucifix with a small cross in each of its four fields.

VENETIAN SPRING

Every Pentecost such men and their womenfolk appeared in Venice, on their way from Spain and France, from Switzerland and Flanders, from England and Germany, to the Holy Sepulcher. As bridge between the Occident and the Orient, gay Venice at its gayest was their point of embarkation for the difficult journey to the scenes of Christ's suffering. Before impressing on themselves a lifelong reminder of the earthly poverty and humility of the Lord, they were regaled with samples of the splendor and power of the rulers of this world.

The Sunday after Pentecost the new Doge, Andrea Gritti, who had just succeeded the deceased Antonio Grimani, sailed out on the Adriatic, enthroned under a golden baldachin, attended by the senators. Eighteen hundred boats, vivid with garlands and with the holiday costumes of their passengers, covered a wide expanse of water. Slavs and Greeks, Albanians, Turks and Armenians chattered, laughed, and gesticulated. Every one understood the language of pleasure even if he was not acquainted with the speech of the pleasure seekers. Gold-embroidered flags waved. The Doge's ship turned. Andrea Gritti rose. In accordance with custom, the ruler of the city built on water threw a golden ring into the deep, thus wedding Venice to the sea. Faithless man plighted the faithless element as if expecting fidelity. Shouts, chants of jubilation, blasts of silver trumpets attested belief in the happy marriage of the two incalculables.

The pilgrims stared. They had come from far-off

villages and small cities. For months they had prepared reverently to hear the Church's most solemn masses. Now they were participating in festivities of unbelievable splendor. For weeks they had imagined only scenes of vicarious atonement. They were treated to visual orgies of spectacles, marble buildings and sumptuous furnishings. Here they forgot the cross, the crown of thorns, the donated tomb to which they were going to pay the tribute of their piety at the expense of hardship and peril. Feeling like rustics, even if they came from communities of some pretension, the pilgrims gawked before the iridescent glass lusters, mosaic floors of Oriental marble, leather tapestries interwoven with silver, gold-inlaid mirrors which mockingly showed them their awed faces. Venice was the garishly lighted vestibule out of which they would venture into the darkness of the Sepulcher. They glutted their eyes with the glories of heaven on earth.

A German servant, attending his noble master on the pilgrimage, explored the wonder city with avid curiosity. The ladies, who got their patterns from the fashion designer Vecellio, Titian's cousin, and their gowns from Messer Giovanni, piqued and exasperated the German provincial. They had black and white silk veils which fastened to their girdles. Nuns in Germany wore a similar affair, but any comparison was obscene, because the ladies of Venice exhibited nudity far below their shoulders and their breasts—the flimsy, gauzy veils only pretended to conceal what they displayed most seduc-

tively. At home, men took pride in great beards and so
they worshiped long fair tresses plaited neatly in proper
braids. These women, to whom nature had not been
stingy, spoiled their hair, then wasted it, hid it. They
dyed it yellow and curled it artificially and coiled it the
way a German hostler would tie a horse's tail. Then they
covered it with what looked like a grenadier's cap, let-
ting just a loop come down over the ears, another
military touch. At that, it was not so bad from the
front, but from the back you would see a knot bulging
out like a red cabbage. Another thing, German women
could walk. These puppets, in their scarlet velvet shoes
with high blocks under the heels, could not get across the
street without leaning on their maids. The Germans
despised every inch of these exotic Eves, with their artificially curled and colored hair, their stilt shoes, and the
strange colors which lighted up their flesh wickedly.
However, when these beauties passed, tripping along
uncertainly, shining to high heaven, the average German
would tingle with a most unpatriotic thrill and for a
moment forget his scolding.

The firm of Bontempelli, which had the contract for
decorating the Sultan's seraglio, had also furnished San
Salvadore with altars and pictures. God, as the richest
and mightiest of all sultans, must have a fitly sumptuous
household. Greatest of testimonials to the splendor of the
Prince of Heaven in this holiday season was the Corpus
Christi procession, in which the pilgrims played a distinguished part. The religious brotherhoods marched

first, carrying green, black, red, blue, and white candles. Then came cherubs carrying silver goblets, full of roses, and colored images of Noah, of David, of Abigail. Parish priests followed, in their richest vestments. Behind the Sacrament were the Doge, in golden robe and golden diadem under a golden canopy, and at his side, Antonio Contarini, Patriarch of Venice and aristocrat of aristocrats. Then followed the legations of the Emperor and of the Pope, of the French and English kings. Every senator had a pilgrim at his right. The long procession paraded around the square of Saint Mark. The ladies of Venice looked down from the windows of adjoining houses. Their velvets and silks, jewels and rings, vied with the celestial regalia of the religious and the state array of the nobles. The Doge stopped in front of his palace. Standing on the steps he reviewed the parade and shook hands with every pilgrim.

Daily, hourly, those bound for Jerusalem received reminders, of a less festive sort, that they had come to the enchanted city not merely to see the sights. On the square of Saint Mark, under the banners announcing arrivals and sailings, voluble agents of the shipowners beset the helpless pilgrims with aggressive eloquence. Pious foreigners were the most desirable passengers. They paid the highest prices to have themselves packed into the dark, hot, stinking hold of some great merchant vessel among bales of goods. The contact men pursued their victims inexorably. The shipowners entertained the prospective customers royally in inns and on board the ships. Jacopo Alberto showed particular persistence. Travel was unusually light this year. The fall of Rhodes into the possession of the Turks, the winter before, had decided many an anxious palmer who had already arrived in Venice to turn back. Jacopo Alberto asked several pilgrims to meet him Whitsunday. The bell founder Füssli of Berne, a most Christian gentleman, would not desecrate the holy day with business. The shrewd shipowner respected these scruples, and invited his customers not to talk business but to drink.

As their numbers did not permit them to charter a big ship—there were only eleven Brabanters and Hollanders, four Spaniards, three Swiss, two Germans, and one Tyrolean—they would either have to hire an execrable little galleon or make reservations in one of the merchant vessels which went to Cyprus and Jaffa. The holy tour was not cheap. It cost sixty or seventy ducats a person. Jacopo Alberto knew his game. He won customers by donning their garb. A fellow pilgrim would take them to the Holy Sepulcher. Who would give them better service than a brother in Christ? Experienced Venetians of every class, from the inn personnel to the Doge, warned them off Jacopo Alberto's sorry crate. The invariable refrain was, "It will drown you surely!" Nevertheless, thirteen of twenty-one pilgrims, thirteen believers, disregarded every worldly warning and actually took passage with the pious shipowner. He confirmed their faith by drawing up a contract which set forth precisely what each party owed the other. Point one: the owner had to take the pilgrims from Venice to Jaffa and back. Point two: the ship must be equipped with the necessary arms and crew. Point three: the owner must stop only at the usual places and remain not longer than three days in the harbor of Cyprus on account of the infected air. Other points specified that the passengers should receive food and drink of good quality twice a day; that each should have a glass of malmsey before meals; that if a pilgrim died during the voyage his belongings must not be appropriated nor his body thrown into the sea. Paragraph eighteen specified that the traveler should have space in which to keep ten or a dozen chickens. The long document concluded with a pledge that all parties formally waived any claim that might arise from an unforeseen contingency or that a distorted interpretation might trump up. That was the most important stipulation, for what did a contract amount to if it did not bind the signers to keep it? Reassured by Jacopo Alberto's pilgrim garb, by the minutely detailed contract, and by the essential specifications that it meant just what it said, thirteen holy tourists yielded themselves trustfully to the mercies of the treacherous Mediterranean.

The cosmopolitan wealth attracted by the festivities had brought thieves and mendicants. Sinister swarms spent the chilly May nights on the stone pavement under the colonnades enclosing the square of Saint Mark. One of these vagabonds bore the insignia of a pilgrim. He looked as if he had been bled. He had no admiration to waste on the majestic spaciousness of the noble bedroom with its authentic star ceiling. As he huddled against the outermost wall of the great patio he made no observations on the little sirens who offered their semi-nudity graciously and artfully to all eyes. This pilgrim contemplated nothing anywhere, on land or sea, in the valley or on the mountain, in Barcelona, Rome, or Venice, but the immutable heaven of his Lord.

The tavern touts, overlooking no pious and therefore profitable guest, hounded him with professional friendliness and volubility, to lure him into the "Mirror," the "White Lion," the "Black Eagle." This was no tourist. He came to the laughing city as to one more station of an agonizing *via passionis*. He bore his cross not as a badge of importance but as the intolerable burden under which his Master had groaned. The way had been long and hard. Venice is four hundred miles from Rome. Six weeks he had trudged through country abandoned to the ravages of plague, through cities and towns which showed no signs of life. People who could not move away barred their doors. Anyone who had to go out into the street hurried along with a vinegar-soaked cloth over his face. Because of the constant raids by the health officers the pilgrim avoided the lodginghouses. He spent the nights in the fields, in the city squares and open arcades, the raw chill piercing his exhausted body. He looked like the walking personification of plague. Passers who glimpsed his dead white face fled in consternation.

If the ghostly wanderer, inaccessibly remote from

the holiday excitement, had eyes for anything in Venice, he looked not at the sights which awed the visitors, but only at the harbor from which ships sailed to the Holy Land. Every year the pious embarked there to visit the cradle of Christianity with every conceivable motive. Some exulted with the spirit of adventure, eager to earn their spurs in the land of chronicled and fabled miracles. Those who calculated heavenly profit computed the merit they would gain. Generals in the service of king and emperor went to spy out the military and political situation of the land to be redeemed. Scholars toured the Orient to collect classical manuscripts for the great libraries. None had mission so urgent, desire so vehement, as the compulsion which drove this man. He had sent no courier ahead to make reservations. He had followed the Master's commandment to His disciples to go forth into the world without purse or scrip.

Only a few days ago, he had received his commission from the Master. Not far from Venice a little band of religious wayfarers had heard the disheartening rumor that nobody could enter the lagoon city without a certificate from the health officials of Padua. The crippled pilgrim, overexerted, could not keep up as the company hastened onward. He felt helpless, insignificant. The faint heart could no longer endure despair. Life was easy when muscles rippled, raiment glittered, women smiled, and men bowed in veneration. How could one live at all when the blood ran sluggishly, when the belly was empty, when one was more lonely on the populous earth than in the coffin? Out of perdition the pilgrim emerged triumphant once again, as in Loyola Castle, as in the cubicle at Manresa. His indomitable will united with his yearning and created miraculously, from the consoling story of the Saviour which his nurse and his parents and his teachers and the books had told him, a personal Master who lighted darkness, reduced distance, and made solitude a precious communion of two. Perhaps the pilgrim on the square of Saint Mark, with all his aloofness, felt some contempt for the prosperous worldlings who thronged before him. What were the Doge and Patriarch and the nobles and the portly business men and the arrogant hetaerae to one whose chief was Imperator Mundi? The servant had Two Wolves in his escutcheon and the fivefold cross on his breast.

He could have had shelter in San Filippo, just behind San Marco. He could have stayed with the Dominicans. His country's ambassador to the Republic of Venice, Don Alfonso Sanchez, would have lodged him. He had not made the inquiries which would have informed him of these resources. Those of little faith prepared for pilgrimage as for any business or pleasure trip. He trusted the Lord, not a travel guide. When he descended from Montserrat to Manresa, his Lord had sent him the pious and wealthy widow Inez Pascual. Shortly before his departure from Spain, the Master had sent him another angel, Isabela Roser. The pilgrim had stood listening to a Lenten sermon in the crowded cathedral of Barcelona, on the steps of the altar, in the middle of a band of children. Suddenly her attention had been drawn to him irresistibly. The distinguished face, the white hands, the proud bearing, the penitential smock, the humility before God, fascinated her. In accordance with the optic laws governing enamored eyes she saw a halo over his head. In accordance with the acoustic laws governing enamored ears she heard a voice whisper, "Speak to him." The pilgrim could rely upon his Protector who had brought to his aid the greatest power in the world—woman.

The patron had other valuable equipment. The rich received this man with open arms. At first he suffered for begging in Venice without preparation, without knowledge of the market. Soon he ran into a prosperous compatriot who knew a Basque nobleman when he saw one, even under the guise of a beggar. The rich merchant took him home, gave him a vast, ornate bed, and had him served with choice food and drink. What, besides the tie of the mother country, drew and held the man of worldly substance to the weird mendicant? The thriving transplanted Basque read the jolly books of the ancients and supped with charming Aspasias. He lolled in a purple-dight gondola on the blue Adriatic and enjoyed the abundance of luxurious days. Even at the height of enjoyment one had strange dark moods. A muffled bell tolled in one's ears; there was a sick taste in one's mouth. One got appalling glimpses of sheer nothingness behind a many-colored web of amusing shadow play. Then consoling indeed were the gracious words of the mysterious

wanderer, arrived from the Unknown, bound for the
Unknown, deeply versed in its secrets. Those balmy
June nights of edifying discourse guaranteed that in the
inevitable times of satiety *something* could not spoil.
The stranger spoke of this imperishable element with
compelling certainty. The merchant, who possessed a
beautiful palace and charming girls, wished also to have
his source of spiritual assurance always with him. He
asked the consoler to remain. The servant of the Lord
was on a mission from which he could not be diverted.

The Doge received the rich merchant and his poor
guest in private audience. Venice did a business with
pilgrims, deriving profit in this world and the next. The
ruler of the merchant city did not feel it beneath him
to exert himself in behalf of a ragged saint. The ship
Negrona would convey the newly appointed military
governor of Famagusta to the island of Cyprus and then
proceed to Beirut where it would lie at anchor forty days.
This would give ample time for the pilgrimage to Jerusalem. The Master had not disappointed the faith of the
true believer. As the holy man had no money for the
passage the Doge got him admitted to the retinue of the
governor. The wealthy Basque induced all compatriots to
contribute what his guest would need on the journey.
While the true believer ministered to the Basque's soul,
their countrymen assembled hams and sausages, smoked
tongue, live pullets, eggs, cheese, garlic, onions, and
dried fruit. A ship's passenger had to establish a little
household on board, providing glasses, plates, dishes,

bedstead, mattress, sheets, pillows, covers, gunpowder and candles, lantern and tinder box, chamber pot, and fragrant essences; the last were especially necessary, in the rueful opinion of the experienced. Bibles and less sacred books were procured. The bell founder Füssli of Berne, and Íñigo, late of Loyola Castle, even provided themselves with pens, ink, and paper. The departure was postponed from day to day.

In the middle of June the plague entered Venice. The health officials closed the most frequented churches. By the middle of July, forty-five fatal cases had been recorded. Finally the owner of the *Negrona* had the white pilgrim flag with the red cross, the papal banner, the symbol of Saint Mark, and his own flag run up on the great square as a signal of readiness for the sea. At this long-anticipated hour the pilgrim lay ill in bed. The fever had subsided a little but strong purgatives had greatly weakened his constitution. "Let him go aboard if he is determined to be buried at sea," said the attending physician. The pilgrim went.

The *Negrona* had six sails. Its staunch, handsome hull was of cypress. A little round lookout basket clung to two masts. The cargo was protected against the numerous pirates of the eastern Mediterranean by two culverins, two falcons, four falconets, all of them on wheels, and by stationary ordnance, nine springals, and six iron bombards of which the two biggest could hurl stones as large as the balls discharged by a cannon-royal. The floating stock consisted primarily of the goods of the merchants, and, less important, of a hundred and fifty travelers stowed in close, stuffy interstices of the hold, among bales and gear. There were favored passengers, the new governor of Cyprus and other high dignitaries of the Republic of Venice, besides women, children, and domestics. However, when the ship set sail early in the morning of July 15 it gave every appearance of having been built solely for the purpose of bearing Christians from the city of Venice to the grave of the Redeemer. All on board drank the "lucky wine" of Saint John. The owner sent word to the pilgrims that they would eat at a privileged table. Thirty-two sailors fell on their knees, invoking Heaven for a happy journey. A strong breeze carried the hundred-voiced amen over the sea. In many languages the hymn arose, "Jerusalem the Blessed."

"Blessing" was only in their hearts.

Diplomatic Notes between a Good Big Fighter and a Good Little One

THE favorable wind held for twelve hours. A series of dead calms followed. The ship lay still with drooping sails at many points along the Istrian coast, off Rovigno, Pola, Lissa. The passengers, glad to escape their stuffy enclosures, looked back at the faint outlines of the Apulian mountains in the west. After many hours a little breeze would spring up.

Pilgrim Íñigo became seasick at once, but recovered quickly. He did not play cards, nor hunt dolphins; he did not listen to the sailors' yarns of fish a mile long. He took no interest in the mountains and islands which trailed shadowy on the horizon. He observed indignantly the lewd behavior of the crew, who decidedly were not virgins nor crusaders. He complained to the skipper that they practiced bestiality. The seamen hated the sour informer. They did not care whether their destination was the Holy Sepulcher or the seraglio of the Sultan. They had to earn their bread with sweat, and they did not intend to let any sanctimonious kill-joy make rules about the way they spent their few moments of leisure.

The *Negrona* glided past Zacynthos, where Cicero was buried, Cythera, where Paris abducted Helen, Candia

here Jason stole the Golden Fleece. Off Candia the sails
ung limp. The fresh water supply had run low. Landing
as impossible. The passengers assembled on deck to
ive the Master of the Weather a piece of their minds.
hey promised six ducats to the Madonna of the new
hurch in Cyprus. A good wind arose at once, bearing
he ship on its way. To the north, in the mist of distance,
ay Rhodes. The pilgrims strained their eyes to catch
he first glimpse of enemy country, which had been their
wn six months ago. Christendom had lost another bul-
ark against the infidel. Did Christendom really exist,
xcept in the hearts of the believers and as a figure of
peech in diplomatic documents? Where had Christen-
om been last December when the Turk Soliman opened
re on the garrison of this little island?

Two years before, the newly appointed Grand Master
f the Knights of Saint John on Rhodes had received first
varning in a letter from the ambitious young Sultan
oliman congratulating him on his accession. "I wish you
rosperity," the Sultan wrote. "May you enjoy many
ears of blessing. I hope that you will surpass in valor
nd fidelity all who have preceded you as sovereigns
ver the island. My ancestors always withheld their
veapons from your predecessors. I wish peace and amity
vith you too. Rejoice with me, therefore, and congratu-
ate me on my triumph. This last summer I crossed the
Danube and conquered Belgrade, the strongest city of
he region, as well as some neighboring fortresses. I put

many to death by fire and sword and enslaved man
others."

The Knight of Saint John did not fail to recognize th
threat under the ironic pretense of courtesy. He retorte
in kind. "I understand fully the letter which your amba
sador has delivered to me. Your amity toward me please
me as greatly as it must displease Curtogli. On my wa
here from France he tried to take me by surprise an
destroy me. Having failed in that attempt, he slippe
into the Strait of Rhodes under cover of darkness to ro
some peaceful merchant ships plying between Jeru
salem and Venice. I prevented this deed of violence wit
my fleet. As the pirate fled he was forced to relinquis
the plunder which he had taken from the merchant
of Crete."

The Sultan, who had ruled just two years, had by n
means satisfied his ambition for brilliant conquest. Th
allusion to the pirate Cutogli, his special protégé, infuri
ated him. Soliman would have to deal roundly with thi
Knight of Saint John on Rhodes. "I cannot tell you ho
delighted I am that you understand fully. You see, I d
not content myself with a victory over Belgrade. Not a
all. I hope for another conquest very soon. Yes, I promis
it to myself. Perhaps you know what I mean. I think o
you constantly."

The Knight of Saint John accepted the open declara
tion of war. "I am glad you think of me. I think of yo
too. You speak again of your victory over Belgrade
You mention your hope of another conquest. You eve

promise it to yourself and proclaim it before the fighting has begun. Beware lest you delude yourself. War has been known to mock fonder expectations than yours."

A fleet of three hundred ships put out of the Dardanelles with a crew of ten thousand. From Scutari an army of eleven thousand marched to the south coast of Asia Minor. What did Christendom do to hold Rhodes, its last outpost? The Pope had no money. The Spaniards and French had other troubles. The union of Christian nations was only a legend. Venice feared for its island possession Cyprus. When convinced that the Turk aimed only at Rhodes the Republic lost interest. Twenty times the infidels stormed the fortress in vain. They laid twenty-five mines, hurled eighty-five thousand nine-inch balls, innumerable stones of tremendous size at the garrison. Where was Christendom? In the hearts of believers like the imaginative passengers of the *Negrona*, and nowhere else.

The Christian tourists, who believed the big words of the kings, popes and diplomats as Gospel, sailed past the lost island of Rhodes into the realm of Sultan Soliman, the owner of Christ's grave and cradle. He was a true believer, too, and for that reason hated the Christians as unbelievers. The Venetian ambassador had reported succinctly to his government upon the character of the young ruler: "He stands as the model of the faithful Turk, keeping his law strictly, hating Christians and Hebrews, who will not receive such treatment in his reign as they had from his father Selim." To this relentless fidelity, the Christian visitors entrusted their safety.

In Cyprus they learned that plague terrorized all Syria. As the long overland route to Jerusalem would be impracticable, the eight pilgrims transferred from the staunch *Negrona* to the crazy vessel of Jacopo Alberto, which had lain at anchor here a long time, in violation of paragraph three. After many days of rough sailing the lookout sighted land, their destination. The pilot did not recognize it. He made off toward Alexandria, far southwestward. Minarets appeared in the distance, the mosque of Gaza. In that city, of old, the mighty Samson had pulled the palace roof down on the Philistines. No strength like that of the blind.

Six weeks had passed since the departure from Venice. On the two towers of the roads of Jaffa the Saracens ran about, vociferous. They hoisted the red banner with white crescent. A shot rolled over the water. The Holy Land offered its guests an impressive welcome. Jacopo Alberto took in sail and threw out the two anchors. The pious assembled on deck, inhaled the sacred air, and chanted, *"Te Deum laudamus"* and "Jerusalem the Blessed."

Picnic at the Holy Sepulcher

THE ship lay in the harbor of Jaffa for a week before the passengers obtained permission to land. Jacopo Alberto rode to Jerusalem to fetch the governor of the city and the Franciscans of Mount Zion, as the holy human cargo could be unloaded only in their presence. Two barefoot monks accompanied the owner back to the ship. Respectfully the pilgrims gathered around the two Franciscans. One, a native of the Netherlands, gave absolution to all who had set out on the pilgrimage without the consent of their wives, their priests, and the Pope. Then he took command of the tour. Did the visitors expect to parade triumphantly to the burial place of their Saviour? Imperative, earnest, the peaceful commander read the articles of war which regulated the conduct of aliens. In Latin, French, German, Italian, he repeated the many variations on the one theme: the crusader must make himself as nearly invisible as possible. Thus the ambassadors of mighty Christendom sneaked into the land where their Lord, the sovereign of all worlds according to their belief, had lived His earthly life.

Jaffa, formerly an important city, was now only a heap of ruins. As the pilgrim vessel landed at the mole, an excited mob greeted the passengers. On foot and on horseback, from far and near, hundreds of Turks and Moors had come to accord the pious enemy the hospitality of pillage and abuse. Saracens armed with bows, lances, knives, scimitars, jostled threateningly around the little band whose sabers were staffs, whose armor was the garb of the pilgrim, and whose knapsacks contained only wine and bread, brush and comb. The journey began with a halt. The pilgrims herded into an abandoned cellar foul with the droppings of men and horses. Oriental Christians, by special license, sold bread and grapes, boiled meat and rice, blankets, rose water and balm. At night the Saracens had great fun throwing filth and stones.

This ground had yielded wealth to its possessors ever since the Caliph Harun al Rashid concluded a treaty with Charlemagne permitting visits to the holy places at a price. For twenty-four hours, while the pilgrims afforded amusement to the worshipers of Allah, Jacopo Alberto haggled with the Emir of Ramleh over the escort fee to his city. Finally the hectored tourists emerged from their first lodging in the Fatherland of their God. One pilgrim after the other was taken before a high commission of the Sanjak of Jerusalem, the Emirs of Ramleh and Jazur, the captain of the escort squad, the supreme scribe, the interpreter. These dignified old gentlemen squatted on beautiful carpets, Turkish fashion. The pilgrim gave his name and rank, or lied if he feared to arouse the greed of the venerable commissioners. "What is your father's name?" The scribe, making the intricate flourishes of the Arabic script with a long reed, recorded the answers and gave the foreigner his passport.

After the sacred rite of booking, the ass drivers put the pilgrims on the beasts' backs and received a tip. Then they tickled the donkeys to make them buck. If rider or pack fell off, the driver not only enjoyed a good laugh but extorted another coin. The inhabitants of the city of Ramleh, fifteen miles southeast, had their fun with the Christians, too. Sharp stakes punched the cassock-men in the sides until they jumped. Malicious fingers yanked the square western beards. The pilgrims submitted to all aggression, according to the ironclad regulations. A Christian must not strike back at a Saracen. He might report to the authorities, but, receiving no satisfaction, he must simply put down the indignity to heavenly profit and loss. "Whoever wishes to visit the Holy Sepulcher," Íñigo's fellow pilgrim Philipps Hagen noted, "should take with him three sacks. He must fill the first with good Venetian ducats, the second with patience and equanimity to suffer shame and injury." Already the pilgrims had dug deep into their supplies of ducats and patience. At their goal they would exhaust another hoard. "The third sack he must cram with faith. Thus when he sees the holy places where Jesus and the saints wandered and suffered he may believe what his guides tell him." In this land a stone was not a stone and a hill not a hill. The evidence of the eyes meant nothing.

At the Jaffa gate of Jerusalem inspectors counted the

little band and rifled the luggage. Then the pious visitors, barefoot, their hands folded in reverence, marched two by two into the blessed city of their visions. The solemn procession halted on the square in front of the Church of the Sepulcher. The peaceful crusaders found themselves billeted to the miserable, dilapidated Hospital of Saint John. Accommodations consisted of a rug and a pillow for each. In the Coenaculum, on Mount Zion where Christ partook of the Last Supper with His disciples, the twenty-four resident Franciscan monks performed the solemn ceremony of welcome. Intoning psalms, the brothers washed the pilgrims' feet. Tables were set in the garden. A great tapestry which represented the sending of the Holy Ghost shut out the blistering sun. Even in this refuge of peace their Dutch guide reminded them that they were at the heart of the enemy's country. No one might enter a mosque, laugh at a praying Saracen, step on the graves of the unbelievers, or write on the walls of the Sepulcher. "Don't give them wine," the Franciscan admonished. "Do not drink in their presence. Do not fraternize with them. Do not forget that weapons and white robes are prerogatives of the Saracens. Do not look at the women. The men are insanely jealous." Through Christ's city, fifteen centuries after His death, believers in Him must skulk like unskilled thieves.

The pilgrims had not a minute to lose if they hoped to visit all the holy places, for here every place was holy. Every broken column, every square inch of ground had its scriptural or legendary association. In that house

PICNIC AT THE HOLY SEPULCHER

Matthew was chosen an apostle. Beside the white stone marked with a cross, in front of the wall, Saint James was ordained a bishop. Over there the Blessed Virgin wept after the Son of Man ascended to heaven. At that street corner, in front of the house of Caiaphas, Mary waited during the trial. A thousand fictions had settled down on a few acres of ground and had thus become tangible. Their yearning for reality satisfied, the pilgrims trod the soil of their legends with reverent gratitude.

The barefoot monks recited, in Latin, Italian, French, German, the narratives connected with every spot. Holding lighted candles they marched from the Chapel of Mary, after revering the whipping posts, to the place where Mary Magdalen saw the resurrected Saviour, from the place where He was kept during the preparations for the Crucifixion to the place where the soldiers cast dice for His garments. Then they descended forty-two steps to the rock under which Saint Helen found the Cross. *"Salve Regina!"* the hymn swelled in jubilant crescendo. "Salutation to thee, Queen, Mother of Mercy, our life, our sweet solace, our hope!" They passed the Chapel of the Crown of Thorns and climbed Mount Calvary. The singing ceased. Prostrate, beating their heads on the ground, they sobbed, groaned, wept without restraint. Fifty great oil lamps burned over the hole in which His cross had been planted. One after the other stepped to this most sacred cleft, lay down, spread out his arms, kissed the edge passionately, rubbed it with cheek and lips, thrust his hands, his arms, deep inside. Every sense participated in ecstatic vicarious suffering of the Crucifixion as if it were enacted then, there.

Pilgrim Íñigo, stern soldier, could not content himself with voluptuous indulgence in imaginary immolation. Soon, now, the respectable cannon and bell founder Füssli of Berne, elected to the corporation of his city by the guild of smiths, would hold his friends spellbound, at their cozy firesides, with tales of the great tour. Only then would his inconspicuous travel companion Íñigo really begin his service, at the lonely post in the enemy's country, to which the Master had called him. This was no atmosphere for a Swiss burgher, an Italian tradesman. Íñigo breathed the heady air of the battlefield. He saw more to conquer than he had imagined, more than the souls of unbelievers. In addition to its Saracens and five hundred Jews, Jerusalem harbored more dangerous, more hateful enemies, a thousand Oriental Christians.

The heretics of the east had arrogated to themselves the Holy of Holies, Christ's grave. On this most sacred site the Empress Helen had built the great church of the Holy Sepulcher. When tourists made the nightlong vigil there, the cold, pale starlight glimmered through the open belfry on an odd conglomeration. Pilgrims huddled on pillows and blankets. Small groups listened to sermons. Some made confession. The night was very long, very cold. Most of the visitors walked about, examining the precious cloths, the silver vessels, the chalices of pure gold, presented by the richest princes of the Christian countries. These tourists had mourned too much,

sustained superhuman emotion too long. They found
devotion in the brisk miniature fair over the very grave
of Christ. Here they bought bargains in crucifixes,
rosaries, relics, confections, and substantial food, ghastly
curios. It is said that an agent of the Sultan sold foetuses
as Innocents of Bethlehem. People ate and drank and
performed their necessities wherever they stood. In dark
corners couples lay together lustfully—"Children be-
gotten in church are lucky." Groups gossiped, talked
politics, boasted, quarreled. Priests scuffled for the honor
of celebrating mass at the Holy Sepulcher.

Íñigo had been scandalized by the lewdness of ordinary seamen. What must he have suffered from the
contemplation of this Christian junket? He found most
disheartening the ever-recurrent illustration of dissen-
sion-torn Christendom. Heretics, who acknowledged and
at the same time betrayed Christ, owned the holiest
sanctuary. When the priests of one sect sacrificed at an
altar dedicated to the worship of a somewhat different
Christ, much holy water washed off the pollution. The
Turks were avowed enemies, at any rate. They would
never have made such progress if the Greeks had not
split Christendom. All other Oriental Christians, the
Mesopotamian Nestorians, the Syrian, Armenian, Egyptian, and Ethiopian Monophysites, would have returned
to the Roman mother church long ago if the schismatics
from the Greek empire had not barred the way. These
false friends possessed the prison in which the Saviour

suffered, the high altar whose many lamps flickere
betrayal.

Thus the pilgrim-lieutenant, at the grave of Him wh
proclaimed universal love, inspected the positions o
the enemy. The most precious treasures were in th
hands of traitors.

No Use for Heroes

WHILE his travel companions made preparations for
departure, Íñigo de Loyola pleaded with Fra Angelo,
who had charge of all the Franciscan cloisters in Pales-
ine. With profound humility and inflexible determina-
on the pilgrim declared that he would never leave the
and of the Sepulcher. If the order could grant him a
ell and a confessor he would ask no more. He had
ound his place at last. Here he could be Amadis and
'rancis, dauntless knight and humble servant of God.
Unfortunately militant devotion to the Saviour com-
letely disqualified a Christian for residence in Jeru-
alem, center of the hostile zone. The Franciscans merely
nade the best of a hopeless situation. It was impossible
to foresee how much longer they could protect pious
isitors. Fra Angelo commanded a lost fortress. His
arrison, so far, had escaped massacre simply by chance.
He did not want a soldier now. Íñigo threatened to repeat
he heroics of Pampeluna.

At any moment the Venetian Republic might have to
uck the Franciscans under its wing and remove them
o Cyprus. The decree of banishment had gone forth. It
ust happened that the officers had not yet executed the
ommand. Months ago a dervish of the Temple Mosque
ad lodged a complaint with the Mufti of Jerusalem

concerning repairs and restoration which the cloister ha
undertaken with the consent of the Turkish authoritie:
The Frankish cloister of Mount Zion, the petitione
related, gave immunity to the godless of many wester
countries. The monks had reported to the governo
falsely, that their cloister was in bad repair, and ha
requested his permission to remodel it. Most graciousl
he had granted the boon. The Franks had dared to re
build entirely, enlarging the cloister by the width o
nine layers of hewn stone blocks so that it extended fa
enough to abut on the Tomb of David. Did the Muft
think it was lawful to erect an infidel temple in th
shadow of the resting place of David, revered by al
Mussulmans? Was it lawful for the Christians to sin;
their godless songs in this place, to drown out the prayer
of the Turks with the peal of their bells?

The Mufti answered that none of these things was law
ful. The dervish of the Temple Mosque journeyed t
Constantinople and laid his complaint, with the Mufti'
opinion, before the Sultan. The mighty Soliman, lord o
all who worshiped Allah and revered King David as ;
prophet, issued to the Governor and the Kadi of Jeru
salem, in the early spring of that year, the decree
"Whereas the tomb of the prophet David stands near th
city of Jerusalem, and the church and cloister of Moun
Zion, belonging to Frankish infidel brotherhoods, abut:
on it, and whereas these Franks, consistently with thei
impious customs, march over the terrace adjoining th
tomb of the prophet, and whereas it is neither right no

94

asonable that every hallowed place remain in the pos-
ession of the unbelievers, that their feet tread the soil
hich we venerate because our prophet made it holy,
e do therefore command that the members of the
rotherhoods and all who dwell with them shall forth-
ith, upon the receipt of this decree, without delay, be
riven out of church and cloister, that the guardian of
ae holy places purify and sequester the sanctuary. The
earer of this document, the preacher Mehdi el Hachimy,
ill administrate the property of the church, its gardens
nd premises. Given in March." Since this decree was
sued, spring and summer had passed.

Fra Angelo gazed at the obstinate zealot with sorrow-
ul sternness. Such a pilgrim did his heart good. Mili-
ant faith like that had animated the battalions of the
rusaders for centuries. If indomitable will to sacrifice
ere all that was necessary! The dreaded baliffs had not
et executed the decree promulgated by Sultan Soliman
a the early spring, but forerunners hovered in the
icinity. Six hundred Janissaries of the garrison of
amascus surrounded Mount Zion. Soldiers had forced
aeir way into the Hospital of Saint John at night, knock-
ag holes in the doors with guns and axes, and had gone
way only when Moslem women and children in the
ervants' quarters raised a fearful outcry. The cloister
as barricaded. The pilgrims could go out very rarely,
nd then had to creep back over the flat roofs. And this
nsuspecting hothead insisted on remaining in Jerusalem.

For Íñigo Jerusalem was journey's end. In the land

of the Sepulcher he would know peace even though h
waged cutthroat war with Janissaries. What did he ca
about politics and policy? He had no dread of cata
trophe, he was tortured only by the thought of returnir
to a world in which he must grope, uncertain, aimles
Fra Angelo had great difficulty in impressing the sorr
facts upon the enthusiast. First he made the mistake o
telling how the front-line pickets here, for centuries, ha
had to brave abuse and death. If a Turkish robber chie
plundered them in the morning, they were at their pos
in the evening, on Mount Calvary where Christ suffere
for the salvation of the world. If word of a new Crusad
reached Jerusalem these Franciscans would fall as th
first victims. If Christians anywhere in the world di
Saracens an injury, if a Christian prince won a victor
over the unbelievers, if a Christian pirate captured a shi
flying the Crescent, the watchers at the grave of Chri
atoned as hostages. Fra Angelo quickly realized that suc
objections inflamed the ardor of the aspirant, who de
sired and yearned to add his name to that long list o
martyrs.

Valor meant nothing. Only wary, guileful prudenc
counted. It would be fatal for the commandant of th
doomed castle to accept the services of a Hotspur. Br
Íñigo was not to be dissuaded, not to be shaken off. Fr
Angelo finally had recourse to his authority, given hir
by the Pope expressly, to excommunicate any Occidenta
Christian who remained in Palestine contrary to th
wishes of the Franciscans. Íñigo's recalcitrance va

shed. He bowed and said, "I obey." Greatly as he longed for peace of mind, for active service, he valued above all else, now as throughout his life, the obedience which he thought the rightful due of constituted authority.

He had not prepared for departure. In the few hours before him, he experienced an overwhelming desire to kiss once again the rock from which the Saviour ascended to heaven. In spite of a stern prohibition, in spite of mortal danger to the others, he went to the Mount of Olives. He bribed the chapel guard with a penknife. He was back in the valley when it occurred to him that he had not impressed upon his memory the positions of the right foot and of the left foot on the rock. Returning, he bought readmittance with a pair of scissors. Meanwhile the Franciscans had missed him and sent an Oriental Christian employee to find him. The native, exasperated at the western fool, threatened him with a huge club, seized him, cursed him, and carried him back to the cloister. The prisoner rejoiced. He too had his Passion. He saw Christ marching ahead of him.

Now he must leave the land of holy presences. From Jerusalem to Jaffa, from Jaffa to Venice, from Venice to Barcelona, he must return as he had come, suffer as he had suffered. He must endure without the hope which had impelled him, must trudge home with nothing to show for his disenchanting pilgrimage but a little wooden box of blessed pebbles, clods, and dried flowers, which he would give to the nun Antonia Estrada of the cloister

De las Jeronimas. The band of pilgrims, with their Turk
ish escort, made off under cover of darkness to trave
remote and devious byways. Yelping fiends in ghostl
white suddenly appeared out of the blackness, barrin
the narrow path. They cut open the pilgrims' sacks
drank out of their gourds, knocked their hats off, hel
knives against their throats. The unarmed victims sa
submissive on their saddleless, bridleless mounts. The
the fiends were attacked by other fiends. The escor
which had crept off at the first onset had formed an
fallen on the robbers' rear. Naturally the honest soldier
and ass drivers would let no rivals seize their legitimat
prey.

The travelers were spared for more and worse. The
had to wait in Ramleh a week while the shipowner cam
to an agreement with the Emir over the escort fee. Ex
hausted, afflicted, many became ill from drinking fou
cistern water. They heard disheartening rumors fron
Jerusalem about the banishment of the Franciscans. I
Jaffa a filthy vault, reeking with excrement, infeste
with bugs, awaited them. A rope stretched in front o
the entrance. The unbelievers crowded along it, mockin
the Christians. Finally the pilgrims were permitted t
run the gauntlet and scramble aboard ship. Covetou
fingers, making the last grasp, plucked them pretty thor
oughly, but they had to pay yet more ransom befor
they left the Holy Land behind. The sea, too, receive
them as if it were in league with the Saracens.

Jacopo Alberto had not even drained the bilge wate

98

rom his wretched vessel. He had not obtained fresh
provisions. One pilgrim died the first day. Five days out,
wo measures of brackish water mixed with vinegar were
ne drinking rations. On the eleventh day, the firewood
ave out. Pilgrims who had supplied themselves with
vine found the chests broken open, the bottles emptied.
ome passengers died. In spite of the contract the bodies
vere thrown into the sea. The pilot lost his course. The
old filled with water. Philipps Hagen's sack of patience
vas empty as his belly. That philosophic traveler had
esigned himself to death by starvation on the open sea
vhen a stiff southeaster carried the wreck to Cyprus.

The *Negrona*, to which the pilgrims wanted to trans-
er, had sailed a week before. The prosperous members
f the party boarded a great Venetian merchantman, the
oorer ones took the little Turkish *Malepiera*. The skip-
ers of both ships refused Íñigo, who had no money.
"What for?" Sier Girolamo Contarini replied to many
leas on behalf of the saintly Spaniard. "If he is so
oly he can walk over the water, like Saint James of
Compostela." Another captain, of a tiny craft, had mercy
n the mendicant cripple who could hardly walk over
lry land.

The mighty Venetian vessel foundered on a rock. Rich
argo went to the bottom of the sea; passengers and
rew barely escaped with their lives. The two little boats
ossed about between the islands of Cyprus and Crete. At
he end of the year Íñigo reached an Apulian harbor.
That winter was bitter cold. A piercing wind drifted the

snow over the roads so that horses sank in belly-deep. Th
Spanish pilgrim shivered in his threadbare summe
clothing, coarse linen smock, knee breeches, short cloak
He had no stockings. He made his agonizing way t
Venice, arriving on the square of Saint Mark in th
middle of January.

It had been almost a year since he left the little cit
of Manresa. He had spent nineteen days in the Hol
Land. What had these nineteen days, and the others
taught him? If suffering sufficed he had added a yea
to the annals of Christian heroes. He had survived hea
and cold, plague and storm, fever, hunger, and thirst
He had felt the fists of believers and unbelievers, th
ridicule of Christians and Turks. He was still helples
and unprotesting in the clutches of the elements, of fate
and of those human beasts who rage at the gentle fo
differing from themselves. Yet his gentleness was hard
his humility defiant, his divine model no weakling. H
had proved that to Fra Angelo. He proved it now. His
route took him through Ferrara across a war area t
Genoa. Although a safe path was pointed out to him he
walked in the combat zone between the Spanish and the
French. His compatriots arrested him as a spy. They
plied him with questions. They stripped him and searched
him for sketches, letters. He maintained a maddening
impassiveness.

The soldiers, dragging him to their captain, hustled
him, half-naked, the image of ludicrous misery, along

100

the company streets. Beside him walked Jesus Christ, keeping his mind free from anything ignoble, reinforcing his resistance. Íñigo had been a soldier. He knew the situation. Captured in the war zone, under suspicion of espionage, he faced not a deliberate, impartial trial but the rack and the gallows. Should he, just this one time, depart from his resolution to acknowledge no distinction of rank, to conform to none of the formalities of courtesy? Had he not better "sir" the captain? His life probably depended on the trivial compromise. The soldiers stared in awe as he was driven, limping, before the petty god who would annihilate him. Íñigo struggled with his common sense. "Why should I give him his vain title? Because I am afraid! Because I am unworthy of martyrdom. I will give him no title. I will not bend the knee. I will not even take off my hat." The debate ended. A Loyola knew no fear.

Imperturbable he stood before the brawny man of iron and of gold braid, who fumed and snorted thunder and lightning. A very few laconic answers blasted long pauses in the tirade. The captain thought, "He is so little I can't thrash him. A spy would lick my boots and whine for mercy. He would tell sixty lies a minute." Then he saw light. "The man is crazy!" the captain roared, relieved as if he had hanged the troublesome suspect. "Give him his rags and throw him out." Honor was satisfied. It was no disgrace not to be respected by a lunatic.

Shortly afterward the lunatic fell into the hands of the enemy, the French.

The ship which took him from Genoa to Barcelona narrowly escaped being captured by Andrea Doria, the Genoese admiral.

The Teacher and the Women

In November, 1526, the Archbishop of Toledo sent his licentiate Alonso Mexia and a notary to investigate disturbing rumors from the university city Alcalá de Henares. One Íñigo, thirty-six years old, who had matriculated at Alcalá after preparatory work in Barcelona, had founded a student brotherhood, known as "the Gray Robes," which inflamed the lay population with aspirations to sainthood.

Holiness unauthorized by the Church was no novelty in Alcalá de Henares. The diocese had long been infested by *alumbrados* (*illuminati*) who claimed to receive divine inspiration directly through silent prayer. A girl from the little village of Piedrahita, calling herself "Bride of Christ," made prophecies and explained theological mysteries at the prompting, she said, of the Virgin Mary, who went ever at her side. The polite village lass would never enter a door without bowing and inviting her invisible companion to precede her. Five years before, *The Spiritual A B C* had appeared. The ordained clergy shuddered at this hornbook of cranks. The author, Francisco de Osuna, depicted the simpleton's paradise: "There love ceaseth not, but the intellect sleepeth, and the will is no more." If any lazy fool could save his own soul, what became of the priest and his hard-earned privilege?

The endangered hierarchy still had its reliable guardians. The austere Alonso Mexia, a perfectly disciplined functionary, had no patience with unlicensed practitioners, the unlettered, the poor, the women, the blasphemous Jews, Mohammedans, Humanists. He would put these Gray Robes in their places.

The episcopal court did not summon the accused. Witness after witness testified to the blamelessness, the humility, of the students, the commonplace orthodoxy of their teachings. Mexia, employing every ruse of the cross-examiner, could not bring out a single damning fact. The vicar-general, Rodriguez Figueroa, passed a mild sentence. He forbade the five Gray Robes, under penalty of major excommunication, to wear distinctive garb. Íñigo and Arteaga dyed their robes black. Callisto and Caceres dyed theirs yellow, Juanico left his as it was. They went on teaching.

Íñigo did not understand the purpose of the investigation. He asked Figueroa if the examiners had detected heresy. "No," the judge answered, "for if they had, you would have been burned." Íñigo still did not understand. Ingenuously he asked the vicar-general, "Would you too be burned if you said something heretical?" Figueroa smiled.

Before Christmas Íñigo received another admonition. He must not go barefoot nor conduct religious services. He put on shoes but continued to instruct his disciples secretly. An investigation in March gave the suspects no trouble. In April the mysterious disappearance of several prominent feminine disciples forced the vicar-general to institute serious proceedings against the unruly saint.

The charming witness Maria de la Flor needed no interrogation. For her the vicar-general was not a judge but a father confessor, an audience, and, above all, a man. Volubly she told of her sins and of her delight in purity. Figueroa listened attentively. Her lively report sounded more convincing than the previous sober testimony. Maria de la Flor had first met Íñigo in the home of her aunt. Mysterious conversations aroused the young girl's curiosity. "He teaches us the right way to serve God," she was told. "We confess our sins to him and he comforts us." Maria wanted comfort too. Íñigo told her to confess and take communion every week and for a whole month to talk everything over with him. He said that at first she would be happy without knowing why. The second week she would be sad, but God would lead her through sorrow to bliss.

The enthusiastic convert who babbled to the vicar-general had long since left sorrow behind. "I used to be bad. I went with many students. I was a lost woman. Then I just had to talk with Íñigo. I fainted because I couldn't see him right away. I recovered as soon as he spoke to me." Maria was not mealymouthed. Her former way of living had taught her the precise words for matters which an inexperienced girl would have been

ashamed to discuss with a strange man. Delightedly she
told tales out of school. "I have heard Íñigo and Callisto
say, 'We have taken an oath of chastity. We are sure of
ourselves. Even if one of us were to sleep in the same
bed with a girl he would commit no sin.'" Once when
she and her cousin Anna had wanted to go away with
Callisto, Íñigo had said, "If anyone should have im
proper contact with you, actually violate you, against
your will, you would not sin. On the contrary. You would
gain merit. You would be virgins as before." Maria de
la Flor could be pure and yet enjoy the flesh, could please
God and yet live in a decidedly earthly paradise. She
glowed as she told the cleric that the holy men brought
their faces very close to hers when they talked to her
"As bridegroom to bride." That was the gospel which
Maria learned from the Gray Robes.

The vicar-general wondered. Had her superior edu
cation in love enabled her to recognize and express with
out shame what the respectable servant girls and house
wives probably did not even dare suspect? Or was her
aroused, tantalized imagination introducing voluptuous
scenes of her former life into the strange new circle of
austerity? Íñigo's audiences were mostly feminine. A
woman always wanted the Beloved for herself alone.
She yearned for unmediated intercourse with God, for
intimacies which would break up the *Civitas Dei* into a
multitude of loving couples. The vicar-general knew
that souls without bodies seldom come together. The
pious and upright Ortiz thought he honored his friend

Francisca Hernandez by the compliment, "In your perfection you have no more need of chastity." Cardinal Ximenes imprisoned a man who thought himself designated by innner revelation to beget prophets on nuns. Evagrius reported that the anchorites sometimes went to the cities, visited brothels and bathed with the women, caressing and embracing them to prove their own chastity. The Gray Robes were pious, but they were men. They could disguise nature, not make it over.

The scatterbrained Maria had given Figueroa an important clue. He followed it to the heart of the same mystery which had baffled Alonso Mexia. Feminine converts now told the vicar-general of sore needs which Íñigo and his comrades had intensified and appeased. The good wives of Alcalá did not know what was happening to them. In all innocence they described enigmatic symptoms of disorder. Anna de Benavente remembered three or four fainting fits. At times she had such pain in her heart that she rolled on the floor and strong hands were needed to hold and pacify her. Leonor had felt better when she could still laugh and have a good time. Now when she remembered that she had renounced worldly delights her throat and breast constricted and she fainted away. The vicar-general shuddered at the successive reports. Women said they writhed in convulsions, groaned under torments which prostrated them, shivered in a sweat of fear. A servant girl swallowed her tongue. One housewife, starting to whip herself, felt as if her hands were held tightly. Another, lying half unconscious on the floor, thought she had seen the devil, huge and black, incarnate before her. Only the married women remained exempt from convulsions and fainting.

The vicar-general could not quite make out what specific power the teacher possessed. Íñigo himself did not know. He taught just what was expounded from every pulpit, but the cold texts caught fire. Beatriz, Leonor, and Maria lived a dynamic romance with Christ as the hero. When they came back to earth the revealer was there to greet them.

None of the witnesses threw any light on the disappearance of Maria del Vado, her daughter Luisa, and the servant Catalina. Figueroa finally went to see Íñigo in the episcopal jail. The teacher had been confined since Easter without knowing why.

Landing in Barcelona from his long pilgrimage of three years before, Íñigo had immediately begun to qualify for ministry. At the age of thirty-three he sat beside small boys in a schoolroom, grinding heroically to supplement the defective education which he had received as a prospective courtier. He was not an apt pupil. The guarantees of his peace with heaven flitted mockingly through his mind when he tried to concentrate on Latin exercises. He did not pass. Dealing with his difficulties in characteristically summary fashion, he declared that he would work twice as hard the second year and requested the teacher to be as stern as if he were a schoolboy and not to spare the rod.

In Barcelona he had been unable to learn without

teaching, and teaching meant fighting. The Lotharios of the city plotted to murder the limping bigot who enticed the most desirable women to make austere vows. He had a narrow escape. Young noblemen insulted him, beat him. However, the Barcelona students Callisto, Arteaga, and Cáceres became his disciples, following him to Alcalá when the schoolmaster finally pronounced him ready for university work. Two years had passed. Alcalá, famous for the brilliant staff assembled by the founder, the late Cardinal Ximenes, had not taught the overmature freshman much. With stubborn diligence he tried to beat into his head the dialectics of Soto, the physics of Albertus Magnus, the maxims of Peter Lombard. How could he concentrate? At any hour of the day or night harassed souls would interrupt his studies to tell him their troubles—or he would find himself in prison. He wanted to be a diligent pupil, but against his will he found himself an adored, hated, persecuted teacher.

The vicar-general twitched with impotent vexation. He could burn a real heretic, but what could he do with an obstreperously loyal son of the Church? Figueroa did not ask about Señora del Vado at once. He still felt strongly the effect which the testimony of the women had made on him. At first he lectured Íñigo on the sensational results of unskilled teaching. As a beginner Íñigo had not yet learned to administer doctrine according to individual capacity. He did not realize, with the master teacher Thomas à Kempis, that feminine psychology presents grave and intricate problems. He thought of Good

109

and Evil and the immortal soul in absolute terms. With perfect equanimity Íñigo replied to the examining judge "When women reform and try to abstain from sin, the devil sends them these attacks to weaken them in their struggle against temptation. If a woman comes to me in such a state I comfort her with the words, 'Withstand these temptations and tortures bravely. You will have conquered them within two months. I can give you this assurance because I myself have suffered.'"

Perhaps the vicar-general smiled at the artlessness of Alcalá's minor prophet. At any rate there was no heresy in the defense. It was difficult to combat an agitator whose ideas were so antiquated. Figueroa did not pursue this line. Without transition he blurted out the question which was the subject of the investigation, "Have you advised any person to leave home and family and make pilgrimage to far distant places?" For the first time, after three weeks of custody, the prisoner learned why he was detained. A professor of theology who fancied himself the spiritual adviser to Señora del Vado and her daughter Luisa had denounced him to the ecclesiastical authorities as accessory to their disappearance. Íñigo asserted under oath that he had always advised the ladies not to go out into the world as pilgrims because of the youth and beauty of the daughter. The vicar-general sighed with relief. His problem child had escaped one entanglement. A few days later the three ladies came back safe. They had been in Jaén to see the Veronica which was exhibited on Holy Thursday. Then they

ad made a pilgrimage to Our Lady of Guadelupe and
heir pious trip cost their hero forty-two days' imprisonment. They made amends by deposing that he was a
good man and a servant of God.

The verdict in this trial really hurt. Íñigo was forbidden to teach religion or any related subject for the next
three years. Also he must quit dressing like a preaching
friar. "I have no money," he said indignantly. "I can't
buy decent secular clothing." He was advised kindly to
avoid making himself conspicuous. He retorted, "I
should not have thought that one could be conspicuous
among Christians by speaking of Christ."

Embittered he turned his back on the city which pronounced piety impious.

Conformity Is Good in the Eyes of God

THE authorities forced Íñigo out of the university as an undesirable. The founder would have acclaimed him the ideal student. Twenty years before, while the impressionable squire played the games of mock combat and light love at Arevalo, the great ecclesiastic and statesman Cardinal Ximenes transformed the backward hamlet Alcalá de Henares into a cosmopolitan center of pious learning. As if he had no burdens of world empire on his shoulders, the tall, powerful old man paced the building sites, taking measurements with a carpenter's rule, verifying plans. He supervised in person the demolition of antiquated structures, the erection of new. At the time of Íñigo's disastrous ministry the Cardinal had lain buried ten years in this university chapel to which he had devoted his most enthusiastic efforts and bequeathed the greatest part of his fortune.

He would have found the exiled troublemaker a man after his own heart. They had many traits in common. Associates spoke respectfully of the Cardinal's resemblance to the hermits of old. Behind his back they called him "the elephant" because of his long face, trunklike nose, protruding canine teeth, and appalling tenacity. He resisted stubbornly when church or state drafted him o new responsibilities or forced honors upon him. "To break the fetters which bound him to earth" he renounced offices and benefices which brought him two thousand ducats a year. As father confessor of Queen Isabella he yearned for the mountain solitude in which he had built a tiny hermitage with his own hands. When he was chosen Archbishop of Toledo he ran away. For six months he refused to accept the highest clerical office in the country.

An ascetic without consideration for himself, he was a stern master. A thousand monks of his order fled to Barbary, finding existence among heathen savages a welcome relief after the regimen imposed by the archepiscopal puritan. The prelates of Spain in the period of false prosperity knew as well as their secular compeers how to appreciate the delights of life. Ximenes, the most august and illustrious of them all, feudal lord over fifteen populous cities and innumerable manorial domains, the omnipotent Archbishop of Toledo, would not have silver on his table, pictures on the palace walls. Even as archbishop he wore the garb of his order. From his kitchen, which could have served a monarch creditably, came dishes fit for a cloister refectory. He made his journeys on foot, like the poorest of his servants, while six asses stood fat and lazy in his stable. The princely palace was a hermitage, ten monks constituting the household and staff of the man who ruled Spain.

More than a thousand years before, the Council of Carthage had prescribed poverty for bishops. The church

of Alexander VI had different ideas of the living stand-
ards proper to a great dignitary of Christ. "Beloved son
Franciscus, Archbishop of Toledo, greeting and Apostolic blessing. The Holy Church, like the heavenly Jerusalem, has many and various adornments. Renunciation
may be error even as excess is sin. Conformity to all
obligations of rank is good in the eyes of God. A prelate
must avoid the suspicion of superstitious abasement not
less than the reproach of vanity and pride. Respect for
the ecclesiastical order is diminished by the one as by
the other. Since the Holy See has raised you from lowly
station to archepiscopal dignity, and we have learned
to our great joy that your inner life is such as to please
God, we exhort you to conduct yourself externally, as
to dress, retinue, and everything that wealth requires,
in accordance with your exalted rank. Given at Rome
under the Ring of the Fisherman, December 15, 1495,
in the fourth year of our pontificate."

Ximenes conformed, outwardly. He equaled the display of his predecessors. Carriages, horses, retinue now
proclaimed their owner's majesty. He set a lavish table
and fasted. Under silk and ermine he wore the coarse
Franciscan cassock, which he mended with his own
hands. He attempted to conceal his abnegation, but
everybody chuckled at his secret. A muleteer, whom he
tried to hurry into making an early morning start, retorted, "Your Eminence may think I can get ready as
soon as you. In the morning all you've got to do is shake

ourself like a wet dog and pull your girdle a little
ghter."

Wearing maroon robes and stoles a handbreadth wide,
ie professors of the great college, founded by the earn-
st monk, paraded their pomp and dignity. In the plain
ew coat which the church authorities had given him,
ie obscure student Íñigo, accompanied by his disciples,
obbled out of Ximenes' city. What was piety in a cardi-
al was presumption in a poor pupil without influence.
'et the all-powerful Archbishop of Toledo, like the un-
icensed teacher, had received a reminder from higher
uthority. Íñigo's rank was that of a placeless aspirant
rho had not yet passed any examination. Ximenes' rank
ad been that of a wealthy prelate. It was not proper
or the archbishop to live as poorly as the apostles. For
ñigo it was not proper to teach without a license con-
erring clerical privilege. The revolutionary Ximenes
ubmitted to the rule that the choirboy should eat little
nd the cardinal much. The revolutionary Íñigo must
earn to be holy without giving the slightest appearance
f wishing to impinge upon the hierarchy which speci-
ied who learned and who taught, what was learned and
vhat was taught, who wore the purple and who the beg-
ar's rags.

End of the World

ON HOLY THURSDAY, 1527, Pope Clement blessed Rome and all Christendom, from the benediction loggia of Saint Peter's. Ten thousand worshipers had assembled in the great square and gazed in horror as a man wearing only a leather apron climbed the statue of the Apostle Paul. Long red hair hung in tangles over the pale, wrinkled face. Greenish eyes, in deep pouches, glared at the snow-white vestments of the "Antichrist" Clement. "Sodomite bastard!" the prophet screeched. "Rome will be razed because of your sins. Confess and reform. You do not believe me? You will see in a fortnight." The monk Brandano, a familiar figure, was mistaken by only five days.

The Spanish and German mercenaries of the Emperor Charles marched through a land which snow and rain had turned into a swamp. Instead of provisions and pay they received promises of booty. Their general, Frundsberg, exhibited the rope with which he would hang the Holy Father. Four months of cold and hunger had made them ravenous. Only their appetites held them in line. When they learned that Clement was negotiating peace with their leaders they mutinied. They wanted Rome and no less. The Pope made an offer. The Emperor's agent demanded ten times as much. The pious grandson of the

116

Catholic Isabella then turned over Christ's earthly residence to his subjects as a prize of war. He proclaimed the "law of Mohammed," unrestricted plundering.

The Eternal City amounted to nothing but a petty Italian principality. Its walls had a circumference of sixteen thousand paces. In his youth, Clement had seen cattle grazing between Sant' Angelo and Saint Peter's. Venice and London contained four times as many inhabitants, Paris six times as many. Even after the invention of gunpowder, excommunication was an effective weapon against believers, but compatriots of Luther now marched to the attack.

The priests' loss of power had weakened the princes. Refractory vassals refused the holy tribute with which the Lord of Peace bought an army from the Italian states. The sovereign of the universal fatherland was a poor old man. The richest banker in Rome would lend him only a hundred ducats. Clement sold a few offices, but had no time to collect the money. The fortress walls could not hold out against cannonade and musketry. Four thousand guards, in artistically enchased shirts of mail, could not check twenty thousand ferocious wild beasts rushing upon their prey.

The great bell of the Capitol rang the storm alarm all night. When the May morning dawned the defenders stared into a fog. The cannons of the Castel Sant' Angelo could not get into the action because of the low visibility. Rome had a bandage over its eyes when it was conquered. Clement stood praying in his chapel when

117

he heard the battle cry. He ran down the covered passage into Sant' Angelo. As he came out on the open wooden bridge between the passage and the fortress hurrying prelates threw a violet cloak over the white papal garment which betrayed his identity. All the non imperial cardinals, the ambassadors of France and England, the papal court officials, many laymen, women and children fled into the Castel Sant' Angelo. On its roof the Angel of Peace made a brave show beside the red war flag. As the drawbridge went up and the rusted portcullis rattled down, about three thousand persons were shut in. Many tried to rush across the bridge too late and fell into the moat.

Desperate fugitives plunged into the Tiber. Boats sank overloaded. In the suburb of Trastevere, where the sea men and wine dealers lived, the populace ran aimlessly through winding alleys, past jutting shop fronts and outdoor stairways. The prosperous hid their possessions in the homes of their friends who favored the empire. The defenders had no time to break down the bridges. The invaders swarmed along both sides of the Tiber visiting first the quarter inhabited by the bankers and the court officials. Twenty thousand fasting and lusting mercenaries, and the scores of tramps who had joined them on the long road, poured into the little settlement around the Tiber flats. The onrushing hordes struck down whatever stood in their way. They murdered the patients in the hospital, the inmates of the orphan asylum. Pools of blood spread before the altars of Saint Peter's.

Plunderers, carrying lighted altar candles, marched from house to house. The Emperor's soldiers took only gold and silver. Robbing with greedy haste, they gutted the palaces, then levied ransom on the servants and on children not yet three years old. They flung babies out of windows, and raped the screaming mothers. Having gutted a building, they applied the torch. Rifled pearls were actually shoveled out to the men. Aristocratic Romans had to dig in the cloacae for their treasures. The Emperor Charles' Spanish and German devils, swarthy, mean, malignant, blond, bull-necked, brutal, marched through burning Rome, in magnificently embroidered silk robes, golden chains around their necks, glittering bracelets on their sinewy arms, precious stones woven into their mighty mustaches, their puffed faces sooty with powder smoke.

Of course they had plundered rich cities before, but Rome was an incomparable delicacy. Even the mercenary did not live by bread alone. Murder and plunder were glorious, but more exciting was the lout's revenge on a superior culture. Horses fed in the Sistine chapel and trampled on papal documents and ancient manuscripts. Dice rattled on the high altars. The Veronica was auctioned in taverns. A mercenary's uniform clad a famous crucifix. A German stuffed into his knapsack the huge rope, twelve feet long, with which Judas hanged himself. Gorged, besotted lechers, wearing the long robes of the princes of the church, the red hats of cardinals, rode through the streets of the conquered city on asses. The Bavarian captain Wilhelm von Sandizell masqueraded as the Pope. His men, dressed as cardinals, had to kiss his hands and feet. He gave them the blessing with a glass of wine. They responded by drinking the toast. The sacrilegious horde marched in front of Sant Angelo with drum and fife and held a lush conclave. In his fortress Clement could hear the drunken conquerors, with boisterous yells, proclaiming Luther Pope.

Profanation of pious ritual and mockery of the servants of God proved more intoxicating than wine and blood. They dragged the Franciscan cardinal, Cristoforo Numalio, out of bed, laid him on a bier and carried him in funeral procession. Mercenaries carrying candles sang the requiem. One ruffian preached a funeral sermon while a squad dug a grave. They would bury the cardinal alive if he did not pay. The ninety-year-old Bishop of Terracina, who could not raise the ransom of thirty thousand ducats, was placed publicly on sale like an animal, a bundle of straw on his head. Soldiers escorted an ass, attired like a bishop, to church, and killed the priest who refused to offer it incense and the host. Nuns were driven through the streets into the houses of prostitution or were auctioned, naked, in the market, at two ducats and less a head. Fashions in desecration, never very subtle, do not change much with the ages. Meanwhile the fine gentlemen who had unleashed the poor brutes betrayed them. The mercenary's fate! The orgy of marauding lasted just a week. It was short and thorough. As Erasmus said, not a city but a world had fallen.

END OF THE WORLD

The Venetian ambassador escaped in disguise as a
pack bearer. What became of marchionesses, countesses,
baronesses who had served the common soldiers? Dogs
worried stinking piles of corpses. Horses stood in rich
shops. Colored frescoes and wise inscriptions made an
ironic display against the black ruined palaces. On top
of the Castel, beside the statue of the Angel, invaders
melted down the tiaras of dead Popes in improvised
furnaces. The refugees in Sant' Angelo would have
thought ass meat a delicacy. A captain hanged an old
woman who tried to smuggle some salad to the Pope.
A Genoese banker and a Catalan merchant offered to
lend money in the imprisoned Clement on ruinous terms.

A great rummage sale on the Campo di Fiore, the
Forum of the new Rome, offered gold-embroidered silk
garments and perfect pearls. The riches of Rome had
trickled away. The mercenaries were poor and hungry
again.

Charles had no trouble getting rid of his bloodhounds.
They starved.

Dinner with the Inquisitor

A FEW weeks after the Alcalá verdict, Íñigo and his fo
lowers faced other judges, in another city, on the sam
charge. The group wandered together as far as Avila
then Iñigo went north to Valladolid, the temporary res
dence of the imperial court, while his four disciple
turned west to Salamanca. Íñigo arrived on the Sunda
when the Empress, attending church, made her first pul
lic appearance after the birth of the Infante Philip
Through a patroness, Doña Leonor de Mascareñas, gov
erness of the newborn prince, Loyola obtained an aud:
ence with Ximenes' successor to the archepiscopal thron
of Toledo. Fonseca received him amicably, listene
benevolently to his report, and managed to get rid o
the crazy malcontent by giving him three gulden. Mean
while, the young apostles, entering the university of Sala
manca, had begun operating among the piously inclined
The women of Salamanca had the same desires, th
priests the same fear of competition as at Alcalá, an
the Gray Robes, though they no longer wore gray robes
used the same methods.

Two weeks after Íñigo's arrival in Salamanca th
Dominican to whom he made confession brought hir
a disturbing invitation. "The monks of my cloister woul
like very much to become acquainted with you. The

want to ask you many questions. Please come and dine
with us next Sunday at noon." The Dominicans could
have only one reason for taking an interest in him. For
three hundred years the order had specialized in the
eradication of heresy. A Pope declared that Heaven had
sent him the Dominicans to preserve the purity of the
Faith. Perhaps the tribute represented a partial payment
of the Inquisition's great debt to the first Dominican,
who invented a most ingenious method of incapacitating
a troublesome believer. According to the saint's prescrip-
tion the naked expiant must be whipped by a priest from
the city gate to the church door three Sundays in succession; eat no meat all his life; keep three fasts a year
without even eating fish; three times a week abstain
from fish, oil, and wine, except in case of illness or
after strenuous labor; wear religious garb with a small
cross embroidered on each side of the breast; hear mass
every day; attend vespers Sundays and holidays; say
the common prayer day and night, the Pater Noster seven
times a day, ten times an evening, and twenty times at
midnight. "If he fail to comply he shall atone in the
flames." Anyone less sure of himself than the apparently
unbalanced Loyola would have been terrified to receive
an invitation from the successors of such a lawgiver. Had
not Íñigo taken Saint Dominic as his model?

Íñigo and Callisto went to the cloister of Saint Stephen
at the appointed time. The monks received them graciously. After refection the Subprior Pedro de Soto conducted them into the chapel. He praised Íñigo's apos-

tolic zeal. De Soto's approval led Íñigo to hope that this man would give the approval which the friendly but discreet Archbishop Fonseca had withheld. Approbation from the most authoritative source, the order which produced Torquemada and exterminated the Albigenses! The Subprior, with kindly interest, inquired about Íñigo's studies. The guest replied ruefully that he would greatly appreciate advice, as he had made little progress and his companions had done no better.

"Then how can you preach?"

"We do not preach," Íñigo answered modestly, "we have informal conversations, for instance when we are invited to dinner."

"What do you talk about?"

"The virtues, the sins ———"

"Who can discuss virtue and sin if he has not studied?" After a breath-constricting pause the Subprior continued icily, "You have not studied—so perhaps you have especial enlightenment directly from the Holy Ghost?" The question was an answer and a judgment.

Íñigo knew enough about dialectic to recognize the classic trap. Thus the Inquisitors entangled an upright believer into implying that he regarded himself as an *illuminatus* and therefore preached that God's intricately subdivided bureaucracy was superfluous. Íñigo had not the slightest desire to be an *illuminatus*. He revered the pyramidal hierarchy whose apex was the Pope. Íñigo's Manresa manuscript did homage to divinely ordained officialdom. "By subordinating every judgment of our own, we must remain willing and eager in all things to obey the Hierarchic Church, our holy mother, the bride of Christ our Lord." The Church misunderstood her true servant. He merely could not endure postponing his mission until he passed his examinations. Why was he persecuted as a blasphemer? What did these canons and vicars-generals and Dominicans want of him, who obeyed the Saviour, the church, and the saints? He could not even contend with his accusers because they did not charge him with any heretical teaching. "Tell me if what I have said is true or false," he implored the Subprior Pedro de Soto, in vain.

The Inquisitor wanted confession, not discussion. With blazing eyes he spoke of Erasmus and a world confused —but Íñigo hated the great Humanist too. The terror caused by the sack of Rome had made the guardians of the divine order unable to tell friend from foe. "Father," Íñigo protested sadly, "I can say no more than what I have, even if my spiritual superiors command me, as they have a right to do." The Dominican jumped up wrathfully and left the chapel. His victim had not let himself be caught, but was not this evasion subversive? Pedro de Soto had the cloister gates locked. The two dinner guests Íñigo and Callisto were forced to prolong their visit.

Three days they remained without news. On the fourth, a notary of the Inquisition appeared and had them removed to a city jail. The two friends were fastened together by a short chain so that each had to follow the other's every movement. They passed sleepless nights in prayer. The occurrence had been reported all over the city for they were popular in Salamanca too. The people had never heard of Erasmus. They did not ask how many degrees Íñigo had. They knew that he was no inapproachable prelate who perhaps spoke Latin by preference and drew a high salary. They simply knew he was a man who cared about them. The burghers and good wives of Salamanca flocked to the jail, bringing comforts and delicacies, and edified themselves by conversations with the two martyrs, who lived up to their roles perfectly. When Don Francisco de Mendoza expressed commiseration, Íñigo gave an answer worthy of Amadis and Dominic: "Do you not long to be put in prison for the love of God? I assure you, no matter how many leg irons and handcuffs there are in Salamanca I yearn for more." Suddenly Íñigo, Callisto, and the other three, who meanwhile had been thrown into cells with common criminals, became the darlings not only of the populace but of the ecclesiastical court. The convicts broke open the jail and escaped, but the five pious students remained loyally in their cells. As pillars of order they received better quarters in the adjacent palace.

The baccalaureate Vicente Frias, vicar-general of the Bishop of Salamanca, examined Íñigo's journal of pious experiences. Íñigo implored the court to pronounce upon his orthodoxy as exemplified by this document and by a dissertation, which he proceeded to give impromptu, on venial and mortal sin. Again he received no answer. This tribunal, evasive as the others, avoided making him the amends which certainly were due him if his teaching was free from error. Like the others it passed on him the severe but untheological censure that he had competed unfairly by teaching without a license, not having passed his apprentice and master examinations. He would yet learn that it was not a question of scholarship but of those who sold it, not of God but of God's functionaries. If a hierarchy tolerated outsiders, the whole structure must one day fall to pieces. All privilege was in danger when any privilege was infringed. Christendom was in a crisis. Many persons not licensed to think were doing so. Examinations presented the most effective check against dangerous ideas, because anyone burdened with the responsibility of learning, of a title, an office, would never get out of line. Anyone who had ascended, step by step, to secure position had no longer the excess energy to make trouble. Íñigo was subversive not because he taught anything heretical but because he taught without privilege.

After twenty-two days in custody the prisoners heard the judgment of their case. Their lives had been found blameless. There was nothing objectionable in Íñigo's exposition—he had been so verbose that the court gladly refrained from further questioning. The fact that he kept Sabbath Saturday, dedicating it to the Virgin Mary, at first gave rise to the suspicion that he favored Judaism, like some Christian bishops. The Loyola could point with pride to his Basque descent. This most indigenous race, whose tiny territory contained virtually no Jews, was certainly above suspicion. Thus the Salamanca judgment repeated, with slightly increased severity, the Alcalá verdict: the student must wait four years before he could expound to his fellow men the distinction between venial and mortal sin.

Íñigo liked influence, not theology. He wanted to be a teacher, not a divinity scholar. He could not live if he could not convert. So he left his fatherland and went into the realm of the national enemy, although a new war between Spain and France was imminent, and although it was whispered that the French delighted in roasting Spaniards on the spit.

The Capettes of Montaigu

THE University of Paris sprawled along the slopes of the
hill Sainte-Geneviève on the Left Bank of the Seine. Two
tower bridges connected the complex autonomous community with the metropolis of which, nominally, it
formed a part. The renown of "the foremost university
in this kingdom and the world" attracted some four
thousand freshmen yearly from every country of Christendom. These newcomers, who might naturally have
expected stately edifices, a formidable citadel, must
have looked with dismay at the disenchanting reality,
a maze of noisy, filthy alleys, a jumble of cloisters,
churches, chapels, bookshops, wineshops, and dilapidated
dormitories.

The first Paris professors, Albertus Magnus and Duns
Scotus, had lectured on the public squares and street
corners, in cloister gardens, on the adjoining fields and
meadows. Sometimes a preceptor had sat in a window,
addressing simultaneously the little group which had
found places in his room and the large outdoor audience
squatting on straw in the street. When Íñigo matriculated,
the Rue de Fouarre, the "street of straw" hallowed by
tradition of that early nomadic phase, was crowded by
lodgings and recitation buildings already so antiquated
as to be unsafe. Each of these belonged to one of the

four "nations" from which the Paris student body had originally been recruited: the French, Picard, Norman, and German. This method of classification had persisted long after it ceased to have any realistic basis. English students were assigned to the German nation; Spaniards and Italians, Navarrese and Savoyards, Egyptians and Syrians, to the French. The use of Latin was compulsory not only as a cultural and ecclesiastical requirement but as a practical necessity. The Latin Quarter was a cosmopolitan city within the world metropolis, an arrogantly independent country with its own institutions and laws.

The little world was a snarl of conflict, contradictions, intrigue. The students had outraged the sensibilities of the monks in the neighboring abbey Saint-Germain-des-Prés for centuries. The youngsters fished in the clerical waters, trespassed on the lawns. If anybody interfered with them they set the whole Latin Quarter in an uproar with the rallying cry, *"A nous, les écoles!"* The "nations" fought each other. The Scots, for instance, did not want to be classed as Germans. The "honorable *collegia*" wanted a monopoly. It had to compete with forty-nine learned institutions and the number of these was not yet limited. Clerical founders and patrons fought over spheres of influence, the bounds of which they guarded jealously. The faculties quarreled about precedence. The theologians, lords of the past, and the philologists, gods of the new era, were at the climax of their furious battle. The *faculté ès arts*, the philosophic, to which the philologists also belonged, demanded that the rector be chosen from their midst, while the theologians would not let their aspiring colleagues out of the scholastic ghetto. At the elections of rectors and student representatives in the little church of Saint-Julien-le-Pauvre and in the cloister of the Mathurins sometimes the tension snapped violently. Church and cloister doors were forced and religious furniture was broken.

At the tip of the university pyramid, the rector, the chancellor (who represented the Archbishop of Paris), and the university judge (appointed by the king) were engaged in a three-sided contest for power. No statute restrained this struggle. A commission appointed by King Francis found "not a single article of the university regulations in effect." "Great extortions and unnecessary banquets" were accepted as routine. The royal commission found it necessary to publish a tariff of examination costs and to limit the number of guests whom a young licentiate might entertain. The university city could still manifest a certain solidarity in common defense of its privileges against attacks from outside, but many an internal dissension was submitted to the Parlement de Paris for arbitration.

Near the present Place de Panthéon, in a rectangle formed by the Rue Saint-Étienne-des-Grez, the Rue des Chiens, the Rue des Sept-Voies, and the Rue des Cholets, stood Collège Montaigu, two hundred years old, famous chiefly for its draconic house regulations. Montaigu had had the misfortune to graduate men who became world-famous and gave their frowzy Alma Mater pitiless publicity. Erasmus, whose stomach was ruined by the student fare, satirized *Collège Vinaigre* in the "Colloquies." "Question: 'You come from Montaigu? Doubtless you covered your head with laurels?' Answer: 'No. With fleas.'" Rabelais caricatured Montaigu as *Collège de Pouillerie*, louse nest, and the poor inmates as *malotrus*, ill-starred ragamuffins, for the delight of posterity.

When Íñigo entered Montaigu the discipline had relaxed slightly. The lads were no longer routed out of bed at midnight to take part in divine services lasting an hour and a half. They no longer had to deplete the scant reserve of their weak constitutions by interminable fasts. Meat was not prohibited at the midday meal. Tyranny over the youthful subjects had been rendered considerably less onerous by anarchy among the dictators. A boy who was expelled by the rector and then turned away by the Carthusian prior, on appeal, could be reinstated by Notre-Dame.

Montaigu was still far from idyllic. Did the roof leak? Did the ragged uniform capes—hence the nickname *les Capettes de Montaigu*—fail to keep out the cold? The *Capette* might take that much more pride in poverty and iron government. Rector Pierre Tempête, *horrida tempestas*, was immortalized by his contemporary Rabelais as *grand fouetteur d'enfants*. He was so famous as a castigator that the neighboring colleges borrowed him in difficult cases. The minutely detailed code ignored cleanliness and comfort. Even then there were commodious lecture rooms in Paris. The master sat on a carved throne, flanked by beadles in full regalia, with long scepters. The auditors occupied comfortable choir stalls which rose in gradually elevated tiers. Some recitation rooms in Montaigu had not even benches. The students squatted on straw. Only the preceptor had a seat, which was raised so that he could see how the boys behaved and rule them with the rod. Filth was removed only once a year, when the winter straw was put in. The contents of the privies still trickled into the adjoining Rue des Chiens.

Duty began at four in the morning. The *Capette* who had slept through the din made by the bells of Saint-Séverin, Saint-Julien-le-Pauvre, Saint-André-des-Arcs, Saint-Hilaire, Saint-Étienne, the master peal of the Sorbonne, was dragged to his feet by a callboy. A hundred and twenty youngsters buckled down to a dreary grind. Those who had dreamed in German, French, Spanish, Italian, English, between six in the evening and four in the morning, must think Latin fourteen hours, in *trivium* (grammar, rhetoric, and dialectic), and quadrivium (arithmetic, music, geometry, and astronomy). They must study the texts of Greece and of the Christian Middle Ages in Latin commentary. They must converse formally two hours a day in Latin. They must whisper in Latin, eat their scanty meals in Latin. *Poculum a dextris! Ad laevam panis!*

Between four and eleven in the morning the *Capette* had nothing to stay his stomach but a dry piece of white bread. Mass and five hours of recitation were thought to

133

replenish abundantly body, soul, and brain. Principal and teachers sat at the first table. A monitor, chosen weekly, sat at each of the many little tables occupied by students. As badge of his office the monitor had his napkin tied under his chin. He kept vigilant watch lest any student put hand to vermin-tormented head during the repast. The group must devour the rationed bread and butter, the unseasoned boiled cabbage, the not very fresh egg, according to every rule of the house code. There was no meat, no wine, but plenty of piety to edify the empty stomach, the insulted palate. Water, black bread, and half a herring were tastefully sandwiched between a preliminary Bible text and a closing "grace."

In returning thanks the chaplain exhorted the anemic pupils to be grateful to the founders and benefactors of the house. He prayed for the soul of pious Marie Parent, who bequeathed her "personal and real property," valued at five thousand *livres*, to the Collège Montaigu. A Paris canon, a noble lady, a doctor of theology, a former teacher of the college, a famous printer had contributed. A glowing passage eulogized the generosity of King Francis. The chaplain did not mention the *Capettes* who went about the city begging for their house. Nor did he allude to the chief benefactors who really kept the concern running. They lived nearby and yet a world away from those whom they maintained in starvation. The rich *pensionnaires* of Montaigu did not eat in *Capette* commons, lodge in *Capette* dormitories, do kitchen duty, wait on tables. They had servants. Their comfort paid for the misery, the whip, the rotten egg, of their poor schoolmates.

Rich and poor had no contact. They were separated purposely, so that the hungry might not catch, as by contagion, the appetites of the nourished. The unprivileged had ample opportunity to earn merit by humility. The front seats of the classrooms were reserved for the well-to-do. At the end of the period those in the rear had to vanish immediately. On the recreation grounds in the Pré-aux-Clercs, the meadows nearby, the two separate species of the *genus homo* kept a proper distance. The divine blessing of poverty must not be menaced. Only those accustomed to rigor could bear the cross.

Íñigo was not quite a charity student, neither was he a *pensionnaire* like Calvin. Íñigo was a "martin," that is, he "flitted" to lectures, recitations, disputations, and at the end of the course was free to "fly away." No word could have been more inappropriate. Once again, as in Barcelona five years before, he sat beside boys ten years younger than he. Once again, dissatisfied with his previous studies, he began at the beginning, with an elementary course in Latin grammar. Even as an outsider he was subject to rigorous discipline. He could be whipped for the slightest infraction of the house rules. Any spare time had to be spent reading a classic so as "not to give the devil a chance to find his thoughts unoccupied." He did not need to pay attention to cleanliness or the multiplication of vermin. These were trivial matters. Humble obeisance to masters was supremely important.

The Humanist Erasmus suffered in Montaigu. He resented the hard bed, the wretched food. The promiscuous whippings revolted him. He was aghast at the agony of comrades who went blind or insane and then died. The Rector, Noël Béda, knew how to obstruct the powerful new movement for humane education and Íñigo, the trained ascetic, scorned gentleness and glorified discipline. He wrote to friends in Barcelona that he was serving as a volunteer until God should order him to another post. No longer worried about the necessities of life, Íñigo found the harsh atmosphere sweetly familiar.

The spirit of Low German mysticism, of the Brothers of Common Life and the mendicant orders, had moved the militant pedagogue Jean Standonck a generation before, when he formulated the rules governing the *Capettes* of Montaigu: "Who loves God must devote his life to training a new generation. We must select the poorest, the most wretched, those of fewest wants, and inculcate in them not only knowledge but love of renunciation, that they may despise worldly pleasures and ambition." The pilgrim to Montserrat and Jerusalem, the teacher of Alcalá and Salamanca would have agreed. The *Capettes* of Montaigu, according to the plan of the deceased lawgiver, must develop into Christian propagandists who would take their mission more seriously than the contemporary clergy did. Íñigo had just such

136

an ideal. Stern Montaigu, which tortured Erasmus and Rabelais, pleased and benefited Loyola. Whip, vermin, malnutrition, compulsory dissension and dispute, prepared a man for life in God.

Paris was expensive. A filthy cubbyhole cost more than luxurious room and board and full tuition in Louvain. Yet Isabela Roser's twenty-five ducats would have satisfied Íñigo's simple needs for nearly a year had he not entrusted the greater part of the sum to a friend who absconded with it. A few weeks after his arrival in Paris Íñigo did not have a sou. The landlord put him out. He found shelter in the hospice of Saint-Jacques in the Rue Saint-Denis, a long way from the college, but the house rules made it difficult for him to get to class on time. The hospice opened too late and closed too early. Begging took most of his working time. He had to find employment which would leave him long hours for study.

A poor student could earn his keep as *famulus* to a *magister*. The word sounds poetic to modern ears. It conjures up the picture of an aspiring disciple reverently handing the master a retort and avidly listening to an interpretation of the cloudy liquor. In reality *famulus* meant a menial domestic drudge. He had to sweep, make the fires, wait on the *magister*'s family and on the rich *pensionnaire*. Íñigo, who had already come to diplomatic terms with a difficult god, identifying the divine will with the pacification of his own desires, had no fear of the indignities which he must expect from a surly master, a termagant housewife, the supercilious young gentlemen whose well-filled purses bought every advantage. He would keep before his eyes not the household tyrants but a gracious personification of the Saviour. He could hear the harshest commands, perform the most degrading chores, truckle to the basest whims, with joy. Human beings could cause no suffering as earth was only a shadowy portal before the reality of heaven.

He would work for any master. No one would have him. Although influential personages interceded for him, the servant of God was not fit to char for the little potentates of the Latin Quarter. He was one of the sights of the district, shabby, unkempt, over-ripe among the immature. Every inhabitant had laughed at him as he ambled down Dog Street. Who wanted the notorious scarecrow in his home? Who could use a cripple as a drudge?

War in Dog Street

THE colleges Montaigu and Sainte-Barbe faced each other across the Rue des Chiens. Military historians assure us that war is periodically inevitable between close neighbors. The traditional feud between the two colleges erupted six years before Íñigo matriculated.

Not a broom had touched the little dirt alley since the memory of man. Mounds of rubbish tainted the air offensively in summer. The city fathers decided to have the street paved. Montaigu and Sainte-Barbe agreed to bear the costs jointly. Who could have suspected that such a praiseworthy action would cause armed hostility? Heroic minds, however, did not disdain even the most insignificant cause for performing deeds of valor. From time immemorial the closets of Montaigu had discharged their contents on Dog Street. The "made" ground, composed of rubbish, had readily absorbed the flow, which now could not sink into the hard surface.

Unfortunately the paviors had not graded the street, which inclined considerably from Montaigu toward Sainte-Barbe. Foul puddles formed on the lower level. Principal Gouvea lodged a complaint. Montaigu apologized officially and laughed at its neighbor's plight. "They are in danger of catching fire from us," said Montaigu. "Yet when we send them liquid to put out the flames they are ungrateful."

139

The house master of Sainte-Barbe proposed a plan of retaliation. By changing the slope of the street Sainte Barbe could send the noisome floods back where they originated. At once the entire personnel mobilized under the strategist's command. They worked laboriously all one long dark night to make Dog Street slope toward Montaigu. Unfortunately they had not finished at dawn

When daylight revealed the attempted improvement Montaigu arose as one man. All rallied to the call of King Béda. Only the blood of the transgressor could wash away the stain on the communal honor. The crisis brought forth a hero from the Montaigu ranks. Its house master, known as Odysseus because of his legendary cunning, assumed command and had the boys gather ammunition, storing it in their rooms, to accord the sappers of Sainte-Barbe a fitting reception the coming night.

The generalissimo of Sainte-Barbe, known as Polyphemus, had only one eye, but he could see as well as the next man. He had not the slightest doubt that colleague Odysseus would launch a perfidious surprise attack on the work under cover of darkness. Polyphemus armed his sappers. The students waited in their beds for the signal which would call them to the front. The second night which was to have been devoted to the alteration of Dog Street, stones hailed down on the Barbiste engineer corps. The Barbistes gave ground, mobilizing in the bed rooms of the dormitory. The house had seen better days In the lumber room the boys found not only broken tools

ots, household utensils, but bolts and crossbows which
ad done duty in the war against the English. They armed
astily but thoroughly. Not a window pane remained
nbroken in the house of Montaigu. Even the crucifix in
e chapel was hit. After this sacrilege, Montaigu waged
crusade. Quarter was out of the question.

Failing to storm the enemy's main building, Montaigu
oncentrated on Sainte-Barbe's bakehouse. The roof fell
n. The bakers fled. The dough burned in the oven. The
arbistes began their counteroffensive with a war cry
hich attested their classical learning: "Let Bacchus pay
eres!" Sainte-Barbe penetrated the empire of Bacchus,
he vineyards of Montaigu, pulled up the vines, and
azed the outbuildings. After both sides had demon-
trated their heroism and sustained losses, the war fizzled
ut. The drainage question was settled peacefully, but a
oreness remained.

Six years after the Battle of Dog Street, the Basque
tudent, Amador, disappeared from the Collège Sainte-
Barbe. He was a model pupil, the great hope of the
nstitute and of the whole Quarter. Doctor Pedro de
Peralta and the baccalaureate Juan de Castro were
nissed too. Excitement reigned in the university city. All
ecalled that they had noticed a strange transformation
n these three young persons lately. They neglected their
studies. They prayed instead of working. They mediated night and day instead of following the curriculum
ind the regulations which provided for every activity.
Any one should have been able to foretell the result, the

determination to sell all and give to the poor—and liv
by begging. Indignation was general on the Left Bank o
the Seine. Could anything be more exasperating than t
renounce goods and possessions and become a burden o
one's fellow man?

Amador's classmates heard that the pious truants ha
landed in the hospice of Saint-Jacques in the Rue Sain
Denis. Hundreds of armed students marched to th
refuge. They called loudly for the fugitives. Amado
and his followers announced that they would never re
turn to the world of vanities. The mob took the statemen
as a challenge, stormed the hospice, forced the doors
haled the rebellious eremites out of their miserabl
hiding place and back to Sainte-Barbe. Teachers an
students agreed that it was less evil to sin against th
commandments than to take them too seriously. Amado
must return to the curriculum and not play saint.

Sainte-Barbe could trace this outrage to the crazy
Spanish student enrolled in Montaigu and living in th
hospice of Saint-Jacques, the scandalous character wh
had given up a great fortune to decline and conjugat
like a grammar-school boy at the age of thirty-seven
Amador's confession implicated the notorious odd fisl
seriously, but Montaigu did not care to go to war agair
over this Basque beggar. Anyway, he had disappeared.
He had not been living in Saint-Jacques for a long time
The Inquisitor, the Dominican Ori, who had to prose
cute the seducer Loyola on the accusation of a master o
arts, searched all quarters of the university city in vain.

142

While Paris was thus stirred by the result of his teach-
ig, Íñigo wandered again as a pilgrim, barefoot, with-
ut provision. Learning that the man who had done him
ut of his subsistence money for the year lay ill and
esperate in Rouen, he had started at once to assist the
ufferer. Íñigo succored and encouraged him, secured
im repatriation on favorable terms, and gave him letters
f recommendation to followers in Salamanca. He knew
othing of the thwarted renunciation until he returned
ɔ Paris. Amador, Peralta, and Castro were his friends.
Ie had tried to teach them because he admitted no
riendship except agreement with his ideals. These dis-
iples, overzealous, immature, had created a disturbance
imilar to those of Alcalá. The teacher still could not
ontrol his pupils.

He went immediately to the Inquisitor. Knowing that
ıe was in harmony with the ruling power, this agitator
ould always go to ecclesiastical police headquarters.
Ie was safest there. Íñigo asked for an investigation,
s soon as possible, so that the incident might be settled
efore the beginning of the new school year. The Domini-
an Ori did not even make inquiries. He simply quashed
nost of the complaints. Íñigo was no rebel, uncovering
langerous truths. He merely made himself somewhat of
ι nuisance by trying to bring down the Son of Man from
he right of the Father to the foul atmosphere of Dog
Street.

The schoolboys avoided him as an uncanny beast. The
rofessors made him feel their repugnance. The whole

university, especially the Spanish colony, accused hi
of leading Amador astray. Unabashed by public opinio
Íñigo de Loyola entered the Collège de Sainte-Barb
center of the storm of indignation against him. The chi
disciplinarian of this famous school was the theologia
Jacques Gouvea, called by the students "the mustai
eater," a near relative of that Gouvea who had playe
a prominent part in the war of Dog Street. He seized tl
first opportunity of humiliating the unwelcome mi
sionary.

To enter the college, Íñigo had to swear that he woul
restrain his evangelical zeal. In spite of the promise I
soon exerted unmistakable influence. Philosophy studen
were required to participate in formal disputations o
Sundays and holidays. Attendance of these fell off wee
by week after Íñigo's entrance. The master in charg
blamed him for the desertions. Following his exampl
the students had suddenly taken to keeping the Sabbai
by confession and communion at the Carthusians' befoi
the Porte Saint-Jacques instead of exercising their min(
by the prescribed scholastic fencing. Gouvea denounce
the pious class cutting, without effect. He now had fu
justification for humiliating the Pied Piper of Paris. Th
Doctor of Theology, Rector Jacques Gouvea, sentence
the philosophy student Íñigo de Loyola to the notoriou
aula—running the gauntlet in the refectory of the Collèg
Sainte-Barbe.

The school bell rang. The doors of the institute close(
All inmates of the house poured into the torture chambe

enjoy the treat. The masters of arts, entitled by their
scholarly degrees to flagellate a delinquent student, were
armed with rods. After the meal they would range themselves in two rows to lash the victim, stripped to the
waist, as he ran between them. Meanwhile the sentenced
student had a talk with his powerful adversary. Íñigo
did not fear the rods of the school executioners. Had he
not whipped himself daily in Manresa? Had he not
sought suffering far more intense, for eight years? For
quite a different reason he went to the principal at the
last moment. Íñigo pointed out to the chief disciplinarian
of Sainte-Barbe the evil effect which a spectacle like the
aula must produce on the minds of impressionable young-
ers. He appealed not to sympathy but to intelligence.
He won his enemy over, completely. The pious legend
has it that condemned and judge walked arm in arm to
the place of punishment, that Gouvea asked Íñigo to sit
at his side at table, that after refection the proud Rector,
kneeling, shedding tears of repentance, publicly asked
pardon. More probably the worthy director of the respectable educational institution "let mercy prevail over
justice" after a long, unctuous moral sermon. A schoolmaster who begged forgiveness of his inferior before a
public assemblage would be much more dangerous than
a student who gave his worldly goods to the poor.

This victory over a powerful enemy deepened the
mystery surrounding the Spanish holy man. Rumor circulated that the enigmatic saint had been condemned by
the Inquisition in his native country. A man nearly forty

just beginning the study of Aristotelian logic, physic and ethics, was remarkable enough. What really mysti fied his schoolfellows was the fact that a man who cam of an aristocratic and wealthy family could wander abou the world begging. Íñigo did not like the role which th popular imagination ascribed to him. He never set him self proudly above the preconceptions of the worl around him. He always preferred the verdicts of quali fied tribunals to the voice of conscience. A compatrio Madera, expressed sympathy for the aristocratic famil of Loyola, shamed by the vagabondage of one of it members. Íñigo submitted to the Sorbonne, the highes court in any moral controversy, the problem: "If nobleman has renounced the world for love of God, ca he beg without prejudicing the honor of his family?" The learned gentlemen searched through the Bible, Aris totle, Thomas Aquinas, and gave the loyal troublemake another certificate of blamelessness. He added it to hi great and growing collection.

He needed the most authoritative testimonials he coul get. No one was bothering him now, while his country man Juan de Pena tried to beat into his head the mys teries of the omniscient Greek philosophers. The unaccus tomed peace did not deceive him. "I am quiet, they leav me alone, but the moment I move they will attack m from all sides." As he made no move, his best disciple came to him unsought. He learned at last to control th effect of his teaching.

Pierre and Francisco

In SAINTE-BARBE Íñigo had two roommates, Pierre and
Francisco.

Pierre le Fèvre tutored the matured and unreceptive
man, fifteen years his elder, in philosophy. As they
talked about entelechy, about subsistent and inherent
forms, a great attachment developed between the Basque
knight and the descendant of poor Savoyard peasants.
The model student of Sainte-Barbe would suddenly drop
his reserve and blurt out the perplexities of naïveté and
inexperience. He had watched his father's flocks on the
Alpine meadows of the Grand-Bornand. A pious and
silent child, he fasted two days a week at the age of
seven. At ten, finding the catechism lessons of the village
school insufficient, he besought a neighboring religious
to tutor him. In the Collège La Roche he heard the
priestly instructors expound the pagan writers as preachers of the Gospel. In vacation Pierre again helped out
at home by tending the flocks. In the solitude of the
mountain pasture he fixed in his mind what he had
learned in school and meditated the lore of the simple
shepherd folk. The fantastic nocturnal light and the
mountain silence oppressed him. The saints above the
mountain tops, near the throne of Wisdom, seemed to
counsel him. At the age of twelve he threw off an in-

tolerable burden by taking the solemn vow of eternal chastity.

From the remote mountain meadow he found himself transplanted to the metropolis, turbulent with the diversities of its three hundred and fifty thousand inhabitants. The great world still rocked from the tumults of the Renaissance which had shaken natures more stable than young Pierre's. Even at "the foremost university in this kingdom and the world" the peasant boy showed his proficiency as a scholar. He was a sound Latinist and had a real familiarity with Greek. When the master De Pena could not interpret a difficult passage he consulted the young Savoyard. Had his character kept pace with his scholastic development? Was he steadfast as in the mountains? The University of Paris had much besides the iron house regulations and the Aristotelian omniscience to offer an ardent, sensitive youth. The balmy summer nights and the dark winter evenings whispered enticingly of enchantments to be found in noisy lighted streets, gay taverns, houses of pleasure. The students of Sainte-Barbe crawled out of their windows, past the proctors, and off to a worldly paradise. The rustic Aristotelian worried over the sins of his fellows. The Latin Quarter flaunted before his eyes what his imagination could not even have conceived at home. A Sainte-Barbe master of arts, who had joined the reveling students many a night, died of the new sinful disease.

The fisher of souls coaxed a complicated tale of woe out of the sad young philosophy student. He was greatly troubled by the knowledge that he was not right with God. He had not gone to confession for a shamefully long time. He used to take communion regularly, but he knew that his former practices conferred no merit on him now. The pride which he derived from his little successes as a student he characterized as vainglorious. He had made presumptuous use of his critical intelligence, sharpened by scholastic exercise. His insecure position gave him great anxiety for the future. The poor peasant boy had no influential relative, no august patron to advance him. Should he become a doctor of medicine, jurist, official, doctor of theology, ordinary cleric, or monk? He was always hungry. Sternly he called his healthy appetite "greed." He found too that it had been easier to lull "carnal desire" asleep in the lonely mountains ten years ago.

There were many approaches to the heart of this young man. Íñigo first ministered to the stomach. Then he sent for Doctor Castro of the Sorbonne to hear general confession. Most important, Íñigo advised his young friend to search his conscience twice a day and bring order to the internal confusion by recording exactly what he found there. The younger man explained to the elder the Aristotelian concepts which still guided the scholastic world. The elder repaid him by drawing up an ingenious chart. Seven columns represented the days of the week, an upper space reserved for an examination of conscience at noon, a lower for recapitulation in the evening. Pierre would wake every morning with the pur-

pose of ridding himself during the day of a sinful habit
which bothered him especially. At noon and in the evening he would take inventory. He would recall whether
he had relapsed, and how often. He would keep score
by a system of dots. Now, checking up in the evening,
Pierre could ascertain whether he had made progress
since midday. On Monday he could make sure whether
he had improved since Sunday. He could see whether
a week's scores were better than those of a previous
week. Thus vague abstractions lost their terror. Confusion vanished.

The teacher, much wiser now, proceeded with tactful
caution, preparing his young adept carefully, thoroughly.
He would have no such results as rashness had produced
in Barcelona, Alcalá, Salamanca, and here in Paris. He
did not drive, he curbed the youngster's zeal. The two
became "one being in wish and will."

Íñigo's other roommate in Sainte-Barbe was the
Basque Don Francisco de Xavier. Fifteen years younger
than Íñigo, like Pierre, of whom he was very fond,
Francisco had the self-assurance of the young gentleman
who knew that he was born to rule and enjoy. He kept a
horse and a servant, and spent more money than his
mother liked to send him. He came from a powerful
house of Navarre which had been brought down in the
world by the Spanish conquest of the independent little
country. When Íñigo de Loyola was wounded as an
officer of Charles, Francisco's brother fought for the

French. When this Navarrese family too had to make its peace with the new master, three years after the storming of Pampeluna, its fortune had shrunk considerably.

Francisco, the youngest, was destined to find his livelihood in the Church. As the family still sympathized with France, he matriculated at Paris, not a Spanish university. After a preparatory year, three years of philosophy, and four years of theology, he would come home a doctor and enter on a prosperous living in the cathedral of Pampeluna. With this settled plan of life the young gentleman, four years before, had left the castle of his fathers, an ancient fortress built on bare steep cliff overlooking the eastern boundary of the former kingdom of Navarre and guarding the pass to Aragon.

Francisco de Xavier was a proud aristocrat, alert, strikingly handsome, with red cheeks, big black eyes, and dark curls. He distinguished himself as an athlete in the student competitions on the meadows. Equally famous for conviviality, he found good use for his fleetness and nimbleness in dodging the proctors who policed the morals of the Latin Quarter. There was one dreadful check on his pleasures. It restrained him when rules and sermons and spies and punishment could not. Loathsome disease marked one after another of his gay associates. "Great pox" was the mysterious horror of the age. In naming it each expressed his chief hate. The Germans, Italians, and English called it the French disease. The French termed it Neapolitan. The Dutch, the Navarrese, and the Africans called it the Spanish Evil; the Asiatics dependent on Portugal, the Portuguese. Pox was Turkish to the Persians, Christian to the Turks, Polish to the Russians, and German to the Poles. How could such devastating evil originate if not in the malice and baseness of the enemy?

Perhaps Heaven had sent it to punish impiety. Had Columbus brought it with him from a New World better left undiscovered? The French, tracing it to their Neapolitan campaign, remembered seeing human carcasses delivered to butchers. A poet sang of Syphilus, who insulted the gods. Astrologers referred to especially unfavorable constellations in the year 1483. Perhaps the evil had arisen from intercourse of men with apes. A popular legend related that a Valencian courtesan, for fifty gold pieces, slept with a knight suffering from leprosy and infected her large clientele. A hundred names and a hundred fanciful origins characterized the horror which kept Francisco from going quite as far as he wished. However, even the compulsion to good behavior did not drive the young aristocrat into himself, into such complications of perplexity as harassed Pierre when the newcomer moved into their room.

Xavier had difficulty remembering that the stooping, limping, middle-aged freshman belonged to his own environment. The comic and dangerous character did no credit to their caste and country. Francisco did not like the idea of sharing a room with a fellow Basque nobleman, fifteen years his senior, who was still grubbing away at Aristotle as a beginner, whom experience and maturity had qualified only to be a greenhorn in Dog

Street. Amador's classmates had seen the results of having anything to do with him. Francisco decidedly had no intention of becoming a vagabond saint. Pointed for a lucrative post in the cathedral at Pampeluna, he was already working hard to realize his ambition. He had to write letter after letter to the authorities of Navarre, who had questioned his nobility, the chief qualification for the appointment.

Francisco had completed his philosophic studies and become a master of arts. He had now the right to give lectures. To obtain a doctor's degree he must present at least one pupil whom he had trained to engage successfully in public disputation. Íñigo brought him a good many promising pupils, so that Francisco was able to begin his teaching activities with good prospects. The young tutor's purse was always empty and Íñigo was always ready to lend him money. The older man did not drag the gay youngster into grim, ugly asceticism. Quietly and humbly the teacher made concessions in order to become indispensable. He had learned something about the human mechanism: one must humor weakness before one could divert strength to one's own purposes.

Resistance gave way. The young gentleman had found a reliable patron in his supposedly inconvenient roommate. Francisco saw that he had misjudged the old fellow. He had thought this despiser of enjoyment would forbid him the delights of life for which he was so eager. Yet no one was so sympathetic, so indulgent, so ready to help him gratify his secret and avowed wishes.

The stranger's influence drew him away from the Humanists, for whose ideals he had once felt great enthusiasm. Without suspecting that he did so, the haughty young nobleman opened his inmost self to the man who still was not his friend.

The day came when the old campaigner knew that success would follow an attack by storm. Francisco still hoped for a comfortable future in the cathedral at Pampeluna. Íñigo, whose personal integration resulted from the wreck of ambitious dreams, mercilessly tore Francisco away from his indicated career. "What shall it profit a man if he gain the whole world and lose his own soul?" The world had now no power, all earthly prizes of victory lost their attraction. The same phrase was different if it was spoken by a despised fool or by a friend to whom one had yielded full confidence. Íñigo's influence had already penetrated so deeply that Francisco could no longer isolate it and thrust it away. Enjoyment and ambitious hopes were consigned to oblivion.

Francisco's sister Maria was a nun in Pampeluna. His sister Magdalena, once a lady of honor to Queen Isabella, had recently died as abbess of the Poor Clares of Gandia. The new retinue of Christ was setting forth in military array from the staunch old castles of the knights of Loyola and Xavier.

On the door of the room in which the friends lived Íñigo fastened a picture of the Saviour. Their schoolmates said it was a heraldic blazon and nicknamed the pious triumvirate *"Societas Jesu."*

A King Cannot Do as He Pleases

Francis I, King of France, was a Sunday's child. We associate him with the lusty Rabelais, never with the austere Loyola. As Prince of Cognac he read *Amadis of Gaul* avidly, but while the Arevalo page developed into the Manresa ascetic, the Jerusalem pilgrim, the winner of souls, Francis came under the genial influence of the civilization that revived in Italy after more than a thousand years' eclipse.

King Francis' severest ordeal, his imprisonment after the battle of Pavia, represented only an off year in the life of a child of fortune. Nor did those months lack romance. Valencia gave lavish festivals in honor of the defeated Prince Charming whom it greatly preferred to the gloomy victor, Charles. The royal gallant had danced with the most beautiful women of Catalonia. A young Spanish beauty took the veil to forget her hopeless passion. The days in prison were not dull, though they were dark enough. The close-barred window high overhead admitted not a sunbeam, not a breath of air. Heavily armed watchmen made the rounds at short intervals to keep the Christian monarch from writing to the Sultan. The Italian captain of the prisoner's watch devised a plan of escape. If King Francis would blacken his face

and hands, he could pass the watch unrecognized in th
clothing of the Negro slave who brought firewood ever
day. The project was betrayed. Francis was forced t
sign the Treaty of Madrid, renouncing Burgundy. H
had no intention of keeping his word.

Freed after fourteen months, he returned to France
A deputation from Burgundy waited upon him, declar
ing, "Your Majesty, the Madrid Proviso is null and voi
because it contradicts your coronation oath and th
fundamental laws of the monarchy. If you abide by it w
will rule ourselves. We will never obey a king whom w
have not chosen." Fortune did her darling the extraordi
nary favor of making his subjects rebel on his behalf
Francis settled hostilities, temporarily, by marryin
Charles' sister. Queen Eleanor was borne into Paris or
a purple velvet throne in a bank of fresh flowers. Th
Church, the University, the City sent ambassadors, wh
mingled pedantry with piety in high-sounding addresse
of welcome. Two thousand students of the University o
Paris marched in the procession. The baccalaureate
wore impressive black capes. Four beadles resplenden
in silver preceded the procurators of the four "nations"
who flaunted red birettas and imposing gold braid
Priests, courtiers, and soldiers could not outdo the mer
of learning in pomp and finery.

The university of Aquinas was fighting for its life in
these days. The isolated Íñigo, unquestioning as if ques
tions were not bursting his world, might teach his friends:
"Man was created to praise God our Lord, to do Him

everence, to serve Him, and so to win the soul's salva-
ion." Outside the room with the picture of Jesus on the
oor, controversy raged about the highly problematic
ill of God and the authority of His servants. The Uni-
ersity of Paris was a decisive battlefield of this struggle.
"The foremost university in this kingdom and the
orld" the unkind Humanists called "the mother of
gnorance." The university no longer held undisputed
uthority. It had passed its zenith a hundred years before.
When Íñigo attended Montaigu and Sainte-Barbe, Paris
ad not a single teacher with a world reputation. Henry
III, it is true, consulted the doctors of the Sorbonne
efore he divorced Catherine of Aragon to marry Anne
oleyn. Paris still arbitrated the moral and legal ques-
ions of the Catholic world, but this was no longer the
nost important part of Europe.

The universe that Thomas Aquinas crystallized had
xploded. The new learning reintroduced Plato and
reek art, Virgil, Cicero and Roman history, the Greek
ods, and the Latin laws. Neither Ptolemaeus nor the
Arabs knew the sky and the earth as did the contempo-
aries of Columbus, of Cortez, of Magellan. Jean Fermet,
he great mathematician and astronomer of Sainte-Barbe,
ndertook to measure a meridian for the first time in
Occidental history. Print freed the layman from scholas-
ic supervision and sent him exploring regions which
were supposed not to exist.

The Paris university was no longer supreme arbiter,
bove all parties. It was now a party itself, defending

the past against the future, against Humanists an
Protestants, against all who investigated instead of a
cepting. The rebels had long ceased to be powerles
They had penetrated the enemy camp. Íñigo had to wi
Francisco away from their wiles. The theological facult
floundered grotesquely in attempting to answer merciles
questioning. "Why," the upstarts asked, "have we ha
to make so many constitutions and decrees? Our la
is sterner than that of the Old Testament. It was Christ'
will that Christians live in freedom."

An era died when the people burst its barriers agains
thought. All attempts to plaster up a cracked heave
ended in failure. Ecclesiastical authorities condemne
the "Colloquies" of Erasmus. An edition of twenty thou
sand copies sold out at once. Precisely the anathematize
sentences of Luther's "Babylonian Captivity" struck th
popular fancy. At one time the judges of the Sorbonn
could have forbidden a work and forgotten it in peace
Now they had to struggle constantly to defend privileg
against the logic of development. A special decree, elo
quently expressive of pride in learning and fear fo
prestige, forbade reading the Holy Scriptures in th
vernacular. Theology professors had no reason for exist
ing if the average person could understand the Wor
of God.

The philosophic faculty presented an even more dan
gerous threat to the theologians. The Sorbonne decree
a tightening of the Aristotelian muzzle, which had slipped
off the philosophers. The Sorbonne tried to bully th

ilologists as if it were still in the prime of power.
You had better stick to your subject and leave dialectics
 dialecticians." Philosophers and philologists realized,
eretically, that the University of Paris had become an
oject of universal ridicule. They replied, "God has not
eased to save His people with sophistry." Was Hebrew
it another dead language, less elegant than Latin and
reek? Should the study be elective? Was not rather
e study of Hebrew, the holy language, imperative?
his controversy kindled the fires in which martyrs
erished. It started Biblical exegesis, criticism of the
ergy. Those who read the original Bible discovered
iddenly that the princely life of the lords of the Church
olated the holy doctrine flagrantly. The Paris Scholas-
cs hated their critics with the righteous indignation
roperty owners feel toward trespassers and burglars.
rasmus accused the Christian lords of "abusing their
ower to avenge their private grievances and to suppress
iences which they could not master." The decried
hoolmen defended themselves like every privileged
ass whose time has passed. They invented strange sub-
rfuges to wangle a few more years from inevitable
eath.

They had an especial grievance against Francis as the
atron of printing. The first book printed in Paris had
ppeared two generations before. The famous printers
stienne, Antoine Verard, and Gilles de Gourmont en-
yed royal protection. King Francis frequently visited
stienne's establishment in the Rue Jean de Beauvais.

Here even the domestics spoke Latin. Robert Estienne made a practice of displaying galley proofs of the work which was on the press and paying a premium to any passerby who discovered an error. Many a needy scholar stood in front of the window and hunted till he earned a few coins. The high and mighty lords of the Sorbonne manifested an interest in Gutenberg's invention much greater than that of Estienne and his king and the proof readers in the street. With the naïveté which characterizes all violent reactionaries they demanded outright the suppression of the devilish sorcery.

They could not frighten the Humanist king. Francis who spent many thousand *livres* a year on women, was not even afraid of syphilis. Friend of Rabelais and Leonardo da Vinci, admirer of Erasmus, sponsor of an anti-Sorbonne Collège de France, he reveled in the invigorating currents which came from Italy. The Sorbonne, however, was expert at ruining his enjoyment. For instance it kept him constantly busy fighting for the freedom and safety of the Humanist Berquin, who had committed mortal sin by demanding the distribution of vernacular Bibles. Again and again Francis rescued his friend from persecution at the hands of the Sorbonnese. They took advantage of a brief absence of the king and accorded his protégé only the mercy of strangling him before they burned him. The wise Erasmus had told his less foresighted friend, "Your enemy is not dead. A faculty is immortal."

Francis and his sister Marguerite, Queen of Navarre

landed in the thick of the fight when Marguerite brought her Humanist preacher to Paris. Noël Béda, the omnipotent secretary of the Sorbonne, incited a tremendous hue and cry. The mob roared, "To the flames! 'Tis God's will." The students in the Collège de Navarre satirized Francis' sister in a Rabelaisian masque. The infuriated king had troops surround and search the college; he banished, the headmasters and forbade all student comedies.

The Humanists made good use of the royal wrath. A philosophy teacher in Sainte-Barbe, Nicolas Copus, son of the king's physician, friend of Francisco, had become rector of the University of Paris. In this capacity he had to find out who had had the audacity to confiscate a pamphlet by Queen Marguerite, *Le miroir de l'âme pécheresse*, during a recent round-up of obscenity and scurrility in the Paris bookshops. Copus knew very well that the theologians had instigated this insult of the Humanist court, but he feigned ignorance in order to implicate the enemy to the utmost. He inaugurated a great investigation. Philosophers and doctors of medicine were able to prove their alibi. The theological faculty evaded responsibility by sacrificing a poor devil who had only carried out their orders. The scapegoat defended himself lamely; he had picked up the pamphlet by mistake while hunting copies of *Gargantua* and similar filth.

The king was enraged. Copus and his tribe congratulated themselves, prematurely, on a great victory. They

had forced the theological faculty to disavow a verdict,
to relinquish a book seized by the censor. The ruler of the
land defended publicly a princess who loved the Humanists. The new day had dawned. Overbold, the rector
Nicolas Copus launched open attack. On All Saints' Day,
in accordance with old custom, he had to preach in the
church Des Mathurins before the entire teaching body.
He arraigned the sophistical theology. To judge by its
style, the speech was written by Calvin. A friend of
Copus, he was then twenty-four years old and had been
an enthusiastic Humanist for a year. The audacious offen-
sive seemed completely successful. The ceremonies proceeded without incident. Copus, Calvin, and their friends
triumphed.

The Franciscans complained. The Parlement de Paris
summoned Copus before its bar. The rector ignored it.
The proper court for him was the academic tribunal.
He convened a general session of all the faculties.
Philosophers and Doctors of Medicine voted for him,
theologians and jurists against. This result, an equal
vote, created great confusion among the learned gentle
men. Suddenly the bailiffs of the Parlement appeared, in
the midst of the conclave, to arrest the rector. Copus
threw off his cloak of office and fled. He did not stop
for breath until he reached Basle. Calvin likewise de
cided "to bow the neck under voluntary slavery no
longer . . . to emigrate without hope of returning." A
search of his house yielded many letters which sent their
writers to the stake.

A KING CANNOT DO AS HE PLEASES

Francis did not come to the aid of his oppressed friends. The situation was too complicated for the royal Humanist. In the last analysis he was not a seeker of truth but "the most Christian and religious prince." He loved art, culture, vigorous life, freedom, but above all he loved the throne. Francis bethought himself of his duties. "As we wish to preserve the name of most Christian ruler, which our ancestors have handed down to us, there is nothing in this world closer to our heart than the destruction and complete eradication of heresies."

Francis had nothing to gain by the overthrow of the ecclesiastical order. He was independent of the Roman court. The clergy paid such important taxes that the confiscation of their property would not have been profitable. On the other hand, it was very convenient for the king to be able to recompense courtiers and soldiers with ecclesiastical offices which cost him nothing. The lover of freedom, the brother of Marguerite of Navarre, terminated the greatest scientific trial of his time with the decision: "It is by no means sufficient to translate the Hebrew of the sacred books according to the profane meaning of the words. They must be interpreted in the spirit of theological discernment."

Shoemakers and printers, shopkeepers and artisans sacrificed their interests to their ideals, as did a very few professors but not a single ruler.

Paradise in Babylon

It was bitterly cold in Paris. The Seine was frozen so hard that loaded wagons could be driven across the ice. Íñigo and Pierre made the retreat in a solitary house just outside the Porte Saint-Jacques. The younger man disciplined body and soul in the snow. At night, in a thin shirt, he slept on the woodpile. He ate nothing for six days. "You progress in proportion as you do violence to yourself," he had learned from *The Imitation of Christ*. During the fourteen-day retreat the new volunteer "did himself much violence," but even under the stern regimen he did not become a malevolent zealot. He prayed for Luther, Melanchthon, and Henry VIII. One must love the heretics and convince them that one worked for their own good. Of all Church Fathers he preferred Pope Gregory the Great. None other had made so clear the doctrine of purgation by fire.

Pierre had just returned from a visit to his home in Savoy. That January, 1534, before returning to Sainte-Barbe and beginning his preparation to be ordained a priest, he sought Íñigo's guidance, far from the distractions of the metropolis, to put his soul in order. The teacher administered the exercises which he had found efficacious in Manresa. He did not cram the pupil with doctrine, "For the soul is nourished not by repletion but by savoring and digesting."

PARADISE IN BABYLON

When going to sleep and in the time it took to recite Ave Maria, Pierre decided what exercise he would practice at midnight, the beginning of his new day. If he awoke, he excluded random thoughts. He saw himself as a sinner loaded with chains appearing before his Supreme Judge. He went out into the snow. He fixed his gaze on the firmament. The Lord looked upon him from above.

Pierre knelt, lay down, sat up. He tried many positions until he found the one most conducive to forgetfulness of self, the entrance of another world into his soul. Then he gave himself over to the meditation which his teacher had assigned for that day and that hour. For instance he saw Adam created on the plain of Damascus and placed in the earthly paradise, the first woman born from the rib of the first man, the temptation, the sin for which all must suffer, the eviction from Eden.

Pierre was not there to dream, to flit through celestial regions free from worldly care. The stern teacher required that the pupil apply to problems of conduct the insight which he gained in supernal vision. Far away as he had flown, he returned to criticize himself.

Pierre conversed with Him who hung on the Cross. "Why didst Thou, my Saviour, make Thyself human, descend from eternal life to temporal death and endure torture for my sins?" With the familiar respect with which an old servant addresses a kindly master, Pierre submitted his questions to the Crucified. Not one failed of answer. Burning with gratitude, Pierre turned upon himself. "How have I deserved infinite mercy? What shall I do to merit loving-kindness? What am I? What are billions of human beings to the angels and saints of Paradise? What are the angels and saints of Paradise to God? Insignificant as I am, tainted as I am, the angels have borne with me, yes, protected me, though they are God's sword. The saints have interceded for me. Heaven, sun, moon, and stars, the birds, and the fruits have served me. Earth has not opened to swallow me. All this forbearance, I, infected offspring of Adam and Eve, owe to my Saviour. My whole life shall be a single ardent thanksgiving to Him." Thus Pierre examined and dedicated himself five times a day between midnight and evening. Love urged action. What could he do for his Benefactor?

Pierre went inside. Windows and doors, shut tight, admitted not even a shimmer from the snow. Pierre murmured the *Anima Christi*:

> *Soul of Christ, consecrate me.*
> *Body of Christ, redeem me.*
> *Blood of Christ, nurture me.*
> *Water from the side of Christ, wash me.*
> *Sufferings of Christ, strengthen me.*
> *O merciful Jesus, hear me.*
> *May Thy wounds hide me.*
> *Let me never be parted from Thee.*
> *In my death hour call me.*
> *Then let me come to Thee*

166

PARADISE IN BABYLON

That with Thy Saints I may praise Thee
Throughout eternity.
Amen.

Íñigo's voice brought celestial splendor into the chill, dark room. The three Persons of the Holy Trinity looked down from their throne. They beheld the motley confusion of earth, the white men, the black, in peace and war, in joy and sorrow, health and disease, birth and death—all, all moving toward hell. The three Persons of Divinity meditated and took counsel. "Let us begin the salvation of the human race." The second of the three Persons, delegated as ambassador, became human and descended to earth.

"What can I do for Him," cried Pierre, "for the ambassador, the sacrificial victim?" Íñigo brought the great plain of Babylon before Pierre's eyes. The ringleader of the enemy sat on a high throne amid fire and smoke, fearful to behold. The hosts of evil assembled around him. He sent them over all seas, into all countries, into all cities and hamlets of the earth. "Set snares!" the infernal commander ordered. "Make men proud, greedy for riches and honors." "Do you smell the smoke about his throne, Pierre? Do you see Lucifer's malevolent grin? Have you heard his words plainly? Then look over there!" Beside Jerusalem the supreme General of all good had taken His stand. That gracious youth, clad in humility, was Jesus Christ. The men who listened to His commands were the apostles and saints. Íñigo's tone was gentle, benign, as if he echoed truly the words of the Imperator of all good. "Teach men so that they shall choose poverty, that they shall desire to be shamed and scorned." Pierre looked upon both generals. He weighed their words.

"Let me, O Lord," he besought, "always detect the imposture of the evil ringleader. Grant me, O Lord, the blessing of service in the army of humility which has taken its stand on the plain before Jerusalem."

The chill darkness of January enveloped again the exhausted teacher and pupil, who returned from vast distances to a bare room in a snowbound house outside the Porte Saint-Jacques.

Heretics to the Flames

PIERRE the humble, Francisco the proud, were not the only catch of the fisher of souls. Simon Rodriguez, a young Portuguese nobleman, had come to Sainte-Barbe on a royal scholarship. Delicate, vacillating, visionary, inclining toward contemplation and asceticism, he offered no resistance to the recruiting crusader. Íñigo no longer needed to court individuals for long years. His name drew candidates to him. Diego Lainez, master of arts at twenty-one, with huge Jewish nose and lively big eyes, an inexhaustible, rapid, and keen-minded worker, a great disputator before the Lord, had heard of the vehemently discussed student in Alcalá, and in Paris joined him at once. Lainez contrasted sharply with Rodriguez. The keen intelligence had no patience with renunciation and misty emotions. Exacting in his demands on the comrades, unsparing of himself, troubled somewhat because his forbears had belonged to Christendom for only three generations, he was the most gifted in the association, and for this reason the master kneaded him with special relentlessness.

Lainez' friend, Salmeron, adept in Latin and Greek at eighteen, did not yield much to Lainez in keenness of intellect, but was ever to retain a youthful spirit which Lainez never had. The third Castilian whom Íñigo received, the twenty-five year old Bobadilla, had studied logic and rhetoric in Valladolid as a boy, had heard lectures on philosophy and theology in Alcalá at thirteen. He came to Paris as a doctor of theology and lectured on logic. In spite of his precocious learning, he was by no means an anemic recluse. Precipitous, combative, he remained a hothead very difficult to manage. He had no means, no influence. He was terrified by his insecure future when he visited Íñigo. The teacher, become wise in the troubles of young men, ministered to body and soul, provided money, and recommended study of proved scholastic theologians rather than of suspected Humanists. "Those who dabble in Greek dally with Luther."

With great care Loyola prepared each soul by itself, according to the peculiarity of its structure. He would have no such catastrophic results as in Alcalá and Salamanca and at first in Paris. Not until he had guided each of the six, by a separate route, to his own goal, did he let any know of his efforts with the others. In those months a dying world was overwhelmed by currents of the new era. Íñigo, nearly twice as old as his disciples, inferior to each of them in learning, welded them together and charged them with energy. A moribund organism caught from them a vitality which was to continue for centuries. The union was ready to begin work in the summer of 1534.

In the quiet of the university vacation, in the early morning of August 15, Assumption Day, the six young

men and their teacher met in the Church of Mary on
Montmartre. Pierre, who had recently been ordained,
celebrated mass. As on all Sundays and holidays, each
received the sacrament. One after the other spoke the
vow which made a single will of seven diverse individuals. "On a specified day I will renounce all my possessions except subsistence money. I will go to Rome and
ask the Pope's permission to make the pilgrimage to
Jerusalem. I will remain in Jerusalem and there serve
God for my own sake and that of my fellow men, be
they believers or unbelievers. Should it be impossible
to make the voyage within the space of a year, or should
it be impossible for me to settle in Jerusalem, I am no
longer bound to go there or to remain there. On the
other hand I am obliged to place myself at the Pope's
disposal and do what he commands me, to hasten
wherever he may send me."

Tempestuous autumn followed the tranquil summer.
Some years before, when a Madonna image was found
desecrated in a suburb, the sacrilege had been expiated
with supplicatory processions and heretic burnings. Now
arraignments of "the abuses of the papal mass" were
posted on the streets of Orleans and Paris, even on the
doors of the royal bedrooms in the castles of Amboise
and Blois. Statues were demolished. Even the destruction
of churches and the plundering of the Louvre were said
to have been planned. Clerical forces mobilized. On
November 13, the lame shoemaker Barthélemy Mollon,
whose room had been a refuge for those inclined toward

protestantism, was burned in the churchyard of Saint-Jean. Two days later the same fate overtook the linen draper Jean de Dourg of the Rue Saint-Denis and a printer who had sold Lutheran pamphlets. On the seventeenth a mason, on the eighteenth a bookbinder who had bound Lutheran books, perished. After a writer, the journeyman of a miniature painter, and a printer from the south of France had been sacrificed, there was a temporary lull in the frenzy of persecution.

King Francis, the widely self-proclaimed Humanist, regarded the writers of the placards as "people who without doubt planned the overthrow of everything worth maintaining." He besought Heaven's pardon, not for the burned human beings but for the defaced monuments. On the day of the great expiatory procession, in which all dignitaries of the realm took part, a tax collector of Nantes, a law writer, and a royal singer were burned in the Rue Saint-Honoré. Before the Halles, a fruit and vegetable seller, a basket maker, and a cabinet maker went to the stake. Two days later a shoemaker's wife was burned because she had eaten meat on fast days. Among others, these suffered in the flames: the merchant in whose house Calvin had lived three years before; a dry goods dealer; a young student from Grenoble; a singer of the royal chapel who had put up the placards in the castle at Amboise. A few Lutherans were publicly flogged, robbed, and driven away. Ten Lutheran women were banished. On January 15, a royal herald rode through the streets of Paris to the sound of the trumpet and invited seventy-three fugitives to put themselves under the ax of the executioner. Many of these were already on the other side of the border. The victims included remarkably few university teachers and students, although the new doctrines had many adherents in academic circles. The learned gentlemen dodged nimbly, justified themselves skillfully, and denounced their colleagues and classmates. Educated, trained, they knew better than the printers, the linen drapers, the vegetable women, the hapless human fireworks.

The new student brotherhood lived on the plains of Damascus and Jerusalem rather than in the streets of Paris. It concerned itself with Lucifer and Christ, not with Calvin and King Francis. Decidedly these squires of the Pope did not favor innovation. In troubled Paris no distinction was made among Anabaptists, Humanists, and Lutherans. Everyone who departed from the norm was considered a heretic. Were seven inseparables, who received the sacrament every Sunday in the Carthusian church and discussed religion constantly, quite normal? Two Spanish students, observing that Íñigo possessed a manuscript which his disciples prized highly and prudently withheld, denounced the head of the mysterious sect. The enemy of Erasmus, the adversary of Luther, the teacher who won his disciples away from the influence of Melanchthon, powerful in the Paris lecture rooms, attracted attention, and therefore incurred the suspicion of being a Humanist and Protestant.

A Paris student must be careful how he associated

with the seven. Nadal, a friend of Lainez, Salmeron, and Bobadilla, saw them frequently, took part in their discussions, accompanied them to church on Sunday, but kept a distance. Lainez and Pierre tried vainly to win him over. Then the master made an effort. One day he went for a walk with the wary young man. Íñigo talked of Spain, of prisons and trials when he, the most loyal guardian of tradition, had been suspected as an innovator. They went into the church of Saint Dominic. The proselytizer read aloud a long letter in which he advised his nephew to renounce the world. "Therefore we must be indifferent toward all created things, so that we do not wish health rather than illness, riches than poverty, honor than shame, a long life rather than a short one." The young man was not to be caught. As they left the church, Nadal held up the New Testament. "I will follow this book. Where you would lead me, I do not know. Please do not speak to me about these matters again."

Íñigo stood in an ambiguous light cast by the flicker of faggots at the stake.

BOOK II

Pope and Emperor

ACCORDING to a Vatican proverb, he who goes into the conclave a Pope comes out a cardinal. Alessandro Farnese, whose election was virtually conceded beforehand, emerged as Pope Paul III. The astrologer Luca Gaurico had promised him the tiara twice before. This time the stars expressed neither favor nor disfavor. The College of Cardinals elevated him, not, by any means, because of his culture, intellect, and diplomatic adroitness, but simply because neither Charles nor Francis objected to him. The sly old gentleman had not committed himself in forty years. Having got along with six extremely different Popes, he seemed well qualified to maneuver the Church away from the storms which had beset Clement. Another circumstance spoke strongly in favor of Farnese. He was sixty-seven years old and had suffered a severe illness the year before. All the other cardinals, much younger than he, dallied with the hope of succeeding him. Paul III did not keep his tacit promise to go soon to the grave. The moribund candidate reigned longer than any pontiff of the century.

To the question, "When is Rome liveliest?" a monk replied, "Just after a Pope's death." The Romans based great hopes on a change. They greeted a new master enthusiastically, lavishing upon him the laurels which

177

he had not yet earned. Leo received tremendous ova
tions—and in his regime Christendom split in two. Poo
Clement, mocked on his bier, had begun his reig
auspiciously enough, eleven years before. The man o
letters who set the literary fashions certified him, i
advance, "the greatest and wisest and most honored Pop
for centuries." At Paul's inauguration the Christia
world rejoiced. Humanists in Germany, Italy, an
France, even those who sympathized with the Protestants
congratulated rapturously the cultivated man of th
world, from whom they expected tolerance.

Rome had an especial fondness for this new master
His luxurious standard of living appealed to a city whicl
had wearied of humiliation and penance. Though bor
near Orvieto he delighted in calling himself "an honor
ary Roman." The city authorities and the nobles o
highest rank marched with the commons and the rabbl
in a torchlight procession to the Vatican. Three tri
umphal chariots represented Rome, the Church, th
Faith. The great square in front of Saint Peter's, th
finest and holiest of the city, devoted at other times t
bull fights and the Papal blessing, blazed with fireworks
A merry-go-round turned in honor of Rome's own Pope
Paul relieved the burghers of the most burdensome cit
taxes. The poor received alms. It was easy to rule in th
first hours.

The haggard old gentleman had clawlike hands, pene
trating eyes, and a flowing white beard. This appendag
would have added dignity to benign features but it onl

accentuated the harshness of Paul's. Old, tired, yet not clarified; sanguine, irascible; he had cynical eyes and a long, pointed nose, which, despite the patriarchal beard, gave him the physiognomy not of a sage but of a fox. Sedateness, culture, increasing moderation tempered the crafty expression. Listening to him, one got the effect, chiefly, of apostolic dignity. He spoke, whether in Latin or Italian, softly, carefully, pedantically, diffusely. He was no more spontaneous in his dealings with people. He had too little life force and too much experience to let himself go wholeheartedly. Besides, the stargazers must sanction every move. If his nativity conflicted with that of the person who wished to see him, the most urgent negotiation would never come about. Diplomats despaired. They could get around a more forthright, less complex person ever so much more easily. To settle any matter with the Pope was considered almost as hard as getting to heaven.

Dealing with him was difficult for another reason, more decisive, perhaps, than his temperamental instability and his dangerous position between Francis and Charles. He became Pope too late. The time was alien to him. He had been a young cardinal under the murderer Alexander VI, the *condottiere* Julius II, the hedonist Leo X, but when he reached the papacy he was an old man. Long ago it had ceased to be proper for the supreme pontiff to put hated priests out of the way with white powders, to enlarge the Papal States in the manner of any reigning sovereign, to admire pretty dancing

179

girls, and to build noble monuments. One of his predecessors, the old, learned, and impotent Adrian, had sighed, "Ah, how much it matters that even the best virtue should manifest itself at the proper time." Paul had the virtues of past decades.

The young Alessandro Farnese had studied under the great Humanist Pomponio Leto. In the home of Lorenzo de' Medici and at the University of Pisa he developed a passion for pagan antiquity. He became famous as a builder in an age of ostentatious building; thriftily he increased the family fortune for the benefit of his heirs, whom he did not hesitate to avow, and in his less important role, his mere vocation, he served for forty years as a dependable, inconspicuous cardinal. If this master at exhuming and restoring remains of classic antiquity had any interest in contemporary matters no one ever heard him express it. He preferred to carry out his plans and ideas in quiet. Leo was amazed when he saw the villa which his taciturn cardinal had built in Bolsena. How could he afford it and how could he refrain from boasting of it? Paul loved only art and his family. In his own time it would have sufficed if he had given the Church his great intelligence and skill, the rich experience of a long life. Now other qualifications were required. He could not forgive Clement for stealing his last decade.

Flourishing Rome had been stripped by storm. The chair of Peter no longer had much attraction for a Farnese. The Pope now might only pasture the sheep, not shear them. In his unregenerate youth, ever since the great Jubilee of 1500, travelers had alarmed the world with their reports of "the Whore of Babylon." Yet the Papal sphere of influence had dwindled importantly only in the last few years. A third of Europe no longer obeyed the master of Christendom. At Clement's death Henry VIII asserted, "I care not who is elected Pope. I will take no more notice of him than of any priest in my realm."

Paul made the English bishop, John Fisher, a cardinal while he was a prisoner in the Tower. The tyrant with broad face and little eyes, who had eliminated the Pope's name from the prayer book and the divine services, jested, "I will send his head to Rome for the cardinal's hat." English and German Popes arrogated Paul's inheritance.

The Imperium Romanum had lost its splendor. Leo, who considered Christianity a myth, had exclaimed with gusto, "Let us enjoy the papacy!" Paul could have no such blithe unconcern. No longer might a Pope revel in the divine office, increase the state, enrich his family, trample enemies under foot, elevate his friends, worship beauty, and ignore the ominous manifestations of world-wide dissent. Catastrophe had made pomp bare and ridiculous. Paul came to the table after the feast, with the robust appetite of his generation.

The contemporary world interpreted the sack and desecration of Rome not as the exploit of a monarch, the orgy of rapacious mercenaries, but as a visitation of the wrath of God. Because the holy city Rome was depraved as Babylon, because the Church was a market of pardon for crime, the Lord of Hosts decreed "the end of the world."

All that was healthy in the pagan tradition was discredited. Cardinal Alessandro Farnese, however, had witnessed the sack of Rome in his sixties. At his age he would hardly swallow a new myth, hardly incur the inconveniences of a moral transformation. Locked in the Castel Sant' Angelo with the weeping Clement and the trembling cardinals, the friend of Leo thought the supposed "divine judgment" merely such a misfortune as might befall any sovereign. Suddenly the whole moral atmosphere changed. Though he could not alter himself radically he managed to change his manner. The more earnest and austere men of the new time spoke of him with benevolent tolerance, as of a grandpa making great efforts to understand the younger generation. "Our good elder," they called him, with kindly condescension.

Our good elder knew nothing of the little company which had sworn devotion to the Pope in matters great or small, on Montmartre, shortly before his accession. News that seven Paris masters of arts yearned to convert unbelievers might not have affected him very seriously when the greatest and finest war fleet of Christendom put out of Barcelona harbor. From the tower of Rocca in Civitavecchia he blessed the Spanish and Dutch, Portuguese and Italian crusaders assembled beneath him. Not only did he give his benediction, not only did he present the Admiral Andrea Doria with consecrated arms, he contributed galleys and money. He thought the expedition against Tunis a prelude to a general war against the Osmans. A religious war would protect his coasts against piratical visits of the infidel, would give the world the illusion that Papal Christendom still existed as a reality, and would keep Charles busy. This troublesome son of the Church was getting too big to handle.

The first booty from newly discovered Peru came to Seville at a most opportune time. Charles confiscated the entire cargo, compensating shareowners with interest-bearing bonds. Before sailing the Emperor obtained the blessing of the Queen of Heaven in the Montserrat cloister. The Holy Father sent him a consecrated sword and a banner embroidered with the image of Christ. Charles flew this pennon from his flagship. "The crucified Saviour," he said to his grandees with arrogant humility, "shall be our leader. I am only the standard-bearer."

The Spanish coasts had been in danger since the corsair Harudj Barbarossa had settled permanently in Algiers in response to an appeal of the Moors. After Harudj's death his brother Cheireddin Barbarossa established the great North African coastal empire extending from Tunis to Fez. His fleets paralyzed Spanish and Italian commerce. Cheireddin did not actually menace the Empire until the Sultan Soliman made him a

Turkish admiral. Then with eighty galleys and twenty-two smaller ships he harassed the coasts of Sicily and Italy as far as Genoa. On the return trip he took Tunis. Charles embarked on a crusade, under a blessed banner, to safeguard his possessions.

The Christians retook Tunis and plundered it righteously. The lock and bolts of the city gate arrived in Rome as a votive offering to "the Keeper of the Keys" and were exhibited in the vestibule of Saint Peter's. Fireworks and processions of thanksgiving throughout the Papal States celebrated the victory of true belief over false. Paul hoped that Charles would now strike the decisive blow at Constantinople, but the victor retired into his Neapolitan realm. He had done what was immediately necessary by taking Tunis, and the struggle over Milan concerned him more deeply. The holy war ended when Charles feared Soliman less than Francis.

For the first time since Charles' soldiers overran the city, nine years before, the Romans held carnival with the old abandon. Paul had given mask license, thus officially ending the long penance. There were races on the field of Testaccio. Mounted lancers skewered boars and bulls. As in the time of Leo the festal procession started from the Capitol, turned into the Via Papale, passed the Ponte Sant' Angelo, marched to the Vatican, then turned back to the left bank of the Tiber, to the Piazza Navona. Paul, the Old Roman, did not catch the holiday spirit as he looked on from Sant' Angelo. He laughed at a nonsensically ingenious play on his papal name: thirteen floats represented the triumph of the Consul Aemilius Paulus. He rejoiced at the defeat of the pirate Cheireddin. Yet Charles perturbed and annoyed him. The holy war had stopped before it started, and it was holy not least because it kept Charles occupied at a distance. Charles' idea of coming from Naples to Rome for a triumph to celebrate the victory over Tunis awakened uneasy recollections. To refute the rumor that he intended to establish a universal empire, Charles had promised to make his appearance in the Eternal City without many troops. What chiefly worried Paul was the fact—on which Charles counted too—that the Pope could no longer refuse to see the Emperor. Paul issued the invitation. He had to.

Despite Charles' request that there be no special festivities—a characteristic wish of powerful and intrusive guests—despite the pathetic state of the Papal finances, great preparations were made. Poets sang the victory of the Emperor. Bombastic Latin inscriptions vaunted the recent deeds in Africa as if they merited comparison with the Republic's campaigns against Carthage. Michelangelo built the triumphal arch. A host of artists worked on the decorations. Paul sent two cardinals to the border of the Papal State to receive the victor appropriately as he marched up from Naples. The College of Cardinals awaited him on the Via Appia beside the chapel of *Domine quo vadis*. All bells pealed as the last German Crusader Emperor marched into Rome.

SOLDIER OF THE CHURCH

Parading rulers almost always disappoint. When the eyes are tired of spectacular display and the crowd expects the grand climax of splendor, the royal personages present a drab contrast to their gaudy precursors. Charles offered such an anticlimax, but most effectively. After the critical Romans had admired four thousand imperial foot soldiers, five hundred horse guards, the ambassadors of Florence, Ferrara, Venice, Spanish grandees, the barons, the senators and the governor of the city, and fifty youths of the most aristocratic families in violet silk robes, he appeared, conspicuous by simplicity. Without jewels, without insignia of his imperial rank, attired in plain velvet, mounted on a white horse, he rode between two cardinals, a quiet, morose, not very impressive gentleman who appealed to the contemporary imagination less than Francis, Paul, or any little Italian potentate. Successor of the Roman Imperatores, he proceeded along the old, narrow, by no means imposing street of triumph, past the Baths of Caracalla, through the Arch of Constantine. In awe he halted before the Colosseum, just recently cleared of the buildings which long had hidden it.

A straight street had been cut through the Forum. Toward the Tiber, in the center of the city, two hundred houses and four churches had been razed to make way for the imperial procession. Cannon thundered as the cavalcade crossed the Ponte Sant' Angelo to the Papal Quarter, which was decorated as during the Corpus Christi festival. On the square of Saint Peter's the Em-

eror dismounted. The Pope awaited him in the portico
f the Basilica. The greeting which followed was elab-
rate, ceremonious, prearranged as liturgy.

Charles wanted to carry his point and get away before
Holy Week. Negotiations dragged out endlessly, fruit-
essly. He found himself, perforce, to his chagrin and
mpatience, participating in the greatest pageantry of
Christendom. Business must wait until Easter Monday.
Safe from Charles' importuning, Paul consecrated the
palms. He blessed the city and the world from the Benediction Loggia. He performed the ceremony of washing
he feet of twelve paupers in the hall of the Consistory.
On Friday he adored the Cross, barefoot, without insignia. On Saturday the bells tolled for the Vigil. The
Emperor, like every pilgrim to Rome, earned indulgences by attending each of the seven cathedrals. Easter
Sunday Charles received the sacrament from Paul at
High Mass. Had the victor of Tunis stayed in Rome for
his pious purpose? He had waited for an opportunity
o out-maneuver the "poor, landless, senile Pope." Easter
Monday his turn came.

An old law permitted the Emperor to attend sessions
of the College of Cardinals. Having failed to attain his
objective by diplomatic negotiations, Charles would now
bowl over the wary Pope by a surprise attack. The coffers were empty. Brother Ferdinand in Germany was
nettled by "the Oriental adventure," which was by no
means liquidated. Francis, the everlasting rival, kept
flirting with Charles' Protestants and vexing Italy by

his claims to Milan. Charles must have the Pope on his
side at any cost.

The Emperor appeared unexpectedly and took his
seat beside the Pope. Charles spoke an hour and a half
without interruption, in Spanish. His peculiar accent
mystified his auditors. With dignified frankness he announced his intention of clarifying the situation. He
would remind Their Eminences of the victories which
he had won against Turks and Moors in twenty years'
rule, and of his merits in combating the German heretics. He painted a dark picture of Francis, the disturber
of peace. Charles touched cleverly on a matter of great
interest to the Pope: only Francis had prevented Charles
from conquering Constantinople and the Holy Land.
Then came the heroics: the Emperor was ready to recognize the result of a duel with Francis as the divine judgment of the case. Infidels and heretics must not profit
from the dissension between true believers. Let Milan
and Burgundy be the prizes. He would give his adversary twenty days to consider the challenge.

Paul could follow Charles' Spanish only with difficulty. He was surprised, but an hour and a half was
plenty of time in which to get his bearings. He answered
calmly, politely, and noncommittally that he deplored
the split of Christendom. Everyone present understood
his meaning: "Leave me out of your quarrels!" Charles'
frontal attack had failed, but he did not give up. In his
impatience he interrupted the Pope. He made another
grandiose gesture in order to soften the effect of his rude-

ess. He looked at a piece of paper in his hand and re-
marked that he had quite forgotten to request His Holi-
ess to decide who was in the wrong. If Charles were the
guilty party, let the Pope support Francis, but if Fran-
is were to blame, let the Pope declare for Charles at
nce. Charles would recognize the Pope as arbitrator.

Paul expressed polite thanks for the honorable post
offered him. He knew that one must never judge a con-
lict between two stronger parties. Paul did not cherish
he delusion of his predecessors that the Pope could
old the balance of power. If his ally suffered defeat
he Pope would be lost. If his ally won a victory, the
Pope would find himself dragged along in the wake of
n overpowerful confederate. Paul had nothing to gain
nd everything to lose by taking sides. He delivered an
edifying sermon. He had faith in the magnanimity of
oth monarchs. He still hoped for peace. He would
mediate, strictly as a neutral. He did not say openly
hat the challenge to a duel could not be taken seriously,
hat the romantic proposal had been made repeatedly,
ow by Francis, now by Charles, and nothing had ever
ome of it. Paul denounced trial by combat as barbarous.
Two such valuable lives must not be jeopardized. Then
he donned his pontifical robes and started for Saint
Peter's, after calming the French ambassador with the
assurance that if he had had any previous warning he
would never have permitted the Emperor to deliver such
a speech.

Charles gave the Pope a diamond worth fourteen

thousand ducats. In return Paul sent him two Turkis
horses. He intended to give the Emperor a prayer boo
with a cover wrought by Benvenuto Cellini but the grea
artificer had not finished it yet.

The French ambassador demanded an explanatior
Charles said that he wanted peace, but if he were force
into war he would defend himself. Even if the Turk
should invade his states, he was resolved to ward o
the attack of the French, the Christian ruler asserted.

Francis had long been dallying with the Infidel. Su
tan Soliman, in a letter to his Christian ally, had eul
gized him as "defender of sovereigns." Christendom ha
ceased to exist.

The Prodigal Son

ÑIGO had been in the saddle twelve days when he turned
:om the highway down the lonely trail leading into the
[rola valley. The Paris master of arts remembered
:uesome stories of the remote and dangerous path. Two
rmed men approached, passed without speaking, then
:rned and followed him. Íñigo then banished his fears
y speaking to the suspicious characters in the local dia-
:ct. He found that his brother, hearing from acquaint-
nces of his arrival in Bayonne and of his intention to
isit Azpeitia, had sent the two to protect him. While
ñigo rode slowly toward Irun and San Sebastian, the
oyola family and its adherents prepared a ceremonious
:ception. Before the city gate of Azpeitia a procession
relcomed the returned wanderer. All the local clergy was
resent. Íñigo's prelate uncle invited him, on behalf of
ie head of the family, to the castle. Íñigo refused. As
sual, he took lodging in the refuge for the homeless.

The splendid reception annoyed him. Azpeitia merely
aid homage to its ruling clan. The prodigal son brought
ome no trophies. Since leaving, thirteen years before,
e had prepared himself in Manresa, Venice, the Holy
and, Barcelona, Alcalá, the Collège Montaigu and the
ollège Sainte-Barbe, and, having taken the oath on
lontmartre, was just ready to begin his life work. He

191

had nothing to display but a master's degree. Empty handed at the age of forty-five, a Loyola without glory he faced his expectant fellow townsmen in no complacent mood. Nor had kindly sentiment brought him back Paris physicians, diagnosing as indigestion the gallston cramps which tortured him for hours on end, though "the air of his native land would do him good." Besides he must notify the Xavier, Lainez, and Salmeron families of their sons' dedication. Íñigo had taken this painful mission on himself, knowing that the young men were hardly to be trusted in the midst of solicitous and practical relatives.

This danger did not exist for him. He knew no homesickness except for heaven, no love but that for the heavenly family. The Loyola clan living in the castle of his fathers not far from his lodging, the refuge for the homeless, simply did not matter to him. He was flesh of their flesh, but what was flesh to kinship in Christ? Martin sent him food from the castle kitchen. Íñigo gave it to the poor. Martin had a magnificent bed brought to the squalid burrow. Íñigo lay on the floor until a hospital cot was provided. Don Martin, chief of the Loyola tribe, had known for three years that his youngest brother had abandoned group solidarity and the ties of affection and pride. "I can still love anybody on earth," Íñigo had written from Paris, "only insofar as he is devoted to the service and glorification of God our Lord. If loved on my own account, not God's, I should no longer love Him with my whole heart." Martin could not expect

at this alien brother would rush into the arms out-
retched to welcome him.

However, he might at least preserve external decorum.
He compromised his family precisely where it had most
to lose. Lodged in a sordid house, under the same roof
with nameless vagabonds, a few steps from the splendid
place of his birth, Íñigo de Oñaz y Loyola went beg-
ing from house to house in the city in which he was
christened, in which everybody knew him, in which his
family had had wealth and honor for centuries. He announced his intention of instructing children in Christian doctrine. Martin predicted that he would find very
few pupils. "One will be enough," Íñigo replied.

Many came, not only children. He did not restrict
himself to private lessons. In the Basque country preaching after Lent was not customary. This preacher out of
season used the most personal data to point his addresses
on virtues and sins, his propaganda for confession and
communion which here, as everywhere else, were quite
out of fashion. The effect was sensational in a community
which had known this remarkable saint when he was still
an insolent cavalier. He had to speak outdoors. No
church could hold the throngs which came from far and
near.

Encouraged by success, the preacher developed into
a reformer. The local Alcalde, thinking, no doubt, that
the great family would appreciate the favor, gave him
complete authority. Íñigo assessed stern penalties for
card-playing, a favorite pastime of his sinful fellow

townsmen. He took vigorous steps to uproot anoth
scandalous custom. Basque girls went bareheaded un
they married, but many a woman, faithful to one m
though not legally married to him, covered her head
if entitled to marital status by holy sacrament.

The theologians of Alcalá and Salamanca, who h
forbidden him to teach the word of God without a licens
would have been amused to find the former rebel a ste
guardian of sanctified prerogative.

Unregulated begging likewise perturbed the holy me
dicant. The poor must receive their dry bread and th
soup according to statute. Azpeitia's son, who had begg
his bread in most of the cities of Europe, formulat
a police code to regulate begging. The priest, Don A
drés de Loyola, read the rules in Basque, at High Ma
The citizens of Azpeitia must elect two municipal ove
seers of the poor every year. These officers would colle
alms in the church every Sunday and holy day. Begga
who continued to go from door to door would be se
tenced to serve six days in jail at the first conviction a
to receive fifty lashes at the second. Citizens who ga
to beggars would be punished too. Vagrants able to wo
would be brought before the magistrate. Failure to r
port them would be punished by a fine of two real
Sturdy beggars would be sent to jail for six days at t
first conviction; at the second they would receive a hu
dred lashes. Loyola's reform resembled a legal opinio
pronounced a hundred and fifty years before, that wh
ever asked for bread, meat, cider, or money must ma

restitution by double the amount the first time, quadruple the second, and be hanged as a thief the fourth. Fourteen years before Loyola passed his social legislation, the city of Wittenberg had received similar aid from its great son who drafted rigorous ordinances regulating mendicants and vagrants. Loyola and Luther, worlds apart in their relations to God, were at one in their views of their fellow human beings.

Also the beggar Loyola was closer to Loyola lord of the castle than the castle to the tramp refuge. Íñigo had written to Don Martin, "In the words of the Apostle, we ought to use as if we did not use, possess as if we did not possess, and even have our wives as if we had them not." Don Martin probably never thought of pointing out to his dear brother the contradiction between that principle and a solicitude for owners so tender as to see danger for them if a beggar even went near them.

The reformer again suffered from his gallstones. He let himself be persuaded to move into the castle where he could have better care. On the streets of his native city he had seen only lazy beggars, time-wasting cardplayers, and concubines masquerading as lawful wives. In the house in which he had been born, spent his childhood, and mended his life, he found no tender associations, but only a scandal. One of the gentlemen of the castle had a sweetheart come to his room every night. Probably Íñigo had already heard gossip in the city. Certainly he was well equipped, by his youthful memories of the ways and means of smuggling a girl into Loyola castle, to act as house detective now. In spite of the pain from his gallstones he lay in ambush at night. Soon the wanton miss fell into the trap. He preached sternly to her, hour after hour, detaining her so as to expose her in the daylight and make sure that she would never come near the castle again. This exploit terminated his brief visit to the home of his fathers. He had had enough of the family, and surely the family had had enough of him.

Loyola pride had still to undergo a dread ordeal. Íñigo wished to go away like a beggar, afoot and alone. Don Martin insisted on a dignified departure. Finally they compromised. Íñigo de Loyola, escorted by his clan, would ride sedately, as a departing lord, to the Alsasua Pass, the frontier of the province. There he would dismount. Past the boundary of his family's sphere of interest he again became the poor pilgrim who had neither home nor kindred on earth.

He followed, in the opposite direction, the same route over the Alsasua Pass to Pampeluna that he had taken as a wounded officer being carried into Loyola Castle. Like the hero of Pampeluna he was still a gallant vassal. Possessing all the qualities of the great general, he could not yet lead, he must follow. As he obeyed Charles in Pampeluna he would now obey the Pope. The vicars of the episcopal courts, the Dominicans, the parents of his friends still considered him a rebel only because in preserving what was going to pieces he often worked more subversively than those who built the future. The lord of Xavier, Don Juan de Azpilcueta, viewed the elderly, unattractive little man who visited him in the Castle Obañoz near Pampeluna only as an unbalanced agitator who had turned young Francisco's head. Don Juan had heard many unfavorable things about the fisher of souls who now brought a letter from the younger Xavier. "That you may understand fully what kindness Our Lord did me in making me acquainted with Master Íñigo, I give you my word of honor, in a lifetime I could never repay my debt of gratitude. Not only has he aided me in need, by lending me money and introducing me to helpful friends, he also induced me to turn from the bad company which, in my inexperience, I did not recognize as such. Now that the heretical nature of their ideas is coming to light, here in Paris, I would not, for aught in the world, have had any connection with them."

The little man had turned Francisco from heretical associates, but also from useful employment. To become a Papal guard! The Pope could get along very well without the services of a crippled tutor and a student corps. Don Juan skimmed the rest of the letter: "I ask you, with all my heart, to seek the company of Don Íñigo, consult him, and give heed to his words. Believe me, his advice and his discourse will benefit you greatly. He is veritably a man of God. Paris, March 25, 1535. Your devoted servant and younger brother, Francisco de Jassu y Javier." Of course the young fellow would never listen to reason. Once settled down to the serious business of life, he would forget the nonsense which seemed all-important to a student. Don Juan must press the authorities to acknowledge Don Francisco's status as an hidalgo and so secure him the post in the cathedral of Pampeluna. Meanwhile there was no use trying to rescue him from the company of fanatics. After all, they were not heretics, and a Xavier knew what a Loyola was.

Íñigo visited the Lainezes in Almazan and the Salmerons in Toledo, with similar results, and took ship at Valencia for Genoa. He was urged not to travel by sea. Cheireddin Barbarossa had recovered from the blow which Charles had struck the year before. In Mahon, on the island of Minorca, bonfires celebrating the victory of Tunis were still burning when a fleet flying the imperial flag put into the harbor. The inhabitants, expecting a visit from the triumphant Charles, were taken completely by surprise and fell easy victims to the crafty pirate. Since then Cheireddin had cruised at will between the Balearic Isles and the Spanish coast. The ship evaded the pirates but encountered heavy storms. The rudder broke. Much of the cargo went overboard. The passengers prepared to die.

Landing at Genoa in the middle of November, Íñigo traveled, by foot, along the Ligurian coast, then eastward through Tuscany and across the old Apennines pass. The descent into the Val di Reno proved very difficult. The autumn rains had turned all the roads into tenacious mud. Often he was in water over his knees. He lost his way repeatedly. Sometimes he crawled on his hands and knees, clinging to stones and bushes along narrow footpaths cut into sheer mountain wall, high over the thunderous river.

Two weeks before Christmas he came to Bologna, where he intended to continue his studies. Entering by a narrow slippery bridge he fell into the moat before the city gate. Dripping with water, smeared with mud, greeted by the laughter of the idle onlookers, the theology student went on into the university city. Ragged, hungry, the former regulator of begging hobbled all over Bologna without receiving a single coin. He caught malaria as a result of the mud bath. Disheartened, he revised his plans and took up his pilgrim staff again.

In Venice, where, thirteen years before, he had merely paused on his way to the Holy Land, he would do pious work among the poor and outcast, while awaiting the arrival of his disciples. The lawgiver who had suppressed gambling, who had upheld the sanctity of marriage, and regulated begging saw Venice as Azpeitia on a vast scale. The city drew enormous revenue from a lottery of which the losing tickets were marked "patience." Counterfeiters drove out good money with bad. Music and literature, according to one who knew whereof he spoke, "provided keys to unlock the portals of feminine chastity." The Greek sin flourished as did that of Eden. Beggars swarmed, without supervision. Concubines even enjoyed considerable prestige. The crusading reformer took a humble lodging in a squalid quarter. He who had tyrannized the morals of a remote Spanish province was not abashed by the wealth, splendor, power of the illustrious republic.

Rosy View of Venice

THE bloom and fragrance of strange plants filled the corridors of Palazzo Loredan. Gilt leather, Flemish tapestries, and brocades covered the walls. Turkish carpets lay underfoot, and velvets embroidered with gold decked the tables. In salons that were already crowded with carved and gold-inlaid furniture, credences stood burdened with majolica from Faenza, Caffagiolo, and Urbino. Throughout the vast palace there was a fabulous display of precious arms, paintings by the masters, rare books, and musical instruments.

The lady of the house, Donna Angela Zaffetta, enjoyed a far-reaching reputation for her beauty and charm. Her movements—when she left the city, when she returned—were eagerly followed. Diplomats communicating with their governments on matters of political importance rarely failed to mention her by name. She was fond of celebrities, and even fonder of birds and exotic beasts. Her walls resounded with the cries of parrots, the chatter of monkeys, the eloquence of the Republic's dignitaries. Her table was superb; modeled on the recipes of Bartolomeo Scarpi, concoctions were prepared with rare spices, flavored with perfume, sprinkled with gold dust. It was there that gold toothpicks were to be found, and, of course, Venice's two proudest products: the fork

—and Pietro Aretino, favorite of the capital, and idol of the world.

That name was fame itself! Aretino was echoed and reflected everywhere. Gold, silver, and bronze medals were struck in his honor. On one of these he was shown seated on a throne, receiving emissaries laying gifts at his feet. The inscription read: "Princes who receive the tribute of nations, pay tribute to their servant." His bust in marble and plaster, his portrait on the façades of buildings, in the frames of mirrors, on toilet cases, and majolica plates, invited comparison with Alexander, Caesar, and Scipio. Troubadours sang his deeds. And it was to him an admirer had once written: "God is the highest truth in heaven. You are truth on earth."

He was showered with gifts like a sultan. Soliman sent him a slave girl. The King of France presented him with a chain of enameled gold and assured him that other objects of value would follow. Charles, the Gracious, urged him to accept a yearly pension. One Pope wanted to throw him into the Tiber, but Paul had granted him blessing and money. What manner of man was this who, right after the plundering of Rome, could through his own resourcefulness set himself up as arbitrator between Emperor and Pope? And at the same time be courted by Soliman and Paul, Charles and Francis!

If one followed the conversations at Angela Zaffetta's, one came away with the impression that he was a legendary character. Malicious stories attributed a variety of monstrosities to him. Time after time, the hetaerae and senile literati who gathered in the lecherously frescoed palace hall improvised new variations on the familiar theme. Girls who begrudged the lady of the house her great love, resorted to the shabbiest old wives' tales. They knew for a certainty that he was the son of a prostitute, that he was born in a charity hospital. His sisters had led lives of shame. He had stolen a silver cup from Agostino Chigi, the banker who had been his patron for years. In Vicenza he had been a street singer, in Austria a servant; as a monk in Ravenna, he had acted as go-between in unspeakable affairs. In Rome he had been court fool for Leo and Clement. The fictitious details seemed inexhaustible.

The literati listened and absorbed it all, but not without first taking precautions against being observed. It would go hard with them if they were caught. Still, they had heavy scores to even with their colleague. He was successful; that—like his talent—could not be denied. But God had compensated them for Aretino's fame and wealth in making him the object of their moral indignation and scorn. How repulsively he flattered the great of the world! Had he not assured Andrea Gritti, ruler of the Republic of Venice, that Gritti deserved to rule two Venices, one Rome, and four Egypts? He had once ridiculed Emperor Charles' pathetic figure and jutting lower lip; an imperial annuity had changed his opinions; in acknowledgment he had written Charles: "Just as God enlarged the world for your accomplishments, so must he raise the vault of heaven: infinity itself is not

as vast as your renown." His letters to great rulers had
just appeared in book form. As the first contemporary
collection of its kind, *Marfisa* attracted wide attention.
The author's gratitude to his patrons was revealed in
a highly ambiguous light.

The greatest stir arose from Aretino's account of his
recent pact with the Pope. The Holy Father required
the deletion of certain passages directed against Clement
and Cardinal Giberti, and suggested the substitution of
more favorable ones; in addition the repentant sinner
was to go to confession like a good Christian; his reward
would be a round sum of money and permission to print
Marfisa. It was a question of striking a bargain with
his hatred, and that was no easy matter. Giberti had
once had him ambushed and wounded. Clement had
known of the murderous attempt. Its instigator was none
other than the Bishop of Verona, the Pope's own minister and intimate. Clement had, nonetheless, ignored
the almost fatal incident. The author had voiced his resentment by writing in the Roman ruler's album: "It is
better to roast in hell than to live in the Roman court."
But now Clement was dead and Paul sat in his place. The
old hatred bore good interest. Why, after all, allow dust
to collect on something that could be turned to easy
profit? Paul's advances filled him with religious fervor;
he repented his sins, tears streaming from his eyes. He
promised to alter his life.

But keeping that promise was another matter if one
lived at Domenico Bolani's, off the Ponte Rialto, in the

richest and most corrupt quarter of the city. The girls were too willing, the music was too wild, the laughter too gay. It was difficult to alter habits and ways that were set in indolence and sensuality. Pietro Aretino's views exactly suited his sybaritic mode of existence. "Live while the living is good!" was his advice, and he observed it implicitly himself. His pleasures were as varied as joy-loving Venice. Yet he was aware of those for whom life was neither sweet nor kind, and he attempted, in his way, to correct the defects of an existence which he found so rosy.

Proudly referring to himself as the "secretary of humanity," he boasted that the marble stair of his own house was as deeply worn by human feet as the pavements of Rome by the wheels of triumphal chariots. Soldiers, monks, and students sought his advice. Turks and Jews, Frenchmen, Germans, and Spaniards, came to see him. He was the oracle of the city. All complaints of injustice and need reached him. If anyone were unlawfully jailed, Aretino was asked to get him out. If a poor woman were expecting a child, Aretino would pay the confinement. If another were sick, Aretino would send for the doctor. On a single day as many as twenty-two women, suckling their young in their arms, found food and sustenance in his house. At Easter, his doors were flung open to the hungry boys and girls of the quarter. Within a few years, Domenico Bolani's house was ruined; it was no longer a home. It had become a crowded passage-way. If the master himself wanted

o work, he had to creep off to Marcolini, the printer,
or visit his friend, Titian. The "secretary of humanity"
divided his money and time between the children of
the poor, hungry mothers, and his women. He practiced
charity, not for any of the reasons Christ had practiced
it, but simply because he was Aretino, the champion of
joy, the enemy of misery. His pen produced no *Ordinance for Beggars*; it produced money to be lavished
on rich and poor, on whore and saint.

Aretino cared very little what the world was coming
to. He had no principles or compunctions. He passed
no moral judgments on his own actions or on those of
his fellow creatures. For him, life was a vital force, and
he stood at the very source of it. His eyes missed nothing, his ears heard all, his senses reacted to every tremor
and movement. He had no more moral character than
a seismograph. His pen was merely the gauge of what
annoyed or delighted him at the moment, recording
every sudden change of mood. He followed no system
or doctrine; no tradition or convention impeded him. In
his room, there were no books—only paper, pen, and
ink. He never polished or rewrote; he had no feeling
about posterity or immortality. The one difficulty, he
found, was in getting a central idea; after that "nothing
mattered but speed and ingenuity." He worked easily
and was proud of it. If he had devoted to his literary
output one third of the time he spent on idleness, he
would have kept all the printing presses in Europe busy.
In reality, he was not unlike those Venetian merchants

who ventured out into new worlds and returned with fantastic treasures.

For some time now, astrologers had been publishing their prophecies in journal form. These *Judica* were brought out in large editions and contained articles on the weather, the imminence of war, the state of affairs between the various princes. It was here that Aretino found the most useful outlet for his talent. Not by following the stars, but by following the movements of the people in power whom he knew. Since he participated in their political and private intrigues his forecasts proved more reliable than those based on the constellations. His *Guidici* resemble a mosaic maliciously pieced together with bits of information and gossip. On the Rialto, they sold as quickly as they came out.

The civilized world was expanding. Man and his tasks were no longer simple. Knowledge had freed itself from the restrictions and narrow order of the old world. "He who does not strive for power, deserves to be a slave," became the motto of the new race which superseded those overlords of Loyola and Xavier who did not strive for power but possessed it. Pietro Aretino, the writing conquistador, had the courage of his hunger plus the sharp tongue and ready wit to benefit by it. His friends said he had the power to bury the living and raise the dead. It was a facility he exploited recklessly, as the first great robber baron of the pen. He conquered more with that weak implement than former generations had conquered with the sword. He showed writers what a weapon they yielded. Hitherto, the literati had been court dependents; no author could live without an influential patron. Aretino set himself up and went into business on his own. He made it clear that his services were valuable, that they could be sold elsewhere, and that they would go only to the highest bidder. He informed the world at large that "the prick of need and not the spur of fame caused him to blacken paper"; that "he would not hesitate to praise those who deserved censure." He lived, "by the sweat of his ink," and at the expense of those who sweated at his words. On the title pages of his writings, he generally described himself as *"per la grazia di Dio uomo libero."* He was not so much "a freeman by the Grace of God" as a free agent by the grace of his sharp, profit-yielding pen. Like every modern slave, he was free only to play off his masters against each other. His pen scratched when payment was not immediately forthcoming; it was tractable when he was paid.

The trick of turning words into money was his chief talent; honors and empty titles held no interest for him. His net of importunity and extortion was spread from Venice over the wide world. He sent letters everywhere; in reply pensions and jewels poured in, trinkets for his women, exotic fruits. He dispatched his agents like pioneers into strange countries where they could prospect for gold and inform their employer where it would pay to dig. Without shame or self-consciousness, Aretino baited his victims, "Although my talent is slight, it will

keep your name alive for the next thousand years, if onl
you give me sustenance for the next twenty or thirty.'
And his great, moneyed clientele responded; no doub
they considered the monuments he set up more durabl
than marble, bronze, and gold.

Somber View of Venice

T IS possible that Aretino while on some dark mission
into remote Venice may have met Íñigo. They were contemporaries in time and place, although, in reality, they
lived centuries apart. Loyola saw nothing but the disintegration of the old order in a world that was expanding and awakening to new hope. He became obsessed
with forcing whatever was fresh and flourishing into the
grooves and patterns of the past.

Perhaps he would never have recognized Aretino as
the Great Adversary, had they met. The famous rake and
confident of whores observed all the religious rules. He
was on the good side of the clergy; he had written books
on Christ, Mary, Saint Catherine, and Thomas Aquinas.
He was no enemy of the Pope, he had merely turned the
ruler's humiliation into profit. Íñigo must have shared
Aretino's scorn for Luther, "the archpedant." If he had
come upon the sensualist of the Ponte Rialto at confession, sobbing and overwhelmed with contrition, begging
God's indulgence, promising reform and forbearance,
even Loyola, who was up to the devil's own tricks, would
never have uncovered the enemy in this pious, gentle
ignore Aretino.

But their paths never crossed. Not because the twelve
ducats which Isabela Roser sent her poor sick friend,

209

and the meager assistance from the Archdeacon of Bar
celona would never have supported an apartment on
the Rialto. The reason was simply that Loyola lived in
a different climate, grew from another root, looked to
ward another heaven. What if the scene from his window
was drabber than the view from the Bolani Palace? The
descendant of feudal lords dwelt on another plane. What
ever existed beyond his damp cellar belonged to the
devil. Now and then, it was true, he would emerge to
track Lucifer down, but the world outside the hole in
which he slept seemed inaccessible and obscure. He
could discern nothing in it but the features of Satan.

He was best able to study these features among the
people who inhabited his own quarter—the low prosti
tutes, the unemployed who lived by theft and murdered
for profit. Yet, he overlooked the causes that produced
prelates and beggars, scholars and prostitutes. He
avoided conversation with seamen who could have in
formed him of the city's shipping traffic. He ignored the
talk on the San Marco, never ventured behind scenes in
the greatest capital in the world. He simply sat in a for
lorn corner of the earth and addressed his opinions to
Archdeacon Jacob Azador: "The divine judgments are
inscrutable; we may not inquire into the causes for His
dispositions; we may only weep and implore Him to
improve our moral systems." Fatalistic Íñigo should have
gone to some intelligent banker or exporter for his infor
mation, instead of ignoring what was happening before
his eyes. He might have discovered that "divine judg

ments" were not entirely inscrutable. He might very well have inquired into the causes of "divine dispositions." Such causes could sometimes be found. Weeping was scarcely necessary when moral systems could be improved on the basis of correct insight. Saintly Íñigo de Loyola who was familiar with all the ramifications of the Christian soul, shut off and isolated from life, should have occupied himself less with the sensual agitations of Sister Theresia Rejadella in the Santa Clara cloister, and more with the machinery and organism of the Venetian Republic. He could have learned on the Rialto, say in the Palace of the Camerlenghi, or in the Fondaco dei Tedeschi, or in one of the powerful banking houses. that:

The state of Venice was strategically situated between four important trade routes. The first led to Alexandria, commercial capital of the Orient. Here, occidental wares were exchanged for Indian treasures. The second led to Constantinople and the Crimea. Here, wax and soap were exchanged for Ukrainian products. The third route crossed Cyprus to Syria and Haleb-Aleppo, then continued on through Bagdad to India. The fourth and western route followed the North African coast into the interior of the Dark Continent. Here, paste pearls and inferior cloth bought the gold and silver required for trade with the Orient and Spain. What was Íñigo's awareness of this system when he attempted to save the Venetian soul? His sphere of activity extended no farther than cardplaying. His only worldly contacts were beggars and prostitutes. What connection did he find between the condition of the Venetian merchant marine and Angela Zaffetta's lavish banquets, Pietro Aretino's lax morals and the godlessness of his own quarter?

The blood stream of splendid Venice was diseased, as any bank clerk could have told him. Venetian commerce had hitherto been nourished on profits made in the exchange of both manufactured goods and raw materials. Business, however, was not what it used to be. The Indian market now belonged to the Portuguese who had rounded the Cape of Good Hope. The next important market fell to the Osmans in Egypt. The Mediterranean trade, which could escape from complete isolation only by going from Venice into the Red Sea and thence into the Indian Ocean, had become small-town stuff. The impractical Asiatic land routes had virtually fallen into disuse. The great western territories were becoming self-sufficient. In the north, England had become a powerful competitor in the very profitable manufacture of wool. France, the leading Atlantic power, was even intruding on the eastern trade. Four years before that, Venice had been forced to discontinue its line to Flanders and England. Even closer home, business was falling off. Florence and Genoa were actively competing in the Levant and in the Adriatic. Did these setbacks concern Íñigo? He had no desire to trade with England or India. He desired only to create faith and morality in his fellow men. The unemployed worker might at least be as honest as the head of a large firm. The hungry streetwalker must

212

guard her reputation just as carefully as the most patrician beauty!

The same year that the English-Flemish line was discontinued, a law was enacted forbidding all Venetians to use alien merchant ships. Greeks, Armenians, and Jews hastily turned to merchantry. The men of Venice shifted their interests from water to dry land. They entered workshops, solicitors' offices, banks. Losses in the world of trade, however, were not compensated by profits in the world of finance which had its own troubles. The state, which appealed to "patriotic duty" in the placing of loans, defaulted both on principal and interest. What made the crisis all the more serious was that the Venetians did not produce their own foodstuffs but depended on Turkey for grain and cured meat, on Austria and Hungary for fresh meat and wood, on Spain for wool. Iñigo, however, demanded no explanations for wealth, prostitution, or thievery. He would have stopped being Iñigo if he had. Yet, all of God's ways were not inscrutable. Nor were all the cries for salvation which echoed through Venice, at the time, His doing. Prostitutes did not differ from virtuous women simply because of their sinful hearts. Iñigo might have come nearer the truth in the city's gilded palaces.

Naturally, if all the souls the disciple of Christ intended to save were as willing as he to go without food and shelter, and to praise their Saviour, Venice's dependence on Turkey, Austria, Hungary, and Spain would have possessed no consequence whatever. But neither the prelates nor their women were anxious to give up their table luxuries for the Body of Christ. Venice was not, as Íñigo thought, a place in which, by God's inscrutable decree, a hundred and sixty-two thousand incorrigible souls dwelt together, some in squalor, others in splendor and wealth. It was more like some earthly organism which had once been too richly nourished and was now becoming diseased. The soul in such a body usually goes the way of the flesh.

Nothing betrays a man more than his limitations. Íñigo was incapable of seeing any specific human being in relationship to his environment. He observed no difference between the man of commerce and the peasant who had never ventured beyond the Guipúzcoa province. Man merely lived in a tragic interval between Paradise and Judgment Day. Here on earth, there were only two kinds of people, followers of Christ and incorrigible sinners. The sinners allowed evil women to pass for respectable ones; condoned prostitution because it reduced cuckoldry. The state itself was sinful when it augmented its educational budget by taxing streetwalkers. How did these evil practices originate when the Church, the headquarters of the Saviour, was founded against them? By a gradual falling away from the Church. Confession and communion were out of fashion. Fast days and holidays were rarely observed. Most Christians did not know the Pater Noster, the Ave Maria, the Ten Commandments, and the Articles of Faith. Few could make the Sign of the Cross. What had caused this falling away? The corruption of the Priests! Íñigo stopped there. That was all he needed to know. The Church must be set in order. But wasn't the collapse of the Church and its institutions merely part of a much greater havoc? What had caused it? Who was responsible? Íñigo did not ask. He knew. God's servants were guilty.

The Church and its servants are never better or worse than the time in which they live. Priests have always been too much derided or too much honored. In the days of Pietro Aretino and Angela Zaffetta, the House of God was, in essence, a market place where toilettes were displayed, where lovers met, where glittering hetaerae made their appearances. Justice was meted out during mass. Jewish courtesans read Hebrew psalms as guests of Christ. The daily routine of God's servants consisted of christenings, weddings, and funerals. Priests could not preach. They could not even read, except perhaps with great difficulty. The few who actually knew some Latin mispronounced it. As for the monks, the spiritual élite, they remained aloof and scholarly in their cloisters, exerting little influence on the world outside. The mendicant monks, on the other hand, who still retained contact with the people, played to the gallery and staged fraudulent miracles with the aid of paid accomplices. Cynics ridiculed and maligned the nunneries and even the great Gasparo Contarini, chief of Paul's ministers, referred to them as substitute brothels.

This was the Church, from foundation to steeple. Ippolito d'Este, who for thirty years enjoyed the title of

Archbishop of Milan, never once set foot in the diocese which supported him handsomely. "Ragged Capuchins" functioned in place of the absentee, worldly-wise clergy, preaching of Jupiter and Juno. What of the Pope? Paul, at the very beginning of his pontificate, had bestowed the purple as well as various lucrative offices upon his two grandsons, aged fourteen and sixteen. When Charles reproved him, he referred to several of his predecessors who had elevated their dependents to cardinalships in the cradle. Íñigo realized that God's servants were to blame. He had, none the less, consecrated his life and blind devotion to God's highest servant. Íñigo knew that God had turned from His world because it had first turned from him. But he did not know that the Venetian patricians, threatened by the rising *bourgeoisie*, had hit upon the idea of shutting their daughters in convents to conserve their doweries. The "sinful" nuns were none other than repressed patrician girls, hungry for life.

Íñigo never saw natural causes. The blinding light of his devotion obscured God's more visible ways.

Pietro Aretino's name was given to a type of glass vase, a breed of horses, and a host of gay young girls. The "Aretinese" were a race of young ladies who had passed through the master's bedchamber and had been ennobled there. Íñigo's name was given to a few wretched masters of arts who now appeared in Venice in the caps and gowns of Paris students, bearing pilgrim staffs in their hands, and wearing breviaries and bibles in scrips at their sides. After a separation of twenty-two months, they had come, reinforced by three Frenchmen, to keep their appointment with the master.

The journey via Metz, Basle, Constance, and the Rescheideck Pass, had been arduous. Pierre, Broët, and Le Jay had celebrated mass daily, but that had scarcely offered adequate protection against the hazards of the war zone. As long as they wandered through France and Lorraine, they passed for harmless pilgrims bound for a destination south of Nancy. If they were questioned where the Spanish were the enemy, the four Frenchmen did the talking. In Germany they passed for pious pilgrims, but en route to Loreto where the magistrate of Strasbourg arrested them as suspicious characters, the Spaniards held forth and the French, who were the enemy this time, kept their peace. The international character of the group often protected it from victimization at the hands of nationalistic bigotry and prejudice.

The band had its first taste of an apostate city in Basle. The church, which lacked both altars and holy paintings, was used as a workshed; heretics buried their dead like beasts, without ritual or ceremony, without candles or prayers. Once beyond Basle, the students waded through snow and abandoned the main highway. By nightfall, they had arrived at an inn where a peasant celebration was in full swing. It turned out to be the wedding of the village parson. The friends couldn't have been more alarmed if they had walked straight into purgatory. They had never witnessed such cavorting, such boisterous dancing and carousing. The priestly groom himself carried a broadsword which he brandished under their noses, from time to time, in none too friendly a fashion.

En route to the Lake of Constance, they made the sober acquaintance of one of these newfangled priests. He was a poorly educated, friendly, and trusting soul. He wanted to sit with the students and proudly introduce them to his children, show them his books. Íñigo's disciples preferred to avoid close contact with the Lutheran taint. The good-natured Protestant took a seat nearby. A conversation, chiefly conducted by Lainez, the dialectician, slowly ensued between the two tables. The shrewd casuists who had been trained at Sainte-Barbe and the Sorbonne, and could resort to Aristotle and Thomas, soon reduced the amiable man at the next table to abject silence. He sat there, paralyzed with embarrassment and ignorance, while they mercilessly made their points one by one. "Why," they finally parried, "do you adhere to these beliefs which you cannot defend?"

The discussion had gone too far. The happy paterfamilias' patience had been more than tested. "You will find out for yourselves," he replied, "when you are in jail, tomorrow, whether or not I can defend my doctrines." The friends might have learned a great deal concerning the nature of truth from this statement.

Their report of the journey to the master, however, did not end on this bitter note. They had another, more consoling story to tell. The world, it was true, had fallen on evil ways, but there was still hope. They had been convinced of this by a poor, old woman whom they had encountered near Saint Gall. She had been driven out of the city to a pesthouse where she lived believing herself to be the last person on earth who still kept faith. The moment she beheld the students in their black robes, wearing rosaries about their throats, she realized her God still prevailed. The sight of the pious men revived precious memories. The old crone joyfully produced an apronful of plaster fragments, arms, legs, heads of saints which the heretics had smashed in their campaigns. The friends kneeled reverently in the snow and kissed the desecrated objects.

The ten, in accordance with their oath, were prepared to begin their journey to the Holy Land. But it was still January and they were free until Pentecost—free, that is, for other services. They had just come through French rain and German frost, but they hardly expected to rest through a Venetian spring. The name, "Íñigo" was synonymous with constant activity. The master attached five of the students to the San Giovanni e Paolo Hospital, and the others to the Hospital of the Incurables. These young, wellborn scholars were required to perform a variety of menial tasks. They made beds, washed night vessels, swept and scrubbed floors, nursed the sick, buried the dead.

They were not merely unpaid nurses. Helping their fellow men was their compensation. They profited in humility. Rodriguez shared his bed with a leper who had been denied admittance at the hospital. The empty gesture scarcely benefited the leper, but the student won a moral victory over himself. Francisco had to massage a man whose back was running with open sores. The young nobleman was filled with dread and nausea but he was well-repaid, spiritually. He smeared his hands with the infection, then touched his lips. He passed the night in horror, convinced leprosy had already reached his throat. It was an experience that paved the way to a wonderful, lifelong assurance. He lost his repugnance to foul diseases; he had passed another stage on the road to freedom.

Within a short time the students had become almost as famous as the "Aretinese." But what were these young men after? Did they expect to change the world? To free themselves from all earthly ties and values? They, themselves, were not quite sure. It sufficed that he who had shown them the way had already gone beyond it. Señor de Loyola, a frail and unwell man, "could endure poverty no longer." He conserved his failing strength for his studies. He would never again squander his energy in asceticism. He was no longer the symbol of piety. Nor did he torture himself to imitate the traditional mode of sainthood. Within the narrow margin of his limitations, he had broadened his beliefs. He was determined to fight the old cause with new weapons.

Courtesans and Ascetics

SIGNORA TULLIA D'ARAGONA, who had written as many poems as she had made men happy, came to Venice from Ferrara. She was no ordinary adventuress of obscure origin. Cardinal Ludovico d'Aragona, a gallant and witty gentleman, famed as a connoisseur of art and feminine beauty, had acknowledged her as his daughter. She had been trained by singing and dancing masters. Scholars respected her knowledge of classical languages. She excelled in the social arts, played various musical instruments, and danced the *rosina* and *pavana* so seductively that she had been compared to Cleopatra. The center of excitement, wherever she was, this calm, oval-faced lady pursued the time-honored custom of favoring and breaking men's hearts.

In Rome, Filippo Strozzi had defended her good name with his sword. He had hardly left the city before slanderous rumors began to circulate again. This time a group of young habitués took up the cudgels. Six youths, led by an Orsini, issued a long manifesto, proclaiming their readiness to defend Tullia's honor. Tullia smiled slyly and took to bed with a German who was very rich, to be sure, but very ugly as well.

When she came to Venice, she was in her early thirties, an awkward age for her profession. Her poetry, on

the other hand, might withstand the wrinkles and ravage
of time. She discreetly established herself as a poetess—
with other accomplishments! The numerous courtesan
of the city, a powerful and respected tribe, deemed th
a contemptible device. They resented the newcome
who had already found champions for her charms an
talents. A Paduan professor had composed a *diagl
d'amore* in her honor. She was acclaimed the Sappb
of the sixteenth century. The whole guild was incensed

Tullia's most powerful enemy was none other tha
Angela Zaffetta, ably supported by Aretino. His polemi
against Tullia revealed a new note. He contrasted th
neglect of the virtuous wife with the extravagant glor
fication of the courtesan. That was the signal. Hatre
and resentment sprang up on a thousand sides. The Vene
tian Sappho was suddenly transformed into just anothe
of the eleven thousand public women of the city. Th
entire tribe were denounced as bloodthirsty she-wolves
harpies, offal, a source of evil and a threat to society
the ruination of man. What formerly had only bee
whispered in secret was now shouted aloud. The hou
had struck. Those who bore any grudge against prostitu
tion or against some specific woman were at last free t
take their revenge. Old stories were revived with nev
interest. Everyone remembered, for example, the tim
when the Spanish ambassador, while being entertaine
by the ill-famed Imperia, spat into a servant's face fo
lack of a more convenient receptacle. Courtesans paraded
through churches in pomp and splendor, heralded by

major-domos, surrounded by page-boys, followed by admirers. There were tales of harlots whom men might approach only on their knees. There were even those who believed prostitutes to be more useful to the world than nuns! Indignant sonnets were posted on the Rialto. Venice, its long arm of commerce already greatly impaired, seemed to be rapidly sinking.

The autumn of the year Tullia d'Aragona came to Venice was marked by the appearance of groups of emaciated young men in the busiest thoroughfares of Vicenza. These groups attracted attention to themselves by resorting to the most theatrical devices. They climbed onto hitching-posts and mounted benches. They waved their hats frantically in the air and shouted unintelligibly to passers-by. They stopped people on the street with words of the greatest urgency. Some paused for a moment, dumfounded, then hurried away. Those who remained long enough to discover what was going on, soon realized that these youngsters scarcely spoke a word of Italian.

No difficulties seemed to deter the young men. If they accomplished nothing more, they at least humiliated themselves before God. They steadfastly continued their attempts to gain an audience. First one person stopped, then another. There were those who remembered what they had heard of these men before. How they had passed the summer in prayer and meditation, living like hermits in the ruins of an abandoned cloister, suffer-

ing hunger, heat, and malaria. Now they were preaching
against fleshly indulgence. No one could doubt that these
creatures, worn to skin and bone, found no delight
in the flesh. The vague unrest which was beginning to
settle upon the aging city gave the street apostles their
first opening.

Rumors concerning their trip to Rome were put to
advantageous use. The friends had visited the Pope
earlier that year to obtain permission for a pilgrimage
to the Holy Land. The expedition to Rome, like most
heroic deeds, had been hard work for the heroes, but
it had also provided an edifying example for the public.
In the wealth of legend that followed there was perhaps
nothing more appealing than the story of Rodriguez
and the prostitute. While the friends were trying to raise
money in Ravenna for the passage to Ancona, their pre-
occupied colleague, who had once before become entangled with a troupe of tightrope walkers, happened
upon a lair of whores. Three charming ladies, delighted
to have found a cavalier at last, even though he seemed
far from adroit or vigorous, greeted Rodriguez enthusiastically. The startled student rushed headlong
down the stairs, not pausing until he had reached safety
in the front hall. There he came to a stop, and turning
his head in the direction of the upper story, delivered a
thunderous penitential sermon. His exhortation was
effective. They came down one by one and stood timidly
in the hall. One of the more melancholy ladies of pleasure burst into tears of remorse. "I want to go to Rome

with you," she whimpered. The young savior hastily withdrew. On shipboard, the wanderer was reunited with his friends. The girl, however, was there too. What were pilgrims to Rome to do with this newly converted Mary? She was left behind, her wails trailing the wind after them. Perhaps she had never accepted Rodriguez merely as a servant of the Saviour.

This was the first year in a long time that a ship had failed to sail for the Holy Land. At Pentecost, Venice had still hoped to preserve peace. The shipowners, however, would not risk sending a ship to the Levant. Late in the summer, Cheireddin Barbarossa had brought the Turkish fleet into Venetian waters to take Corfu. Earlier that spring, the Pope, allied with Charles and Venice, had anticipated trouble. He had received the little company of students with open arms, offering them blessing and money. Then, in careful Latin, he had added somewhat skeptically: "I gladly grant permission. I am afraid, however, that you will never get to Jerusalem." His prediction had come true.

They would wait another six months until the next spring. Time would pass quickly. No matter where they were their cause was the same. Íñigo divided the little band among the five university cities of Upper and Central Italy. The students of Padua, Ferrara, Bologna, Siena, and Rome sat in church annexes and heard theories expounded that were not in strict accordance with the Bible. Gian Battista's navigation followed a geography that corresponded more closely to the Spanish and Portuguese discoveries than to the reveries of the Church Fathers. The historians received instruction from politicians and diplomats, not from the creators of legend and the prophets. The Paris scholars would now go to these students and inform them that world history began in Paradise, that the Evil One still set his snares on the plains of Babylon. Had he not just recently inspired the engineer Vittore Fausto with the heinous idea of making men fly!

Íñigo went to Rome. Sadly, he made his way through the city of his master. All doors seemed shut to him. In Padua, Ferrara, Bologna, and Siena, his disciples stood before closed doors, too. The students had not even looked up from their books.

Audience in Frascati

THE Austinian hermit, Fra Agostino, preached at Santa Maria del Popolo. The sixty-year-old Piedmontese was a great favorite of the Roman Lent. Throngs attended his sermons. Agostino knew how to hold his audience spellbound. He had already won the admiration of prominent members of the clergy.

But two young men sat by, unimpressed, taking notes with marked disapproval while their neighbors fairly swooned at the speaker's ardor. Pierre le Fèvre and Lainez, who at the Pope's behest were preceptors of positivist and scholastic theology at the University of Rome, ignored the emotion around them. Dispassionately they analyzed the friar's fiery eloquence, subjecting it to a rigid conceptual scrutiny which it could scarcely withstand. The monk's definitions of predestination, grace, and faith were more than suspect.

Le Fèvre and Lainez waited until the sermon was over, then, in private, they took the Austinian friar to task. Six years before, preaching Lent at Asti, he had been accused of heresy. A papal brief, however, had declared his doctrine orthodox. Fra Agostino brusquely rebuffed his two critics.

The friends on whom no one could palm off heresy for dogma proceeded to an open attack. They went from

227

church to church denouncing this false teacher who was also one of their greatest rivals. Fra Agostino's popularity won his less-known adversaries an immediate audience. Was he really a renegade? This question could hardly be answered now that traditional ideas were fluctuating. Even in the College of Cardinals, the very substance of Catholic ideology was in ferment; perhaps the counselors closest to Paul were unwitting Lutherans. Thus the Pope might regard a man as orthodox when the Church's truest servants affirmed him guilty of serious deviations from doctrine. The friends were more papal than the Pope, and perhaps better versed scholastically, too. A conflict of ideas, however, is never settled in the realm of ideas.

Fra Agostino's patrons struck back with a counteraccusation of heresy. They had a ready witness at hand in the person of Miguel Llanivar. This man harbored an old grudge against Íñigo and would testify to almost anything. He had been deprived of his duties as famulus to the wealthy Francisco in Sainte-Barbe when his young master, instead of choosing a course at the end of which a bishopric rose magnificent, had strayed along the shameful paths of poverty. In the heat of his indignation, Miguel had broken into his master's room to seek revenge. Later he had followed Íñigo and sought to ally himself with the man he could not destroy. Rejoicing in the sinner's repentance the master had written to Paris: "Miguel is here in Venice and leading a new life." The new life, however, soon proved to be Miguel's old familiar one. Íñigo, disillusioned, parted company with him. But Miguel could not endure being dismissed. He followed the friends; his dislike for them was so intense that he could not live without them. Now in Rome, he ran into the unexpected luck of playing an important part in the battle waged against the enemies of Fra Agostino.

Even before his most recent patrons had felt the need for a suitable witness, Miguel had attempted to alienate one of Loyola's intimate friends. Lorenzo Garcia, the better to draw Llanivar out, had attributed various fictitious statements to the master. Miguel incorporated this false report with his own, and took an oath on what now comprised his accusations: Loyola was a blasphemer since he claimed God would grant him greater glory than the apostle, Paul; Loyola had founded a new order without authorization from the Pope; this order consisted of a band of fugitives and disguised Lutherans who had already been condemned in Spain, Paris, and Venice.

The friends, who had spent half a year working in the residence of the Pope, had not gotten off to a bad start in Rome. They taught in churches and public squares. The Romans, who believed only monks could preach, were confounded by these strange laymen. Hitherto, persons who took communion each week had been the subject of town gossip, an interesting topic for letters to friends out of the city. These men now successfully propagandized weekly confession and communion. Yet they were not firmly entrenched in Rome. The storm of protest might uproot them entirely. Many adherents, as though by command, had already turned against them. "When a wolf makes himself known," said Cardinal de Cupis, inciting the attack, "he can often be fought off; but a wolf in sheep's clothing is really dangerous!" Even Íñigo's worthy landlord was warned against him by a solicitous cardinal; it was hardly pleasant to house a man who would go directly from his lodgings to the stake, a convicted Lutheran.

The accused conducted his defense the familiar way. He went straight to those in authority and demanded with the forcefulness of an attorney of state that the complaints against Íñigo de Loyola be investigated as quickly and thoroughly as possible. The investigations merely confirmed his loyalty to the prevailing order. The chief prosecuting witness was easily discredited. A letter which Miguel had written Íñigo conclusively revealed the motives behind his slanderous assertions. Llanivar was banished from Rome forever, despite the intervention of those slandered. The victor was congratulated. But this was merely the beginning. Under cover of Llanivar's action, Fra Agostino's partisans were busily plotting and pulling wires. Those under cover were more difficult to catch, because, as Íñigo knew, they were "personages"; "one with a revenue of ten thousand ducats a year, another with six hundred, and another of even greater considerations." Thanks to their connections they could long evade investigation. Once cornered, they played innocent; certainly they had attended the sermons and discourses of the Inigists, but without taking exception either to their behavior or doctrines. The victor was congratulated once more. Even his comrades were satisfied with the outcome. The accused, however, still did not consider himself sufficiently vindicated. Perhaps he feared that the vague rumors of his difficulties in Spain, Paris, and Venice would continue to cause friction unless his orthodoxy were certified with full formality by the Pope. Perhaps, he thought, too, an official trial would best publicize the purity of his life and teachings. The Inigists were in grave need of a strong push forward. Their sermons and catechetic exercises had been poorly attended ever since the investigations. Íñigo again took his place in the prisoner's dock and insistently demanded a judge and prosecutor, but no one would hear of conducting a trial without a plaintiff. The decision lay with the Pope.

Paul returned from Nice in excellent spirits. In spite of everything, he had managed to effect a reconciliation between the hostile brothers, Charles and Francis. That must have been a strange encounter! Charles' suspicions prevented him from visiting the Pope at his quarters on the edge of the city. So Paul, who came alone, and Charles, who brought a bodyguard of five hundred men, met in an orange grove on the coast between Nice and Villafranca; the imperial galleys lay within easy distance of the fortified tent. Paul negotiated now with Charles, now with Francis. The two rivals refused to see each other. The give and take was lively; three cardinals, functioning as *legati volanti*, darted back and forth between the hostile rulers. There were many difficulties to be ironed out. Who was to make the first move? Should Charles make concessions because of Milan? Or should Francis first contribute to the Turkish war and consent to the Council? A matter not easily settled —since the one who delivers first is always in the position of being cheated by the other. Diplomacy, even at that time, had already hit upon an excellent solution, armistice; during the truce everything was to remain as it was. After the cardinals had been sufficiently shuttled back and forth between Villeneuve, the quarters of the Frenchmen, and the ship off Villafranca where Charles lodged, a ten-year armistice was agreed upon.

Paul paraded into festive Rome in diplomatic triumph. The Porta del Popolo bore the welcome, "To Pope Paul III whom the senate and Roman people wish health and happiness; his wisdom and authority are to be praised for peace among Christians and war against the Turks." But these publicly announced successes were not the only ones Grandpa Farnese had to his credit. In Nice the betrothal of his grandson Ottavio to Charles' natural daughter, Margaret of Austria, had been arranged. And in order not to lose the equal balance of papal power he had also negotiated the marriage of a French prince to Vittoria, the daughter of his son, Pier Luigi. The head of the family was more than pleased with the ascendancy of his tribe; his commission as agent would be far from insignificant.

Gasparo Contarini, Paul's prime minister, who was favorably disposed to the Paris scholars, recommended Íñigo's petition to the recently returned victor of Nice. Paul reviewed the case, and the Loyola document sank to the bottomless pit of some papal dossier. Íñigo, however, knew how to promote his affairs. The two university professors, Le Fèvre and Lainez, participated every two weeks in disputations at the Vatican. Paul found stimulation during his meals in the keen exchange of conversation and argument between his scholars. On one such occasion the friends reminded him of their situation. Paul's response was so encouraging that the leader of the group now dared to press forward himself into the presence of the supreme master.

In August, Loyola was received by Pope Paul III, in a one-hour audience in the bishop's palace at Frascati. The haggard old man may have fixed his cold, analytic glance upon this petitioner with no more intensity than he usually bestowed upon the thousands of petitioners who had come before Loyola and would follow him. There were petitioners and requests every day. This one, at any rate, was distinguished by the fact that he not only asked but offered as well, offered himself and nine comrades. Paul probably realized that he could do no more with the gift of ten learned ascetics than he had already done. They served their purpose as intellectual spice for his frugal meals. Beyond that, he was pleased to accept the offer of the "company of Jesus" as a gesture. It was the kind of overture great lords customarily receive with gratification.

Back in Montmartre, the students had pictured this first reception differently. Perhaps as a great holy spectacle, a ceremonial scene in which the Pope took over their command. Instead, the company leader now appeared in the suspicious light of someone bearing a gift which was scarcely welcome. Long-winded, and in Latin which came very hard, Íñigo rendered an exhaustive account of his life. Such a confession usually interests the petitioner more than it does the petitioned. Yet Íñigo went into detail about his past not merely out of a desire to hear himself talk. He yearned to make his lord familiar with every seam and wrinkle of his soul. Let no one ever say to the Pope, "Your servant, Loyola, did not tell you this or that." He had spent forty-two days in prison in Alcalá, twenty-two in Salamanca. He had been investigated in Paris and Venice. How often had everything about him been sifted and resifted! Yet, neither his doctrine nor conduct had ever justified the slightest cavil. Vindications had never prevented new accusations. He was accused because he accused. It was precisely because he wanted to fight for the endangered order that he required incontrovertible testimony. He might be called ignorant, a poor speaker; he took such censure lightly. But any word against his faith and purity was a word against Christ and the Church. And so, once again, a man identified himself with eternal truth.

The man who sat before Íñigo de Loyola was an individual, not a deputy of God. He was neither Heaven's pawn, nor the pawn of his own desires. He was no saint, no Leo. He did not live in Christ. He did not believe that he was truth personified. He was merely responsible for the heritage which had fallen to him. Íñigo had pledged himself not to Paul, but to his Holiness, the white papal vestment trimmed in ermine. Now he knelt before his Holiness, not Paul. The Pauls would come and go. But his Holiness reigned eternally over all mortal men. Many things were said in Rome; Íñigo, who had also forsaken his kin for the brotherhood of Christ, must have heard that the man who was named Paul had been known to the Romans before he became Pope as "the petticoat cardinal." But flesh and bone were immaterial to the consecrated vestment which the body served only as an armature! If this vestment ordered him, Íñigo de Loyola, to set sail in a boat without equipment, he would eagerly obey. "What wisdom would there be in that, Señor de Loyola?"

"That concerns him who commands, not him who obeys." And the Pope was the supreme commander of the world.

Paul did not demand his petitioner to put to sea in a rudderless ship. He merely praised his servant's talents and zeal and then dismissed him in grace. Three months later Paul's formal verdict was issued; Íñigo and his company were good Catholics. It was fairly simple to arrive at this conclusion. At the time, all the specialists in the Loyola affair were in Rome: Doctor Figueroa of Alcalá, Doctor Ori of Paris, and Doctor Dotti of the Papal Legate. None were in a better position to testify for the rebellious defender of order than those who had already accused and acquitted him.

A General Is Drafted

CHARLES had little feeling for Margaret, his daughter by the Flemish Fräulein Vomgest. At the age of twelve, she had been forced to marry the twenty-seven-year-old Alessandro de Medici. Widowed now, she was anxious to accept Duke Cosimo of Florence who proposed marriage. The Emperor, however, preferred a connection with Grandpa Farnese, and so his sixteen-year-old daughter had to take the Pope's grandson, aged thirteen and tainted with syphilis on his father's side. The marriage took place in the same November that Paul III certified Íñigo's innocence. Margaret, who had come to Rome still in mourning, was so repulsed by her uncouth and immature bridegroom, that she could not bring herself to utter the word, "yes" at the ceremony. Banquets, balls, fireworks, horse, bull, and buffalo races marked the happy event. Twelve gilded chariots were drawn from the Capitol to the Piazza Navona; the triumphal rites of ancient Rome seemed once more revived. But Margaret, to the great amusement of the Roman populace, did not admit the green youngster to her bed. Her marriage, promoted by Loyola's master, created nothing but town gossip.

The winter was a very hard one. People in the outlying territory, who had neither food nor shelter, came

to the city. Of Rome's forty thousand inhabitants, two
thousand had nothing to eat at all. Wasted gray hulks
lay in the streets and public squares, perishing in public
view. No one seemed concerned, and the Pope, who had
spent too much money on his grandson's marriage, could
not help. The friends went out night after night salvaging
the unfortunates and giving them refuge in the Frangi-
pani court near the Capitol. They built fires out of wood
which they had collected piece by piece. They made
pallets out of straw which had been donated to them.
They washed the feet of the weary and fed the starving
with begged bread. Their landlord was called, Frangi-
pani, "the bread breaker"; his pious tenants did his name
justice.

Hunger and cold have their effect upon the spirit. The
pious troop which still operated by shock attack, promising heavenly bliss or threatening the cruelest tortures of
hell, made their impression on these battered creatures.
The homeless accepted the word of God along with straw
pallets and bread. The Romans, too, who as yet were
neither hungry nor exposed to cold, proved vulnerable
to the germ which the friends were spreading. There
is a season for prayer and morality, even in Rome. The
venereal plague, perhaps less violent than at the beginning of the century, now raged throughout the city. It
contributed more to anticarnal propaganda than all the
blandished punishments of hell. Diseased prostitutes
roamed the streets. In the salons of courtesans, filled with
the frivolous chatter of cardinals, artists, and bankers,

the fear of infection hovered like a threat. Fear always unleashes old superstitions. The glittering, red-slippered ladies, only so recently admired, once more became temptations out of the inferno. Their priceless necklaces turned into Satanic nooses. The perfume of their boudoirs, once so voluptuously inhaled, now reeked of the very sulphur of hell.

Íñigo's seed proved fruitful. He had complained not long before that Rome "was a soil sterile to all good, fertile to all evil." He now discovered that want and terror had fructified the barren ground. He immediately took up arms against the old enemy, conducting his campaign from the house on the Torre del Melangolo. He first struck at the erotic "fences," procuresses who began their day's work at nightfall, haunting the cloisters and courts, the brothels and taverns. They were the guardians of the lust exchange procuring waiting women for bankers, and nuns for land stewards. Their lists included widows and virgins, courtesans and respectable wives. The friends kept on the trail of these agents like bloodhounds. They lurked in doorways like spiritual policemen waiting to catch some matron who hoped to slip out unseen. No trouble was too great so long as these men, who had renounced their own virility, could hinder the erotic freebooting of the Romans. Íñigo would willingly have given up his life to prevent some prostitute's sinning for a single night. The rewards of his quest were no longer a matter of remote, provincial success. The trial had been excellent publicity for the strangers and

now they were working in the limelight. Íñigo's seedling
was shooting up.

The road to the land of their longing was still barred.
The "Holy League" which Paul had formed between
Charles, the Venetian Republic, the Knights of Malta,
and the Italian princes, ambitiously planned to defeat
the Turkish fleet, to conquer Constantinople, to create a
new Latin Empire under Charles and a great colonial
empire for Venice. The pilgrimage to the Holy Land,
endangered by war, was finally abandoned. The friends
had long since discovered infidels in Europe; there was
enough work for Christ's servants within Christendom.
They were already in great demand. The imperial ambassador wanted them as missionaries to Mexico. The
King of Portugal tried to send them to India. The Pope,
however, refused to let them go. There was more than
enough for them to do in Rome. He commissioned them
to give Christian instruction in the schools. He sent Broët
and Rodriguez to Siena to reform a cloister. They could
already proudly say of themselves, "Even if there were
four times as many of us, we should still be unable to
satisfy all the demands made upon us." Although these
men were now known from Rome to Madrid and Lisbon,
they themselves did not know where they were actually
heading. A band of comrades with a common interest;
tomorrow, perhaps, they would be scattered helter-
skelter over the face of the earth.

The Pope had just concluded a fine carnival season.
The coaches of the procession for the first Thursday of

Lent were so huge that each had to be drawn by four buffaloes. For the first time all the municipal authorities appeared in ancient costume, and for the first time the obscene Testaccio festival was celebrated on the square of St. Peter's within the purlieus of the Apostle's Church. Some pious souls grumbled. But Paul had paid the costs. Looking on from the Castel Sant' Angelo, he prided himself on the lusty vitality of his city. Meanwhile the students were working out the most difficult of their problems: What are we really? All through the day they prepared themselves with prayer and meditation for the solution. Assembling in the evening, remote from the thousand petty trials of the day, they sat down and analyzed their existence, point by point. The subject the first night was: "Shall we remain together at all? Or shall we place ourselves at the Pope's disposal as individuals?" The answer was unanimous, "We will remain together and create a company which will not end with us, but outlive us. Since God has brought us together from so many lands, we will preserve this unity; in united activity there is double strength." The second subject presented more difficulty. Should they create an order of the usual kind and so choose one among them as their superior to be obeyed on oath? The holy men debated whether, in view of this decisive problem, they should not retire in solitude for forty days and await Divine inspiration. But they could not desert their numerous practical tasks. They were so involved in their work that they could no longer spare even half a day

241

to eternity. They would objectively weigh the problem that confronted them, ignoring personal interests. They would not exchange opinions with each other until they assembled for the final decision. At that time, however, they would openly present their conclusions.

These crystallized into three objections against a strict alliance: (1) Most orders were in bad repute; (2) if they formed an order, the Pope might impose alien rules upon them; (3) if they were headed by one of their own members who would command absolute obedience, perhaps pious recruits who had no concern with absolute obedience would be discouraged. Those were the reasons contra. The following night the pros were discussed. The Paris students were accustomed to analyze everything dialectically, both for and against. Perhaps the objections arose from nothing more than tried and true dialectical habit. In the first place, their contras were very weak and very easily refuted. In the second place, they had already, and without statute, obeyed that strictest of officers, Loyola, for ten years. Since they were dialecticians they invoked not fact, but logic. Could a society exist without obedience? Did not obedience beget heroic virtues and deeds? Was it not the root of humility? The officer Loyola and his company brought obedience to the fore, and decided, in contrast to the older orders, to elect their *praepositus* for life. Why was obedience to be the supporting pillar of their structure? Why did God inspire them, in 1539, to form a close company, and not a loose group of individuals, each pulling a different way, like the first Egyptian and Syrian monks? Or a pious, idyllic family waiting before the gates of cities like the Benedictines?

Solitude, it was the opinion of the old oriental hermits, is the latitude of monks, just as water is the element of fish. Those who enjoyed the company of human beings lost the company of angels: that was the belief of the Eremites, who sought God in the wilderness. At that time among these Christian anarchists there was obedience only to God, and indifference toward the fellow monk. But the Occident had a different concept of Christ. "Set not your contemplation above the needs of the church," Augustine had preached. Since the time of the Greek Basil, monks, too, saw their task as the common aid of their fellow men rather than as an exclusive preoccupation with their own souls. The promotion of obedience as a binding social force gained importance when the cloister ceased to be a wall surrounding various individual souls, independent of each other, and became an actual community in Christ. In May, 1539, what seemed to Íñigo and his comrades a divine inspiration—no society of monks without obedience—developed out of the thousand-year-old occidental monastic practice.

The obedience which the friends decided upon was to be different and even stricter than the one St. Benedict had introduced. The founder of Monte Cassino had created a cloister which was a small self-sufficient state, a communistically conducted enterprise. The cloister was to have everything, Benedict arranged, so that the monks would have no need to go out into the world. Íñigo's friends, however, definitely wished to go out, far out, into it. They no longer lived in a provincial Europe, in rural seclusion. They worked in the big cities, in a society which had arrived at an era of world economy. The Paris students would not remain together; they would go on missions to the Turks, the Lutherans, to India, and America. How much more difficult it would be to hold such an expansive group together. It was not, after all, a pious family which would meet within a small area, day after day, decade after decade! A family scattered over the whole world can no longer be ruled by paternal frowns. In the Benedictine abbeys, the abbott was the "living rule," like the lord in his castle, and the master in his shop. In the vast empire which was now arising, the general would be the highest member of an administrative staff, like a sovereign in Portugal, a banker in Rome, a merchant in Venice. The authority of the new order would be more impersonal, practical, rational, and mechanized, than the patriarchal authority of former orders. "The better the subaltern, the better the command," became the motto of this newest Christian society; it was more a postulate of the growing empires than a promotion of Christ.

The company worked for three months on its constitution which looked like nothing more than a statute divided into five modest articles. Actually, it was an illuminating self-portrait of Íñigo de Loyola, not of an immortal saint, but of a mighty force in his time, nurtured by all the elements of the epoch. Even at first glance, this portrait, which is also a miniature constitution, reveals the soldier. The only language Loyola could speak was the language of the warrior: it was always the banner and the battle, obedience and command, company and militia. At second glance, however, one finds this soldier a remarkable example of his kind. There is nothing of the swashbuckler about him; he seems unaccustomed to killing enemies or celebrating riotous victories. He has a severe, disciplined gentleness. There can be no genuine warrior without a thirst for blood, a love of havoc, a desire for booty. This soldier was not a true one. He demanded the virtues of a soldier but renounced the conditions that fostered them. The soldier desires to defeat the enemy and sacrifices comfort and security to this aim, but he also wants to kill, plunder, and humiliate. The goal of soldierly asceticism is the soldier's excess of enjoyment. Loyola required the superhuman. His soldier never achieved the rewards of hardship; he had to be ready day and night, without pay, without triumph, without the trophies of victory. This leader even dammed the sublime source of all bravery, "worldly advancement." The soldier, because he risks more, must also gain more. Íñigo fought to keep the possessors in possession and his troops in poverty. A peculiar commander!

One also discovers that this man was not merely a peculiar soldier but an anomalous saint. What do men of God cling to? The Benedictine is exalted by the glorious image of Christ as King. The Franciscan is edified by the images of the appealing Child in the cradle, and the Man of Thorns bearing the sufferings of the world to the grave. Did Íñigo's troop renounce all earthly possessions for the enjoyment of such a vision? Their asceticism went so far that they did not even grant themselves the solace of the pious. Greatly as Íñigo loved choir singing, his men, in order not to be distracted from the duties of love to which they had devoted themselves exclusively, were not required to sing *in choro*. For the same reason they had no music, neither organ nor psalm singing. Thus they renounced even the most immaterial compensations for their lost comforts.

As a soldier, Loyola was all saint; as a saint he was always the soldier. On the wall of Pampeluna, he was the complete officer. In the ascetic cubicle at Manresa he was the direct descendant of those old monks who went into the desert and mortified themselves before God. His life combined a contradiction in terms. The soldier forbade the saint the honors of his profession, fasting, self-flagellation, going barefoot, wearing hair shirts. The saint forbade the soldier the honors of his profession—ambition, debauchery, booty. To what end? The man, his enjoyment, his salvation, were no longer involved. Production had become objective and holiness, too, was now impersonal.

The Papal government had its doubts. There were enough orders already. It would be more practical to decrease and merge them than increase them. A division which opposed fasts and castigations, the organ and singing had almost the savor of Lutherism. What was the reason for a special oath of obedience to the Pope when all Christians owed him obedience? The friends calmly set about combating all objections. They vowed three thousand masses. They also employed less pious means to gain their pious end. They connived for the intercession of Donna Constanze Farnese, illegitimate daughter of His Holiness by one of his mistresses from Bolsena. This lady was no model of virtue. She was avaricious and had a talent for obtaining benefice for not very deserving persons, but the priestly soldiers thought less of reproving her than of utilizing her mediation with Father Paul. They were not simply innocent holy men, but holy conquerors of the world. "With all our trust in Divine Providence," Íñigo decided, "we must still set to work as though everything depended on our own efforts." It was better to play safe. "While we exploit all natural means we must nevertheless look only to God." Security doubly secured. Paul signed the letter which was based on the portrait constitution of Íñigo, on September 27, 1540, in the Palazzo Venezia.

Six months after the Pope had raised the student alliance of Montmartre to the rank of an order, the friends were scattered over the wide world. Paul, delighting once more in a carnival, invited his favorite nephews and their ladies to the Vatican and regaled them with a masked ball and the jokes of the Buffone Rosso. Meanwhile, Paul's soldier, Íñigo, working with Salmeron and

Codure in Rome, summoned the fathers still engaged in Italy—Le Jay, Lainez, Broët, and Bobadilla—to their first assembly. They proceeded to elect a general, following the method chosen by Íñigo—for had he not been elected long ago? On the fourth of April, the vote was taken by sealed ballot. Two days later the friends cast their votes into the urn which already contained the votes of the absent Le Fèvre, Xavier, and Rodriguez. The nine ballots (Bobadilla was prevented from giving his) remained locked away for three days more. No haste, no curiosity. They must not hurry a decision which would come out of eternity. They must approach it with measured steps. The result, which no one could have doubted, might have been established in a few seconds. The election took six days.

The man elected declined. In his heart, he said, he was more prepared to be ruled than to rule. He was unable to govern himself, how could he govern others? He had bad habits and many sins. His health was poor. He was still really setting himself apart from the others. First, he had decreed a ridiculous election. Then, individualistically, he exempted himself from the right to vote. More than that, he presumed not to acknowledge the result of the vote. Anybody who accepted election after this refusal would be admitting himself less ready to obey than Loyola, less conscious of his own sins. One of them stood apart and the friends accepted him as an example. After his refusal of the command it seemed more inconceivable than ever that Loyola would obey and not command.

A GENERAL IS DRAFTED

Three days later, the second election took place. It lasted four days. Five of the six present chose Ignatius de Loyola. Again he declined. Which other one of the six would have dared such insubordination? Then Lainez pulled a trump, "Father, submit to what God imposes; if not, the society may break up, for as far as I am concerned, I am resolved to acknowledge no other supreme commander than him whom God wants." Loyola demanded a third vote. He would, he decided, retire to the cloister of his father confessor for three days. The decision that the Franciscan Fra Theodosio would hand down to the comrades would be irrevocable. They submitted to Íñigo a third time. He had long been the commanding authority.

The budding general made his confession in the Minorite cloister, San Pietro in Montorio. He referred to his sins and inadequacies. His physical transgressions were many. He had even required dispensation from the regular performance of the Canonic Hours, which affected him so profoundly that he wept at every word. He was very weak and already felt the proximity of heaven. Is a dying man placed at the head of an army which is to conquer the world? Three days after he had returned to the friends, he was ordered to accept election. Power came to him as a command; as a man of obedience he could not imagine authority originating in any other way. He obeyed; humbly, he accepted the order to be a dictator.

THE IMPERIALIST MONK

THE house stood next to the church with the shrine of Our Lady of the Highway, not far from the foot of the Capitol. It served as both a laboratory and administrative building.

When the Company was still small and housed in a rented lodging, it operated as a refuge for baptized Jews. The Hebrews were not to be driven out, but saved. In order to convert the children of Israel to the Jewish Saviour, unusual regulations were passed: the baptized were not to be deprived of the money which they had earned through usury. The prospect of loss was decidedly no inducement to baptism. Also, poor proselytes accustomed to living on the wealthier members of their race would be compensated by endowments from the purses of the more stubborn followers of Moses. The newly initiate Christians could not be expected to give up the advantages of their old faith along with the faith itself. The Order next door to the Maria della Strada, from the beginning, reckoned with a fundamental law of human nature: on this earth one does not fight unscathed against the Golden Calf—and for an invisible God!

250

BETWEEN IRELAND AND JAPAN

The new Company planned large-scale conversions and succeeded brilliantly in dramatizing itself for the spectacle-loving metropolitan Roman public. From the first, the wise maxim of its founder was followed: "An appeal to the populace is more successfully effected through the eyes and the emotions than through refined speech and careful rhetoric." Often christenings and weddings were efficaciously turned into attractive public spectacles. Invited cardinals sat on the stage. The crowd, obsessed with the theatrical, packed the Piazza Navona. The company for spiritual commodities, which was not above any dramatization of popular notions, was thriving.

Another reform which in its early years kept the Company before the eyes of the Roman public, was the refuge for repentant adulteresses. Roman antiquities had been discovered on the site which the Company had obtained. The hundred ducats for which these were sold formed the basic capital for the Home of Saint Martha, in which twenty-eight converted sinful women were maintained until they returned to their husbands, got new ones, or became nuns. From time to time, the Romans would see the founder of the Home heading a procession of these ladies toward the house of an aristocratic patroness or to a cloister, while his subordinates collected charity for the holy prison. The Company became popular. The greatly publicized baptizing of Jews, the colorful parading through the streets of interned female transgressors, the public assembling of the orphans of Rome, the consistently opposed plan to gather all the beggars together for communal sustenance and employment, focused public interest on the undertaking

It also invited attack. A certain Mateo of Santo Cassiano, who had seduced a married woman and then been deprived of his prey by the Martha Foundation, tried to break into the hateful place. When he did not succeed, he slandered the morals of these guardians of public morality, causing an investigation of the inmates of the Home. Another, a Spanish monk, made the accusation that the Company intended to do away with all married women in Rome who had ever exhibited frailty. What did the men next door to the shrine of Our Lady of the Highway want? Jews consecrated to Christ? Rehabilitated adulteresses? Organized beggars? Adopted orphans? Was this Company an evangelistic army believing in a mixture of ineffectual Christian charity, a bit of timid gospel propaganda and a great deal of vulgar, street sensationalism? For now it was impossible to gain the attention of a Christian when speaking of Christ without first raising an uproar. Or were they out "to reform the whole world"? as the monk Fray Barbaran of the Holy Office asserted. The Chief replied that the accusation had "neither head nor tail." Perhaps he was too modest.

Now, in the eighth year of its existence, the Company had become a world-wide enterprise. Its representatives occupied posts in the cities of four continents. They toured Ireland and Germany, Austria and France. In Italy they had taken firm root in Venice and Padua,

Florence and Tuscany, Genoa and Bologna, Modena and
Ferrara, Naples and Sicily. They met with their greatest
success in Spain and Portugal. Francis Xavier, their
ablest man, was now working on the south coast of India
and in the Malayan east. The year before, a branch in
Abyssinia had been considered. The plan for a settlement among the Brazilian cannibals had just been concluded.

Before the travelers left the main office they appeared
before the Chief for final inspection. They carried no
sample cases. They were not out to exchange a com-
modity which they had and others needed, for a com-
modity which they lacked. "All those under allegiance
to the Company," read the rule of their house, "must
remember to give as freely as they have received."
"Keep your hands out of money matters," the Chief instructed. They were traveling in a field more difficult
than trade.

The administrative office in Rome directed its representatives the world over. It plotted their courses and
instructed them generally. It was important for the agents
to personify the Company's principles. They must also
treat their prospects in a way that would make the goods
they offered seem most desirable. The apostles must be
constant to their abstract model and yet adaptable to all
classes, ranks, and characteristics of peoples from England to China. The agent had to be both a wily salesman
and a testproof sample of an intangible ware.

The reports streamed in from Ingolstadt, from Lisbon,

from Goa. The central office examined the incoming data and sent out new instructions. Its branches were set up in remote territories. Its local bureaus offered specialized services and would take care of the next generation. In Cologne, in Messina and Palermo, in Valladolid, Valencia, Gandia, Barcelona, Alcalá, and Coimbra the future personnel was trained. The central office had to supervise this chain closely. The general line, laid down in Rome, must be strictly followed.

The chief of this complex bureaucracy sat in the administrative offices in Rome. They consisted of three low, dark cells furnished with an uncovered table, a wooden chair, and a "library" that included only the New Testament and a Thomas à Kempis. He was the monk imperialist, inventor, and organizer of the Company's product, a small, frail man of sixty, with a broad bulging forehead, high cheekbones, and a strong, curved nose. The lower part of his face seemed strangely youthful with its firm, sparsely whiskered chin.

The man who drove his followers on, over the face of the earth, had himself left the city only once in the last eight years. From day to day he had become more and more the omnipotent god, invisible behind his throne, making himself only known upon occasion by a flash of lightning, a thunderbolt, a rainbow. Was he sadly alone, an elderly gentleman whose wife was dead and whose children had deserted him, whose friends had been taken from him by various circumstances? His oldest brother was dead. Fifteen years before another

brother had informed Martin, head of the family, that
ñigo de Loyola had no kin on earth. Pierre, the first,
best, truest comrade, the successful laborer in the hard
German field had died three years ago. His lonely
General had buried him with the indifferent words:
"We have no reason to mourn. God will soon bring us
a substitute for Le Fèvre. Indeed, He will give us a man
who will be even more useful to the Order." Francis
Xavier and Simon Rodriquez had been away in foreign
lands for ten years. The General longed more for new
triumphs than for old friends. He had trained a band
of men who "even rested with one foot ready to march."
He had grown great alone. No one was bound to him by
fate or circumstance and he missed no one in his isolation. As others build nests he had created around him a
desert solitude. He had secluded himself not in Egypt
or Syria or the outskirts of human society, but in the
heart of Rome. The monk imperialist dwelt at the center
of a world industry.

Few friends had remained true to him. He had even
driven away the most loyal, Isabela Roser. Twenty-five
years before in Barcelona, she had taken the beggar
from San Maria del Mar into her prosperous house. She
had supported the pilgrim and student, obtained new
friends for the youths' alliance. After the death of her
husband she brought the General a gift for his Company.
The wealthy widow did not come to him as a disinterested
friend; in the intervening twenty-five years pious Isabela
had become an erudite lady. Now in Rome before an

audience of cardinals she discussed the most difficul
questions of dogma. What irritated her old protégé, th
General, even more, were the eternal spiritual trouble
which she and her friends piled upon him. This circl
of wealthy ladies gave him more to do in three day
than the whole Company did in a month. When h
cautiously tried to shake them off, the ambitious widov
from Barcelona, incited by her nephews, raised a lou
and tearful hullabaloo in the palaces of the cardinals

This Jesuit-warrior refused to admit Amazons to hi
fold, despite the examples of the Benedictines, Ciste
cians, Dominicans, and Franciscans. He secured a papa
brief which rid his Company of any further troubl
where women might be concerned. They might still b
given what no priest could refuse any person. "Bu
wherever you can, my comrades, avoid women. Espe
cially if they are young, beautiful, of doubtful reputa
tion, or low rank. Conduct religious conversations onl
with aristocratic women, and never with the door shut
Dispatch a female penitent who powders and prinks
with a quick exhortation. If she continues to be vai
let her find another confessor." Lonely Loyola was no
poisoned by a hatred of women. He had always bee
successful with them. They had always indulged hir
with money and flattery. But they had also always endar
gered his position. In Manresa there had been scandalou
gossip about the wealthy nurses at the bedside of th
invalid pilgrim. The combination of convulsions and
band of hysterical girls had landed him in jail, i

Alcalá. Now, in Rome, he was brought to court because
an incensed Isabela demanded her money back. One
could not conquer the world and at the same time cure
the spiritual aches of lascivious and foolish ladies. Nor
could one demand continence of soldiers and then put
women in their care. The General was not a misogynist,
merely a man who distrusted men. Whatever had once
existed between the page and Queen Germana had long
since disappeared below the surface of more than thirty
years' renunciation.

The hermit next door to the church of Santa Maria
had no masculine friendships to take the place of women.
He was aloof and reserved even with his closest associates. He discussed current business with his colleagues,
impersonally, and retained the same businesslike equanimity when they revealed their secret spiritual troubles.
Proximity did not breed familiarity. He kept the intimate experiences of his life to himself, even though
they were the material of which a precious essence was
distilled for export over the world. Even his old comrades were denied the right to familiarity despite the
long years spent working together. He dismissed a father
confessor who had dared to praise him publicly. Only
in his association with the younger ones, where there
was no danger of unwelcome advances, did he sometimes
for the sake of encouragement describe what a bad subject he, the General, had been as a youth. He absolutely
refused to sit for his portrait and even forbade those
living in the house to look him straight in the face. He

was not a father who rejoiced and grieved with his flock.
He was a father only in the allegorical sense of the
word. A god who showed neither personal vices nor
virtues. A mysterious man, even to those who saw him
every day, whether he spoke to them about money, the
menu, or the cleaning of toilets.

This mysterious man spent his days in the soberest
uniformity; this tireless organizer ate and slept in his
workroom. His daily routine, however, did not begin in
strictly conventional fashion. At morning mass he saw
the Holy Ghost in colors of flame, and conversed with
Him until tears and sobs left him speechless. The Lady
of Heaven, supremely gracious beside God, the Father,
offered the rapt worshiper assurance that her flesh was
also present in the flesh of her Son. The monk was over
whelmed by this signal act of grace. He was impelled,
Sacrament in hand, to declare to Jesus, his dictator, that
His vassal Loyola would never "desert Him at any price
of Heaven or earth." He was still shield-bearer for a
conqueror.

If the day was fair, the chief sat in an adjacent garden
which a Roman burgher had deeded to him. On the
table before him were ink, pen, and paper. For forty
days he meditated whether his churches and sacristies
should acquire property. Although he knew that God
did not spare a holy company the necessity of seeking
revenue for inevitable expenditures, he had the feeling
"with extraordinary clarity, that partial possession was
disgraceful and complete possession, vexatious and a

degradation of that poverty which was so pleasing to God, the Lord." Thus, after prayer and meditation, he described the conclusions which would become the law for his Company. He placed the newly written memorandum on the altar at which he had celebrated mass and offered the first fruits of his meditations to God.

The hours before noon were spent in office conferences with the hundreds of people whose affairs busied the firm. He conducted interviews as efficiently as any director who has never looked up from his papers to heaven. Saint Arsenius' eyelashes had dropped out with weeping and when he worked he had to wear a cloth over his chest to catch the tears. Abbas Schnudi wept such floods that the ground upon which he stood became fertile. Loyola's eyes were dry enough in the morning to see through his wiliest business associates. He preferred to listen rather than speak, constructing his sentences very slowly and with great care. He never said anything which he could not at any time publicly affirm. When a garrulous visitor wasted his time, he would innocently talk of Purgatory, Judgment Day, and other unpleasant eventualities, until the unwelcome guest beat a hasty retreat.

He was no luminary at the dinner table either—merely a well-trained executive with a bad stomach. His secretary, old comrades, and, often, guests from the outside world, sat at the table which was spread in his cell. Because of the guests food was served with special care. To strangers, the General was the respected representative of a world-wide firm just as to the Virgin Mary he was a poor sinner in desperate need of salvation. True, he himself often ate no more than a handful of chestnuts all day, but he was not abstinent to please Jesus nor to parade before the eyes of his contemporaries his personal relationship with God. He pleased Jesus by being a wise administrator. Unfortunately, in his misspent youth he had so depressed the capacity of his stomach that the maltreated organ now refused to function. The accomplished starveling and boarder at tramp hotels had lost his sense of taste. The General turned this difficulty not into a personal virtue, but into an advantage for his men. He saw to it that the Loyolas who were growing up, in a thousand places, to succeed him, would not develop into good Christians with bad stomachs. He was pleased when his table companions enjoyed their food. He was especially fond of dining the young, corpulent Benedetto Palmio, a thorough and lusty eater. *"Ridere, fili mi, te volo!"* he encouraged the young ones who often thought a Jesuit initiate had no business being jolly. He was, despite the infirmities of his years, still the same Íñigo who had once broken into the Basque national dance before an overly ascetic friend in the Monte Cassino Cloister.

In the evening he became the proctor of the institution. The General had the cardinal virtue of a good administrator. His interest in his men had no limits. He would have liked to have known at first hand how many fleas bit the novices under his roof each night. Although in the early morning he saw and spoke with the Holy Ghost, in the evening nothing interested him more vitally than providing for the inmates of the house: the color, cut, and material of their coats; the height of their collars; the length and width of their waistbands; the weave of their stockings; the shape of their shoes; the position of the nightcaps under their pillows, and of the slippers and night vessels under their beds. As a pilgrim and student he had enjoyed slovenliness—neglect and disorder to the glory of God. The Íñigo of Manresa had rolled in filth and dressed in rags. He would have been immediately ejected from this house where spitting and even the smacking of lips were strictly forbidden.

At that time, his beard had grown wild to honor God. The General now, in God's name, prescribed the length of beards. At that time, the pilgrim and student lodged in refuges for the homeless. The General now kept an immaculate house in which even the toilets were inspected each evening—and woe to the saint who left a drop of urine on the seat. Not long before, the Paris students had wrapped themselves in disease-infected sheets and slept with lepers. Now the General had his laundry checked piece by piece. Once the wounded officer of the guards had served his God by eating out of the plates of the sick and the filthy. Now this head of the house of Jesus, in the service of a more hygienic God, instructed the cook never to touch meat with his fingers. The mendicant who had thanked strangers for every spoonful of soup, no matter what the ingredients, taught his kitchen staff, as chief, how and when food was to be seasoned. God's beggar had become God's nobleman.

A private secretary followed the administrator. Juan de Polanco, a Spaniard of Jewish descent, formerly a member of the College of Papal Secretaries, had become the General's adjutant. He served as audience for the General's monologues and as pen for the ever-increasing correspondence through which the General daily drilled his company of traveling agents. "What," the General had asked Polanco, "is the principal virtue of a secretary?"

"Keeping secrets inviolable," the candidate had answered and passed his examination. The discreet amanuensis had other virtues than secrecy. He had the ability to be an involuntary and yet active tool, a servant whose independent will and thought coincided with his master's. He became a literary ghost whose letters were often not to be distinguished from the General's.

In Germany "a wild boar sought to uproot, and an evil beast to devastate" the vineyard which the master's hand had planted. Progress, there, was much slower than in the more southern countries. The representatives stationed in Ingolstadt would have to be thoroughly drilled in fundamentals again. Polanco had only to repeat the business principles which had long since become an integral part of the old seasoned travelers like Xavier. The guidelines issued from a very cautious, very wise master who was so distrustful that he always sent his men out in pairs. Thus, for the dangerous expedition to Scotland and Ireland he had coupled volatile Salmeron with clear-thinking Broët. The supreme virtue of his travelers must be guile. As a model, he suggested the Guileful One, himself. "A member of the Order must have many eyes," like the devil.

The managing director was not squeamish. His inspirations in the mornings revealed what was going on in heaven. In the evenings, instructing Polanco, he followed the revelations which came to him from Satan. He could see through Satan better, in any case. The man in Rome knew which levers set men in motion and he manipulated them as dexterously as only Lucifer and Pietro Aretino could. How did the Devil really go about getting his good booty? The General, long trained in probing the inner mysteries of life, finally arrived at the secret of the Devil's more successful tricks. The Evil One crept into his victims' houses, lured them toward the door and then suddenly sprang his trap. The technique of this notoriously successful hunter appealed to the unprejudiced managing director. He exploited it thoroughly in advising his representatives. They might graciously acquiesce to the customs and requirements of their clientele —even flatter them though these customs and requirements were abhorrent. There was no point in being squeamish where one was certain of one's objectives. The first rule of the house next door to the church of Santa Maria became: "In through the other man's door but out through your own." Getting into other men's doors required an accurate knowledge of what opened them. The managing director offered systematic instruction in the methods of burglary. There was, for example, the gentleman of lively temperament who enjoyed conversation. He would never yield if approached earnestly, solemnly, or indifferently. On the other hand, a steady reflective person of few words would make a much better impression on the sober type of man. The least talented burglars were the irascible ones. They roused the victim instead of putting him to sleep. The General in Rome had no use for the impetuous and foolhardy. He would have rejected the officer of Pampeluna and the courageous volunteer of Jerusalem.

Polanco scrupulously copied his chief's diabolic rules, applying them appropriately to each specific case. He had followed the old models in devising the letter to Germany. Under twelve heads, he had sketched the strategy which the representatives were to follow. "Make yourselves liked by all, becoming all things to all persons in humility and love, and adapting yourselves to the customs of the people." The Chief even advised the Jesuits stationed in Munich to drink Münchner beer for love of Christ. The emissaries of the house next door to the church of Santa Maria were to be courtiers in a social gathering, authorities on drafts and quotations in the company of business men, sophisticates in the presence of harlots. "Twelfth," the secretary concluded in his letter to Germany, "when defending the Apostolic See and in your efforts to keep people under its allegiance, do not become overzealous and be decried as Papists, for you will only lose people's confidence."

The General's desk was his field marshal's post. In the silence of the night he reviewed his strange army of traveling representatives. He who commanded everything no longer took the battlefield in person. From the letters piled up before him he gathered the position of the enemy and the action of his own men. There were reports from the Provincials and the heads of branch houses. He was an exacting correspondent. He had no use for irresponsible accounts of religious victories. The crafty monk preferred exact lists with the statistics of the entering, departing, and discharged brothers. True, he still retained patriarchal habits, vestiges of past times. He corresponded not only with the officers. Every soldier had to establish direct contact with him, state his age, background, what talents he possessed, what he wanted. The General had the superiors inform on the subordinates, and the subordinates on the superiors. Sometimes he even directly commanded a pupil to report on the superior. Then it might happen that he would send the complaint to the accused for his own information, with the request not to bear a grudge against the informer.

He wrote thousands of letters to thousands of persons. This correspondence was a rite as sacred as the exercises of the soul, for the unity of the scattered Company was based solely on the exchange of letters. First he sketched the outline. Then he spent many hours in correction. Each word, each sentence, must be unassailable. Only then did he have the text transcribed. None of his men knew, until taught, what a sacramental procedure the transcription of a letter was. "Improve your writing," he urged again and again. Pierre, gentle as ever, acted at once on the command, but scapegoat Bobadilla dismissed this aberration on the part of comrade Íñigo with an ironic retort. The father, reflected Bobadilla, must have a great deal of spare time to elaborate his letters so handsomely. The father, however, tirelessly sent circular after circular on the subject of correspondence to his personnel. After all, letters were also a means of soliciting contributions and he wanted to be able to submit them to patrons of the Order as proof of his firm's accomplishments. But the miscellany which landed on his desk, the hodgepodge of practical report and private triviality, would have to be carefully edited before it could be used for publicity. For that reason all employees must always write an official and edifying main version. Whatever was intended only for the eyes of the addressee might be added in an appendage. In the supplement they were free to talk their heads off. The main body of the letter, on the other hand, was a public document which would have to be composed with pious care.

The managing director's letters to his men were not, to be sure, always edifying. They were the long, strong arm with which, from his cell in Rome, he directed his subalterns in Vienna, Paris, and Portuguese Indian Goa. Such a letter now reached over to a small Spanish residency ruled by his most powerful patron, the Duke of Gandia, former Catalonian viceroy and intimate of Emperor Charles, a healthy scion of the diseased Borgia stock.

It was from this beloved Gandia that the General now received word of an upheaval which threatened to terminate his work. He was under suspicion again, as he so often had been in the last twenty-five years. Attacks had not ceased even after his enterprise had gained Papal recognition. The renown of his Company had frightened away many old enemies and attracted as many new ones. Bitter words were aimed at the rising Jesuit troops: "If the Turk had sent his own men to Spain to destroy morale and strength, to turn soldiers into women, knights into tradesmen, he could not have chosen better agents." Yet what threatened the General in Gandia was more dangerous than this hatred of Professor Melchior Cano of Salamanca who inveighed against "a certain new society," the meeting ground of all *alumbrados* and hypocrites who themselves denounced their General as pompous and self-important, the forerunner of the Antichrist.

In Gandia, the past had risen against him. The ascetic of Manresa had cast his shadow over the work of the General in Rome. He had already conceded his men two hours for daily prayer, and they were praying six to eight hours. They fasted much and slept little. They had no sense of serving their fellow men. They stormed the heights of perfection and along their precipitous way ran counter to the dictum of their leader: "There is no room in the Company for the man who desires only his own salvation and consecration." A quarter of an hour was enough time for a pious man to unite himself with God in prayer. The ardent, not the lax, were the plague of the empire which he had founded.

Francis Borgia, Duke of Gandia, disillusioned by failure after a brilliant career, lived estranged from the world. After the death of the Empress and the loss of his wife, he had fallen under the spell of asceticism and the influence of his visionary court chaplain. Andrès de Oviedo, rector of the Jesuit college at Gandia, had requested his General's permission to promote piety with two or three private masses daily. When the request was refused, he and the French Father Onfroy petitioned for a seven years' leave in the desert. They wanted to pray themselves out, once and for all. In Gandia there was much dissatisfaction with the obdurate managing director. Had not his Company given up cloisterly garb and prayer in chorus? Was not the Societas Jesu already dubbed the "Business Order"? Loyola even begrudged the time for mass which he limited to no more than half an hour. The impious Chief actually stood beside the priest, playing timekeeper with his hourglass, and severely admonishing every early or late arrival. If they lived up to cold theory his personnel would be a troop of angels without wants. They would in no way be concerned with themselves. They would devote their entire working strength to the firm. Thus in Gandia, the

ghost of the man of Assisi rose against the practical
management of the reigning imperialist, who as a
wounded hero had once written the name of Saint Francis
on his banner.

The judgment which the General's Commission of
Fathers had handed down on the Gandia case lay before
him. Onfroy had had thirty-two revelations to the effect
that the Chief and his Society were on a false track.
The General, too, had once, by means of a supernatural
communication, received his vision of the war which
Christ desired him to conduct. Now, when a new prophet
threatened to destroy Loyola's work, the Commission of
Fathers passed an extraordinary commentary, anticipat-
ing many scientific deductions of later centuries:

*The more a being endowed with reason isolates him-
self from the external world, the more dependent he
becomes upon his own speculations. It frequently hap-
pens that such a person, especially when the ardor of an
emotion blurs his clear vision, may become the victim
of fixed ideas. The danger of delusion is further increased by his physical weakness, the result of excessive
bodily and mental exertion. We conclude this from the
descriptions of blood expectoration and other symptoms
of illness. Thus the whole idea borders dangerously on
hallucination.*

An unexpected, dangerous, candidly materialistic interpretation of the origin of inspirations. The verdict
might apply to the General with equal justice. He, too,
had shut himself off from the external, blinded by an

emotion, his body debilitated and his mind overstrained, when he had beheld that vision from which his Company originated. Why was Father Onfroy "a victim of fixed ideas," a "prey of hallucinations," and General Loyola, who had drawn and still drew from the same source, in possession of the truth?

In the quiet of the night Loyola restlessly paced the three bare cells. His right foot, wrapped in two socks, still hurt at the slightest touch. The cane which eased his weight a little tapped along on the floor. Heaven drew back. The earth bound its son even more closely to itself. Time—master of earth, not of heaven—no longer granted this most pious man opportunity to consider his eternal needs. Kings, businessmen, and the monk imperialist must think only of conquering the world. Those who still mawkishly dreamt of heaven had long since ceased to matter. If the Company next door to the church of Santa Maria had followed the course of the God seekers of Gandia, it would now, after four hundred years, be buried in the deepest oblivion. Instead it grew mighty in posterity. A cross-fertilization of the seed of Assisi and Machiavelli. And Machiavelli was the stronger.

After midnight the spectral shuffling and tapping of the three unequal feet ceased. For the next four hours the light of a holy managing director would be dimmed.

The Agent in the Far East

THE junk of the Chinese Ah Wong, a square box with a wide projecting fore-and-aft deck, glided along the jungle coast of the Straits of Malacca into the narrow and winding channel of Singapore. On the island of Pulo Timon, a hundred miles beyond Malacca, timber for repairs had been taken on as a precaution against the violent storms which might be expected in the China Sea.

The company on the Chinese junk, so eager to reach Japan that they were willing to risk the storm, consisted of Francis Xavier and two Spanish men of God, a Portuguese whom the commandant of Malacca had sent along for their protection, three baptized Japanese, the Chinese servant Manuel, and the Malabar servant, baptized Amador. The Christians had brought their religious goods with them: the image of the Virgin with the Child Jesus and the necessary paraphernalia for celebrating the mass, a keg of sacramental wine, and the Japanese translation of the Gospel of Saint Matthew. The great gift for the Emperor of Japan was stowed in the water-tight cabin alongside the ballast space, next to the treasury for the journey, which consisted of one hundred and twenty hundredweight of the finest pepper.

The Chinese god beside the helm was hard at work. It was his duty to exorcise the hurricane which raged against the tiny craft. The mat sails had already been taken in. Two bamboo masts stood stark against the sky like stripped trees. The Chinese servant, baptized Manuel, lost his balance and fell into the flooded hold. The captain's daughter was swept overboard. The yellow slant-eyed sailors, wearing wide pantaloons and smocks with sleeves narrowing toward the hands, prostrated themselves before their supreme lord. They touched the deck with their foreheads so that the god could discern only the round little caps with their gay buttons in the center. They killed the birds which the mighty one liked to eat. They nourished him with ceremonious attention and care.

The water had actually become calm. The junk peacefully glided on, past the high steep coast of Cochin China. But the god was invoked, none the less. Should they now sail on to Japan? The Chinese skipper had a great desire to lie up for the winter in a home port. Had the mighty one beside the helm the same desire? They burned incense to him. Flaming strips of paper floated over the sea. Little sticks scrawled with enigmatic characters were thrown on the ship's deck. The oracle spoke through the weaving smoke and fire. They would get to Japan safely enough but would not come back. The owner of the junk decided not to sail across the water again that year.

The passengers would not accept his decision. It was contrary to their previous agreement. But the wishes of his customers made no impression on the skipper. He yielded, however, to a more forceful circumstance. The dreaded Japanese "butterflies" which owed their poetic name to their narrow fluttering flags, occupied the Chinese harbor, Chin-chu. While he was seeking other quarters for the winter, intending to return to Canton, a perverse wind tossed the junk in a direction which neither captain, crew, nor the devil, wanted to go—toward Japan.

For two and a half centuries Occidentals had dreamt of these islands. Marco Polo had never reached them. He had been told at the court of the Mongolian Khan in Peking, of the "Land of the Rising Sun," Zipangu, and he had repeated the tale to the peoples of the old world. The imperial palace on Zipangu was covered with gold. Even the floors of its rooms were pure gold. Gods with the heads of oxen, pigs, dogs, and sheep ruled the island. Gods who had a thousand hands and three heads. Columbus too had failed to reach Zipangu, though he yearned for it as the goal of his journeys—a fabulous land of gold lying off the east coast of Asia. This obsession tricked him all his life. Once when he thought he had finally reached the island of his dreams he landed at Cuba. Another time it was Haiti. He was, in any case, spared a great disappointment. While he gilded his imagined Zipangu with his boldest fantasies, its hundred-and-second Mikado died so poor that his corpse remained before the palace gates forty days, for lack of enough money for a conventional burial.

The motley company on the Chinese junk were as

feverish for the magic island as Marco Polo and Colum
bus had been. The mysterious place had been discovered
in the interim by white men, too. Six years before, a
Portuguese ship carrying a hundred men had been
stranded on its southernmost islet, Tanegashima. The
headman of the village on whose shores they had landed
using a stick to shape Chinese letters in the sand, had
written: "I do not know from what land these men have
come. How strange they look." Goho, one of the seamen
who understood the Chinese characters, had answered
again using the stick: "These men are merchants from
the southwest barbarian land. They know the difference
between master and servant, after a fashion, but I do
not believe there are any strict rules of courtesy among
them. They drink from a glass without handing it to
another person. They eat with their hands instead of
chopsticks. They permit themselves to be ruled by their
passions. They are not familiar with the alphabet. They
are migratory people, now here, now there, with no fixed
abode. They seek to exchange that which they have for
something else which they have not. All in all, they
are harmless."

The "harmless" white men endeared themselves to the
yellow men in a short time. The Portuguese had an
object on board ship which greatly impressed the Japa
nese. It was a straight and very heavy affair, hollow on
the inside. At the breech it had a secure lock, at the
side, an aperture. The white men inserted a magical
substance into the opening and, with it, a small lead ball

A white disk was then fastened to the edge of a rock. The marksman who held the instrument in his hand stood upright, closed one eye, lighted a fire through the hole, and then instantly hit his mark. The spectators learned to their astonishment that iron walls could be crushed with this instrument, men and beasts killed. The Prince of Tanegashima sent word to the merchants of the "barbarian land" that he would like to learn the use of this instrument. The merchants replied, "The whole secret lies in remaining sincere at heart and closing one eye." When the Portuguese returned to their station their report on the newly discovered people was celebrated with festivities. A thanksgiving procession marched from the church of Our Lady of the Conception, to the church of Saint James. A special mass was read. Then junks were hastily equipped with goods for barter in the new territory. They were all anxious to be the first to bring muskets and wine to "The Land of the Gods."

Xavier and his comrades brought neither Occidental muskets nor Indian spices with them. Six years after the white weapons had been introduced, they were going to introduce the white God. While the bureaucratic monk wrote flaming and upbraiding letters, letters which traveled the wide world as proxies of their writer, Francis Xavier, his best commercial representative crossed the China Sea and the sea of Japan to conquer a new market for the export house next door to the church of Santa Maria.

It was not easy to maintain communication between the central office and this outpost. In Indian Goa, Xavier had authorized entrusting the European mail to the two royal ships which came to Malacca in September and April. Now, it was his advice, that as many copies as possible be made of the letters and sent by all possible routes. The General in Rome could not expect an answer to a communication directed to the Moluccas in less than three years and nine months. How long would it be before the representative in Japan received the decision of his firm on a question which he might ask today? Yet this distance was less than the smallest fraction of a second. Ignatius Loyola had already crossed the sea in the person of Francis Xavier.

Only restlessness distinguished the disciple from the master. The noble, intended for the sedentary life of a place holder in the cathedral at Pampeluna, could at no time call a halt to his activity. He had been on the road for ten years now. Between Lisbon and the Moro Isles he had proclaimed his God of love and sternness to many peoples, to the forsaken Christians of the East African Island of Sokotra, enslaved by a Mohammedan garrison, as well as to the pearl fishers of south India. The "great Padre" was honored and feared on the fishing coast. He treated the sick who wasted away in the pestilential atmosphere of rotting pearl oysters, and left behind him in every village an outline of his doctrine of salvation written on palm leaves. Sometimes, too, he sent out the village jailer with the instruction: "There will be a silver coin for you, for every woman you catch drinking palm wine, and three days in jail for the woman. People will either mend their ways or spend their days in jail." With such love and sternness, he won and drove souls to the fold. When luck was good as many as ten thousand at a time were set on the road to salvation. He conquered Ceylon. He prayed at the grave of the Apostle Thomas whom he revered as the patron of India. He pushed on into the Malayan Archipelago, a thick, primeval forest inhabited by a barbaric and treacherous people, more heathen than the Mohammedans. He even functioned as a matrimonial agent, and with great success. The godless would see what blessings his God brought.

Yet because he lived without patience, he also lived without peace. He overcame all obstacles except the one that can only be conquered by waiting. If immediate success were not forthcoming, if reverses beset him, he was overcome. The reports to his central office were just as facile as his Chief had ordered, empty gestures which might cheer the brothers far and near. But for the inner sanctum the letters interspersing the announcements of converted provinces and converted civilizations struck a more faint-hearted note. The word of the Saviour reached no farther than the Portuguese muskets. The sinful natives hated the holy doctrine. They became fierce if one so much as mentioned it. The reason? The foreigners who should have led the lives of exemplary Christians were no credit to the Saviour, nor did they make His religion desirable.

Here in the East, Xavier was fighting against Christians for his Christ. They tore down whatever he built up. An official with a salary of three thousand ducats a year bled two hundred thousand ducats in two years out of the poor Paravas. Besides, these natives paid tribute to the Portuguese court and their local landlords, and contributed to "the slippers of the Queen of Portugal." In addition to all this, they were also bled by the resident Christians. "These stockings will enable you to walk into the kingdom of heaven," Xavier had jested when he was permitted to draw on the "slipper" fund. Did this messenger of the Redeemer know that he was proclaiming the legend of the Saviour at the expense of the miserable pearl fishers? It was here that the gentle Xavier now preached the God of kindness, the God who permitted a man only one wife. Meanwhile His Christians, before these same natives, testified to a God of greed, a Christ whose followers kept harems of twenty women, Siamese, Peguan, and Negro. Xavier arrived at a simple, logical conclusion. The rich and powerful Christians of the Occident must be the first converted to their God. Xavier upheld the rights of the native princes and peoples. He commanded the bishops to excommunicate abductors of girls. He threatened a higher functionary with the inquisitor. He wrote to the king in Lisbon: "If you do not threaten your officials with chains, prison, and the confiscation of goods, and do not also carry out this threat, all your attempts to advance Christianity in India will be futile. It tortures me to look on

patiently while your captains abuse the newly converted." Was the missionary turning revolutionary?

Such a logical and antagonistic change of heart would
have been contrary to the practical principles of his
Company. The Master would, no doubt, have dismissed
his dearest Francisco without notice. Perhaps some
energetic colonial official of the Portuguese King had
already spoken to the rebel who had traveled to the
royal lands with royal gold pieces and by royal ship:
"Look here, my good envoy! You are expected to do no
more than substitute Christ for this Mohammed who has
been a nuisance to us ever since he came into power
here sixty years ago. On the east coast of Africa, in
Arabia, in Persia, in India, on the far Moluccas, the
Mohammedans were in possession until we came. We
have driven them away. But our empire is unsteady: it
depends heavily upon our fortresses, our guns, and our
fleet which is the only connecting link between the lonely
stations lying hundreds of miles apart. You, my good
missionary, need not trouble yourself with the inclina-
tions and shortcomings of our administrators and merchants. You are merely supposed to use God to reinforce
our constantly threatened army."

Xavier was a dreamer who kept his eyes open. He
dropped his untenable project and continued onward.
He triumphed over his setbacks with even greater plans.
He would not despair until he had traveled around the
world. There were still many countries where Christ had
never been heard of. A few years ago Japan had been

discovered. The merchants reported it inhabited by a courteous, intelligent people, eager to learn. Immediately Xavier, the poet, sent his Chief in Rome the most alluring reports of this land of great promise. Soon the Chief would receive the letter in which his representative described Japanese calligraphy: "The Japanese differ significantly from other people in their way of writing. They write from bottom to top. When I asked the Japanese Paul why they did not write as we do, he answered, 'Why don't you do as we do? It is proper that men begin with the lowest and work up to the highest.'"

The same Paul, who was now returning with his two servants on the Chinese junk, was Xavier's guaranty of great future victories. The Japanese were anxious, too, to accept the God of the white men after having accepted their muskets. The Japanese Anjiro, the first of his country to travel with the Portuguese into the "southwest barbaric land," became one Paul of the holy belief in the college at Goa. His two Japanese servants now bore the Christian names, John and Anthony. Paul, born Anjiro, sighed deeply. He was sorry for his compatriots who still worshiped the sun and moon. He knew those at home would welcome the Christian belief with joy, for it was written in Japanese books that a time would come when all men would have the same law. Xavier had learned from his Japanese pupil, from the sea captain, Alvarez, and from Portuguese traders, that the Japanese were different from any of the peoples he had previously encountered on his journeys. They drank a

280

wine fermented from rice. They ate from earthen bowls which were black on the outside and red inside. They were very proud and easily offended. They loved weapons and had a weakness for Kaffir-bread. God had given the different peoples different figures, colors, and customs. The varied exterior was interesting but had little importance. All that mattered was how ripe the spirit was for Christ and these Japanese were riper for Christ than any people between Lisbon and the point on the world's surface over which he now stood. Such, at any rate, was the belief of this dreamer whose will was as firm as a tree and whose mind was as clear as water.

The Chinese junk sailed into the bay. Anjiro's countrymen sat in fisher boats with high sails. They wore loincloths and broad, pointed straw hats. Grayish-brown, fragile houses covered with straw and weighted down with stones stood on wooded hills surrounded by high, blue, smoking mountains. High-storied pagodas with soaring roofs towered over the settlement. This was the harbor of Kagoshima, Anjiro's home. His mother, his wife, and his daughter offered the strangers a hearty welcome.

The room was a vacant area, confined by sliding walls of paper, its floor covered with mats. Squatting on their heels, men in colored embroidered jackets of unbleached linen, armed with sword and dagger, sat in a circle, side by side with women in long flowing robes gathered at the hips. With deep bows and nimble genuflections, the guests were offered hospitality. The white strangers accompanied by their black attendant aroused curiosity on all sides. Anjiro's friends desired news of the "barbarian southwest land." The master of the house enthusiastically reported the extraordinary discovery he had made in the unknown realms, the new God. What might the Samurai of Kagoshima not have concluded from this well-intentioned but untrained convert who translated incorrectly and improvised unskillfully, putting the words of his yellow countrymen into the mouth of the white God! His teachers were familiar only with the instructions they had given him, not with the distortions of his translation. Anjiro's relatives and acquaintances were eager for information. Of what material had the Invisible one, who had now landed on their shore, created the soul? He had created it like the sun, the moon, and the other attributes of the world without material, by His will alone! What color was the soul and what shape? If the air, which really was corporeal, had no color, how could the soul which was without body have color? Yet the Christian doctrine could not be true because it had remained unknown to the Japanese until then. Why had the Christian God, if He was really omnipotent, kept the Japanese in ignorance till now? The yellow men's skepticism struck at the white Creator's weakest spot. If this God was truly benevolent why had He created the Devil? Why did He permit his beloved children to sin? Why did He make it so hard for them to reach paradise? Why was He so cruel to those who had departed this life with-

ut knowledge of His magnificence, that they were required to roast in hell forever? This severe God must
either be impotent or the worst of all devils. One could
never tell, the Great Unknown might very well be a
devil. The yellow men became greatly perturbed over
the fate of their dead. They implored their countryman,
His interpreter, to put in a good word for the innocent
Japanese departed. But Xavier was as inexorable as his
God was sympathetic.

The yellow men who despised loud speech whispered
excitedly about the white men standing among the de-
baters like statues. The three Spaniards understood no
Japanese. They were the inarticulate symbols of a strange
God. But it was unwise not to speak for their own
candidate. Xavier had an account of the Creation translated, Lucifer's fall, the sin of Adam and Eve, the
Saviour's life history. He recorded the Japanese words
in Latin letters. Then, twice a day, on the temple terrace,
he repeated sounds which he did not understand. The
Heavenly One, the preacher informed his public, had
not permitted Adam and Eve to procreate until they
had been united by their Creator in the holy bonds of
matrimony. There was as yet no wanton Christian life
on the island to give his statement the lie. The Christian
God, he said further on in his address, forbade the
peasants, the artisans, and the merchants of Kagoshima
to continue praying to His wooden and stone competitors,
or to tolerate the practices of Sodom. "Whoever commits
such sin is filthier than the swine." In Kagoshima, there

were as yet no Christian swine to antagonize the new
God's recruiter.

Despite the good luck of being able to teach the work
of Christ without the living example of Christians, the
white man's argument was not wholly convincing. An
invisible God, as yet untried, was being offered in exchange for the visible gods with which the public was
familiar. Besides, this Unknown prohibited favorite native customs. The very poor were almost the only ones
to give Him a trial. They had nothing to lose by giving
up their old god. Perhaps the foreign One sympathized
with the wretched. But even this scant harvest was denied
the representatives of the Company. Like God the Father
and God the Son, the yellow princes of heaven, too, had
a varied and numerous retinue, servants learned and
unlearned, pious and impious, adroit and blundering.
Xavier would have to best them all before he could clear
a path through the island for his Lord.

What did it matter if he had not a glimmering of
Japanese theology! What harm was there in his knowing
nothing of the complex world of gods which existed
here? At the Sorbonne, Francisco de Xavier had scarcely
been informed of the Indian Nihilist who had set up a
new race of gods in Japan on the old Shinto ones. Like
the Japanese people and like the bonzes, he knew nothing
of his God's great competitor, or merely what he could
make of the gold images, flashing from the inner obscu-
rity of the temples; evil, wild demons, and saints squatting on lotus leaves. He had studied none of their innu-

nerable bibles. But neither had the public. The holy
books were not even translated into the language of the
country. Xavier's ignorance was of no disadvantage to
his Company. It was not the philosophy of the yellow
people's heaven but their functionaries' fear of competition that barred the Christian God's way into the hearts
of the Japanese.

Xavier must have found the bonzes with their shaven
heads and black-robed figures very familiar. Had he
not seen all this before? They slept with the nuns. They
seduced aristocratic youths entrusted to their cloistered
protection. They sold amulets and holy water, consecrated sand and shrouds stamped with sacred characters.
They arranged ceremonies for those in sorrow and those
in joy. These pursuits brought them a fairly good living.
Only the costumes were different than those at home.
Four or five fathers might come to the temple escorting
an old woman. From the tabernacle, there would be
brought a drum, a hoop with bells, a woman's gown, and
a multicolored scarf. The woman would put on the dress,
tie the scarf around her, then, in honor of her dead husband, sing and dance to the bonzes' music. The care of
souls was one of the thousand ways of making a living,
no more holy or unholy, sometimes more simple, sometimes less so, than any other business. As everywhere
under the heavens, the special claims made by the men
of this profession provoked scorn. "Before a bonze
becomes Buddha," the Japanese people said, "dung will

turn into bean soup." The white agent met many old
acquaintances under the yellow man's heaven.

The bonzes fought back hard. Here was a new God
with a new following who wanted to take their customers
away. The white competition was something to be
reckoned with. The foreign priests resorted to the trick
of desiring nothing for themselves. They were cheaper
than the cheapest since they could underbid the most
modest demands of their Japanese colleagues. The bonzes
had to fight or be bested. They crept from house to house
crying down the Christian God and promoting their own
stock. Why should the Japanese people forsake the gods
of their fathers and trust to the Unknown One who
tolerated none besides himself? What did this new association have to offer? They, the bonzes of Kagoshima,
had at least proven their merits. They had equally
shared the burdens of this earth with their fellow citizens.
It was impossible to comply with all the commandments
of the gods in this life. Yet, had they not performed their
clients' duties, balanced the sins of others with an excess
of priestly perfection? Would anyone reproach the
bonzes for eating at the expense of those whose spiritual
burdens they took upon themselves? Or would anyone,
misled by the unfair white competitors, hold it against
the bonzes that they did not concern themselves with the
poor? Were the bonzes of Kagoshima to join hands with
the peasants who repeatedly resisted and violated the
divine order? Those who could not pay had no right to
hope for Paradise. Heaven had abandoned the miserable

rtisans from the beginning, else why did it refuse them
what it granted the rich so freely? And now here came
his Xavier with his gospel for those who had nothing.
He taxed nothing. Indeed, his Kingdom of Heaven was
more accessible to the beggar than to the gentleman.

Here in Japan there were as yet no rich Portuguese
to tempt the natives' eyes with the treasures salvation
would bring. The yellow men, however, could very
quickly realize that this God of Bounty ruled as im-
potently over the powers of the earth as their domestic
gods who preferred to admit no servant to heaven. The
bonzes resolved on a measure which was not especially
Japanese in character. They applied to the prince of
their country and roused him against their competitors.
They threatened the sovereign who had protected their
rivals, with the wrath of the gods of his country. The
daimio Shimatsu Takahisa had been favorably disposed
to the new men at the beginning. When Xavier paid his
first visit, the lord of the country, sitting on an elevated
stage, offered due reverence to the image of the Virgin.
The princess mother and her ladies prostrated themselves before the unknown saints; they requested repro-
ductions which no painter in the country could execute.
The prince's heraldic device, a white cross, served to
reassure the white men. They were unaware that this
symbol of their devotion represented the bit of a horse's
bridle. The prince asked Xavier to keep for him carefully the books in which the doctrine was set down. One
day, convinced of the rightness of the new God, he would

turn to him and the devil would be beside himself wit
rage. A year later, the lord of Kagoshima went over t
the hostile bonzes. He forbade any conversion to Chri
tianity under penalty of death. Had the welcome fo
eigner committed some blunder in the meantime, or ha
the bonzes convinced their prince of the superior merit
of their laws? The ruler of this province of Satsum
on the southernmost coast of the main islands, sought t
extend his dominion over all the island of Kyushu. I
was for this reason he had considered the white Go
How had the ungrateful foreigners reciprocated the gr
cious prince's hospitality? The ships of the Portugues
landed not in the harbors of Satsuma, but on the islan
of Hirado, a rival territory. Could Takahisa be on th
side of a world ruler who took sides against Takahisa

After this contretemps Xavier resumed his pilgrimag
He still kept faith in the Japanese as in the Gospel. "The
are the best people we have come upon yet, and it seem
to me we shall never find any other among unbeliever
to excel them." The heart of the old Navarrese militar
aristocrat beat warmly for a people who took deligh
in weapons and set great store by them, who were de
sirous of honor and respect, whose bourgeois honore
the nobles, whose nobles deemed it an honor to serv
the prince. Francisco de Xavier had not forgotten hi
origin, and because of it, he loved the Japanese even i
they did not reciprocate. The people refused his god
The bonzes intrigued. The prince asked him to leave
The Spaniard still did not understand the Japanes

anguage. He wrote (*quia absurdum*): "It is quite clear o the Japanese that the Christian religion is the true ne and the one inherited from their fathers is false." Ie continued his pilgrimage in this belief. "The illus-rious grandson of the sun," the prince over all the rinces of the islands, was enthroned at Miako, the mperial city. He would accept the new god. He could vith his power overthrow the old gods. Like the Chief n Rome, Xavier the traveling representative, was con-inced that Christ must always ally himself with the nightiest earthly power. Such an alliance did not work ut well for the passive ally. Christ's diplomats, Ignatius f Loyola and Francisco Xavier committed, in this con-ection, the same significant error which had under-nined their Lord for centuries.

Xavier made his way over the highways and seas of he world with all the valor of his master's pilgrimage to erusalem and Paris, to Venice and Rome. The mission-ries to Japan carried their worldly possessions over the ostile island in two wallets; a priestly robe, some shirts, n old cover for the night. The bowl of rice, which was heir food, was contained in a little bag hung at the girdle.)n sea, the moment a suspicious ship appeared, they vould hide below deck. On land they were mocked, and toned by children. Xavier wandered barefoot over icy oads and waded through freezing streams. His feet welled, burst at the veins and bled. Yet the very thought f being permitted to bring the message of salvation to hese distant regions caused him to leap for joy. At

Miako the missionaries would build a church to the Mother of God so that Christians who came to these islands in the future would be able to invoke the Virgin of Miako during the frightful storms of the Chinese archipelago. The alliance between emperor and God would be concluded at Miako. The General desired not only what was Caesar's to be rendered unto Caesar, but that Caesar be rendered unto God. To what end should the emperor be God's ally? So that God might reign over the entire world! Why did the Company not leave it to the Almighty God Himself to establish His rule over the earth? Obviously because they did not trust His omnipotence. Yet they depended on Him to curb His powerful allies to His own ends.

Francisco had heard a great deal about the illustrious grandson of the sun goddess, Amaterasu, to whom he intended to propose two business matters which apparently had very little connection with one another. The first concerned the monopoly for the white god, and the second, the sending of a Japanese agent to the "southwest barbarian land" to purchase Indian products. Xavier actually knew very little about the future ally of his Saviour. He was unaware that the great Boo was pope and emperor in the same person; that when the moon waned he withheld himself from his wife and promenaded through the palace in a white robe, wearing a broad crown on his head; that he must remain chaste till the end of his life if his wife died after his thirtieth year.

Unfortunately his informants forgot to advise the Occidental exporter that the trip to Miako would scarcely be worth its cost. Behind its mighty walls, the old imperial city lay shriveled and ravaged. The metropolis of the "land of great peace" constantly resounded with the war cries of contending factions. For generations, the grandson of the sun had met with nothing but disaster. Powerful vassals diverted public taxes into their own coffers while the emperors starved. When Grandfather Go-Tscuchimikado-Tenno died, his descendants had not enough money for his funeral. The heir to the throne could pay for the coronation ceremonies only with the aid of Buddhist priests. The ruler whom Loyola's traveling agent now visited lived in a neglected peasant's hut behind a bamboo hedge, fortified with bushes. The emperor of Japan lived by copying songs, and as his customers, who were also his subjects, were not permitted to see the "illustrious grandson of the sun" face to face, they left their orders and honoraria in front of a curtain. An audience with the imperial copyist cost six hundred ducats. Perhaps the copyist might have been persuaded to accept the princely gifts from the "southwest barbarian land" as payment, but he was no longer even able to send an agent to India or drive away the defenders of the Japanese gods. Of what earthly use to Christ was a day-laboring grandson of the sun?

Xavier was not at a loss for what to do. If nothing could be accomplished with the emperor, one turned to where the power was, to the prince of Yamaguchi. This favored individual received the artistically inscribed parchments of the Indian governor and the bishop of Goa, as well as the thirteen presents which likewise had been intended for the man behind the bamboo hedge. The gifts argued their cause more eloquently than the Japanese version of the Gospel according to Saint Matthew. There was a delicately wrought clock which struck every hour, twelve times a day and twelve times a night. There was a musical contraption which sang without a voice. There were a pair of little round glasses with the aid of which an old man could see as clearly as a young one. And finally, there was the great symbol of white renown in Japan, a richly decorated harquebus with three barrels.

Utchi Yoshitaka was greatly pleased; he wished to make princely return for the precious and unknown wonders. The Roman Company, however, accepted neither gold nor silver. It reckoned in another coin, in concessions for its goods. Entrance could not be refused a spirit who had proven himself so noble. The subjects of Yoshitaka read a proclamation in the busiest squares of the city: it had pleased their authority to give the new lord a chance. The people of Hamaguchi had just as much curiosity as those of Kagoshima. The empty Buddhist cloister, which had been assigned to the white man, was overrun by natives from early morning till far into the night. The Company's representatives could hardly fight off the intruders. The missionaries no longer had even time enough to say the breviary and to eat.

They were, to be sure, an attraction to which no great respect was accorded. On the street people shouted after them: "Look at those priests. They claim it is wrong to have more than one wife." But Xavier, an accomplished propagandist like all the agents of the Roman house, was well satisfied, "Thus with mockery and scorn they become impressed with the fundamental teachings of our religion."

Progress was made in several other ways. A ruffian spat in the face of Xavier's companion. The spectators were indignant. Only the victim remained unperturbed. He wiped his face casually and continued preaching with perfect equanimity. Self-mastery made a strong impression on these people who idealized absolute control over the passions. The new God had won a victory. Even among the bonzes He met with some success. The white men taught that the earth was round. They explained the course of the sun, the origin of rain and hail, the causes of the moon's eclipses. In Yamaguchi, too, the parasites of the gods defended their monopoly tenaciously; but the learning of the foreign priests impressed a race which knew how to value the intellect.

The first new souls were hardly won over before restless Xavier moved farther on. A Portuguese ship had landed in Bungo. It carried mail for him, letters which had been sent from the Indian college at Goa a year and a half before. Father Antonia Criminale had suffered a martyr's death in the north of the fishing coast; he became the first martyr of the Society. The four Japa-

nese whom Xavier had sent over to Malacca from Kagoshima had been baptized on Ascension Day. The governor of India had died. New representatives had not
come, unfortunately, because the Company needed six
agents for the settlement among the Brazilian Indians
alone. Gomez, the Rector of Goa, had dismissed twenty-
seven native pupils and replaced them with Portuguese
novices. This Gomez was really no good at all! The students belonged to all nations where it was at all possible to spread the faith: Malabars, Canarese, Tuticorins,
Malays from the Malacca region and the Moluccas; Chinese, Bengalese, Peguese, Siamese; Kaffirs from Sofala,
Mozambique, and the Saint Lawrence Island, as well
as eight Abyssinians and ten Kanarese from the vicinity
of Goa. Gomez was a bad governor, more a defender of
the white race than a Christian. Xavier must go back to
India at once and set things to rights. Then he would conquer Japan a second time, indirectly through China,
because the island would at once worship a God recognized by its great, respected neighbor. Xavier would do
one more thing before his departure. He would make
his overtures to the Prince of Bungo.

When the Portuguese fired four salutes in honor of
his arrival, the sound broke on the rocks with such an
uproar, that the prince mistook his guests for pirates.
At the news that a mighty and revered bonze had come
to visit business friends, the lord of Bungo addressed
an ingratiating letter of invitation to the padre. It was
delivered by a young relative of the ruler, accompanied

by thirty samurai. When the delegation departed the Portuguese fired fifteen shots. They knew what they owed their Saviour.

In India, Xavier had worn faded and filthy rags in the service of the humble Nazarene. Japan demanded of the servant of Emperor Christ a wardrobe befitting his rank. So the traveling representative strode past the high volcanoes to the Funai Residency, to the tune of festive music, in gala uniform and accompanied by a Portuguese bodyguard. The houses were jammed to the roofs with sightseers eager for the spectacle. Thirty boys, in holiday regalia, with gold chains glittering about their necks, headed the procession. The august Signor Xavier wore a black soutane with a white rochette and a stole of green velvet bordered with embroidered brocade. Next came the commanding officer of the ship, a truncheon in his hand. Five of the most respected merchants brought the presents: a book in a wallet of white satin, a pair of black velvet slippers, a Bangalese cane with gold head, an image of the Madonna, wrapped in violet damask. Thus Christ's caravan paraded through the nine main streets of the city to the palace. Here the gentlemen in the suite of the august prelate spread their precious cloaks for him over the mat-covered floor. The ascetic had assumed the role of a proud majesty.

The high volcanic peaks of Bungo disappeared into the distance. The junk, Duarte da Gama steered southwestward. Xavier had spent two years and three months laboring on the island of his ambitions. If Xavier, once again at sea, reviewed the Japanese adventure he certainly could not rate the success of his operations against the sage men of God very highly. Only in three localities had he left behind him little Christian communities. What Christians! They could barely make the sign of the cross. Perhaps they could also parrot one or two prayers in their own language. Many of them had been baptized on the same day they had learned of the existence of a God other than their own. Xavier, however, was too romantic to examine his Japanese experience objectively. His only reality was what he imagined. The future had always meant more to him than what was past. Yet this wanderer was no ineffectual poet, but rather a shrewd business man. Beside him sat two Japanese Christians whom he had brought along as the first fruits of his harvest. He sent them to the General in Rome with the message, "I hope they will be amazed at the might and wealth of the Christians." It would only be necessary to show the Japanese what treasures and powers favored the new God. Then the yellow men, returning home with their reports, would themselves be the best propagandists. Don Francisco de Xavier was no idle dreamer.

He would have done credit to any export house in the world, this adaptable fanatic. If soldiers stopped gambling when he entered their canteens, he encouraged them to continue. Soldiers were not monks, he was glad to see them enjoying their game. He reminded the Viceroy of India that, "he who would be first to seek the Kingdom of God would not want for material advantages." The king subsidized the transactions of the white God with more than a thousand gulden. The enterprising patron must be shown that his gold pieces would bear good interest. Saintly Xavier knew the profane mainsprings of human beings as well as his holy General did, and exploited them just as unscrupulously. He reported to the Portuguese officials not only on the advantages of building a church to the Blessed Mother of God in Miako, but also on the key position of the seaport Sakai, Japan's chief commercial city. "With the help of God, the King of Portugal's agents should easily obtain the right of settling in this city." Xavier was not merely an exporter of religion; he was a pioneer in Portuguese commerce as well. It was not that he wanted to make money on the side, but, "because the spice was to be suited to each individual appetite; those who are used to reckoning in temporal gain are unimpressed by the promise of spiritual advantages." The devil might have employed the same argument. The merchant was as dangerous an associate as the emperor. But the ambassadors of Jesus Christ did not mind.

"Follow the other man's course to your own goal." Thus spake Loyola. Thus Francisco de Xavier, doctor of the Sorbonne, volunteer of Christ, served as Portuguese commercial agent and diplomat—following the other man's course. He arrived at a better understanding with princes and merchants than ever he had had with priests and scholars—following the other man's course. Thus he, who touched no money himself, concerned himself with enriching the rich—following the other man's course. Thus this dreamer, whose present existed only in the future, trained himself along the courses of others to the extent of understanding that his God would be tolerated on commercial ships only as a kind of deadhead passenger. "We shall rejoice when Christ is preached even if only incidentally, and shall count it a gain if the Kingdom of Heaven is regarded at least as an adjunct to temporal prosperity." Would the adjunct really one day outbalance the massive temporal prosperity to which it was merely incidental?

A year after his departure from Bungo, the aggressive missionary of Japan was waiting on one of the little islands before Canton. Innumerable ships lay in the harbor of Sancian. A row of huts hastily constructed out of branches and straw, and extending to the beach, was occupied by the Portuguese merchants who had come for contraband trading with the Chinese. Beyond these huts, on the other side of the labyrinthine island thirty miles away, lay the great commercial city. Elegant and sedate gentlemen in white pantaloons and loose jackets secretly exchanged silks, lacquer, and porcelain for pepper, spices, and aloe wood. The captain, George Alvarez, received his friend, Francisco de Xavier, in a reed hut. With a yearning glance the missionary surveyed his new love, his latest promised land. The stone houses in the distance appeared large and well built. A single lord

298

ruled over these devoted and obedient subjects. Admirable laws governed an intelligent people who respected knowledge and loved peace, who were not troubled by civil wars like the Japanese. Perhaps the island was already inhabited by brothers in Christ. Xavier might not have been informed at Sainte-Barbe that Christ had entered the middle empire nine hundred years before and three hundred years ago a Great Khan had petitioned the Pope for a hundred learned followers of the Occidental Saviour. This Great Khan on whose birthday Christians, heathen, and Saracens prayed their respective gods to bless their ruler, was in the habit of saying: "Four prophets are honored by the four creeds of the world. The Christians worship Jesus, the Jews honor Moses, the Mohammedans Mohammed, the heathen Buddha. I honor and revere all four and ask him who in reality is the greatest among them to help me." Certainly Xavier would have found this Great Khan too eclectic. Even in the land of serenity, this magnanimity never became part of the permanent order. If the missionary crossed over to the island now he would seek his Christians in vain.

He discussed various problems with the merchants. Hesitantly he revealed to them his wish to be taken to the mainland. The risk was great. The smuggling of aliens was severely punished. Finally, however, he found someone who would sail him across for twenty hundredweight of pepper. The man would conceal him in his house for three or four days and then, under cover of

night, lead him to the gates of the city. Xavier, armed
with letters to the Emperor of China, would go to the
governor of Canton. If he could then make no headway
he must arrange to accompany the emissaries who each
year went from Siam to Peking. But bad news arrived.
The Portuguese men had again fallen into the hands of
the Chinese. Terror spread over the island. Xavier's
Christian attendants deserted him. The Portuguese captain whose approval was required for every trip to the
mainland asked him to postpone the excursion until business transactions were concluded and the ships had sailed
away. Xavier was resolved to go to China despite all
odds. China must be won just as once the Roman Empire
had been won. If the emperor were converted, his people
would follow.

The Portuguese burned their huts and sailed south-
ward. Alvarez went away without taking leave. No doubt
he felt no reconciliation could take place after the separation. The little island was quiet once more. Xavier
waited in vain for the Chinese who were to take him
across. The involuntary delay forced the habitual pre-
visionist for once to look back. He had just recently
learned that Pope Paul had died more than thirty months
before. He had also received the first letter in four years
from brother Ignatius. The aloof man in Rome had sub-
scribed himself, "Wholly yours, who can never forget
you." Xavier wept for joy. Portuguese India and the
neighboring regions (with the exception of Ethiopia and
West Africa) had been designated by decision of the

main office in Rome as a special province of Portugal. Xavier was now Provincial of the southeastern empire. More than these honors which he felt as a burden rather than a distinction, those last words sank benignly into his restless heart, "Wholly yours, who can never forget you." Nor could Francisco ever forget his companions of Paris—Íñigo, Pierre, Diego, Alfonso. Like the oath sworn in St. Paul's Without the Walls, he wore their signatures on his breast as priceless relics. The image of "the father of his soul" burned in him with an eternal flame. It was for him that Francisco traveled around the world. To him, before every new voyage, Francisco confided his most ambitious plans. Before setting out on his Chinese campaign, he had written "the father of his soul": "I am assured that one can travel from China to Jerusalem. If I find this to be true I will report to you how many miles it is and how many months it takes. Your most insignificant and farthest banished son."

Now the farthest banished son waited in vain for the smuggler who was to take him into the paradise beyond the northern horizon. Loyola's most insignificant son who was satisfied with the rice of the poor pearl fishers and the bitter herbs of Japan, who for a thousand nights had rested his tired head on an anchor rope or a wooden pillow, who fared through the world in the guise of a poor priest unless he must don the masquerade of pride, saw in the distance his last Promised Land. He was destined never to reach it! The great arraigner of human self-sufficiency, the nimblest juggler who ever fought for

Jesus Christ, Francisco Jassu y Xavier, born the son of a lord forty-six years before, now lay down to die on the threshold of a new great hope. In Tamil, Malay, Japanese, and Basque, he still muttered what was ever-present in his mind. His servant understood not a word. As the morning of December 27, 1552, dawned, the faithful Chinese Aman with the Christian name of Anthony lighted the dead candle. He placed it in the hand of the departing Father Francisco. An icy wind rushed through the joints of the hut.

More than half a year later, at the end of June, General Ignatius decreed Xavier's return to Rome: "You can send others to China and instruct them so that your purposes will be realized. Thus you will really be multiplied and will be able to do in many places what you could personally do in only one."

Francis Xavier had been the best duplication of Ignatius Loyola.

Purge in Portugal

THE General maintained in Portugal, one of the most affluent provinces of his wide empire, a spiritual garrison of two hundred and thirty-five warriors for God. Thirteen years before, shortly after the Company's inception, he had sent two of his best officers there at the suggestion of the King. They immediately attracted great attention. The populace marveled at the strange men who remained poor and modest in the midst of a rich and magnificent court. The courtiers overwhelmed them with reverence. The thirty-eight-year-old John III, son of Manuel under whom Vasco da Gama had discovered the ocean route to India, declared after his first audience, "My greatest wish is to have all of the Society of Jesus in Portugal, even at the cost of part of my royal possessions." What did the sovereign and the court of the mightiest colonial empire get from these "apostles" who lived on another earth and under a different heaven? What attracted people of pleasure to the men of renunciation?

The products of all continents accumulated at Lisbon. From Brazil to the Congo and to the east coast of Africa, from Persia to India, to the spice islands of the Moluccas and to China, it was a common proverb that all the treasures of the world flowed toward Lisbon. But Portu-

gal which was weak and small had bitten off more than
it could chew. Like its neighbor Spain, it wasted away
while strutting in finery. Prosperity is never a question
of surplus, but of equitable sharing. Portugal was both
overnourished and undernourished, and suffered at the
same time from malnutrition. The most industrious strata
of the population, the Moors and Jews, had been driven
out. In their place twelve thousand Negroes were brought
to market each year. The Portuguese masters had cheap
slaves. The Portuguese workers starved, however, in ex-
pectation of the treasures which regularly sailed up the
Tejo. Sometimes they served as overseers of the blacks,
in the hope of becoming white masters, themselves. The
court, the nobility, the landowning Church, all flourished
without roots. Portugal's great era was characterized by
a magnificent unfruitfulness.

The lord of this hollow splendor conceived a great
need for these Roman men of renunciation and discipline. They preached the solace of abstemiousness to a
glutted court. They were a moral chastener for the riff-
raff from America, Africa, and Asia with whom Lisbon
was thronged, as well as for the white slaveholders who,
grown prosperous abroad, dissipated their booty at home.
The royal quarters became an elegant cloister. The Fathers were permitted to give exercises to the Queen, a
duke, and many nobles. Loyola's traveling representatives offered them, despite their personal fortunes, security in that other world which had no gold standard. The

ladies of the court crowded the confessional, tempering
the delights of sin with the joy of forgiveness.

Simon Rodriguez, who had remained behind in Portugal when brother Francisco set out for the Indies, had
not remained as true to form. In thirteen years, the conqueror of the East, had never lost his integrity of purpose nor identity no matter how many roles he assumed
and dropped. In those same thirteen years Simon became
a caricature of the archetype which Íñigo had coined in
Rome. Simon Rodriguez was not of stern enough stuff.
He was an easygoing, rather than a soldierly man, who
conceived of Christ more as a friendly comforter of
souls than an austere field marshal. The lax confessional
practices in Portugal soon became a matter of common
gossip. The main office in Rome which pumped its inexhaustible energy into its farthest outposts by means of
thousands of little letters, began at once to resuscitate
its weak son Simon. "Be constantly on guard, Simon
Rodriguez! Never forget yourself. Always remember
that we are surrounded by enemies! I never permit myself complete peace of mind," the worried father confided to the wayward child. Father Ignatius knew human
beings. Many cultivate our friendship without being our
friends. The wise "children of this world" time and again
find "the children of the light" imprudent and loose-
tongued. The child of light seated at his desk in Rome
had become a guileful saint. Jesus Christ's model diplomat could hold his own with the best Venetian ambassadors. But the child in Lisbon stumbled into difficulties,

not because he was a dreamer, remote from life, but because he was weak. The soldier Simon lacked all military virtues from self-discipline to the power of keeping subordinates firmly in hand. His piety vacillated from laxity to hysteria, from comfortably prolonged sojourns at court to mad, unprecedented performances of mysticism and asceticism. He had adjusted himself too well to the sybaritic atmosphere of the Portuguese court. The King and the General's delegate were on very cordial terms. This accord, however, which was definitely favored in Rome lacked one detail: the archetypal identity behind the diplomatic mask. Beelzebub has no better servant on earth than the holy man who believes himself to be following a star when in reality he is turning his back on it.

Here in Portugal, Loyola's strict campaign had become a comic opera. Every Friday the friends of the order assembled for a nocturnal penitential and flagellant procession. The courtiers were edified by the grimly beautiful spectacle, and crept out to visit it at night, although attendance of the sacramental circus was a violation of etiquette. The young preachers developed great skill in creating disorder at the popular festivals which according to old custom were held in churches. If these disturbers of the peace were thrown out, they became all the more zealous in creating disorder outside. If they were violently suppressed, some particularly ardent young man would fall to his knees and pray God's mercy for the blasphemers. Now in Portugal a second crop was growing up, giving the lie to the saying: "Other orders fish with a net, the Jesuits use a rod and line." The college at Coimbra admitted them indiscriminately. Instead of pursuing their studies, the students made pilgrimages to Santiago and Guadalupe. Or, preparing to be eremites, they ran off to hide in the mountains. Sometimes, an especially ambitious adept was inspired to stroll through the streets naked, to challenge the world's ridicule. Was it possible to serve God constructively in this way? Was a soldier, so burdened with weapons that he could not use them freely, fit for service? Pierre had once observed, quite in the spirit of the man in Rome, that self-denial consisted in witnessing manifestations of self-denial. But Pierre's old friend Simon still praised his pious clowns. Under his régime, it was possible to become a saint of one's own accord. Until the man in Rome drastically intervened.

Loyola did not travel. He sent letters and representatives out into the world. He dispatched Miguel Torres to Lisbon with two authorizations in his pocket. It was up to the delegate which of the two he would use: the honorable recall of the unworthy Provincial or, in case of the King's partisanship for the insubordinate agent, the General's resignation. Was the General dependent on the King? He obeyed only the Pope and no one else in the world. The General's arm, to be sure, was very strong and far-reaching, but it had one great shortcoming. Perhaps for tactical reasons, it trembled before crowns. Loyola might have believed that God could thrive only in the shadow of the king. He certainly was aware of the impotence of any idea which could not be substantiated with muskets. This attitude was deeply rooted in the traditions of the feudal lords of Loyola and the successors to Peter. The servant of the princes in Rome was fond of citing the text of Saint Paul to the Ephesians: "Servants, be obedient to them that are your masters according to the flesh, with fear and trembling, in singleness of your heart as unto Christ." The General could not have been a pupil at the Sorbonne without proving philosophically that the salvation of the King of Portugal was more important than the salvation of his cook. "Just as the body is affected by various states of mind, subjects are affected by the well-being of their prince and to that extent the spiritual aid offered a prince is of first importance." Yet surely not all Portuguese subjects were affected by the well-being of the prince. Loyola, who in his own sphere proceeded implacably, proved himself a foil in the hands of his worldly colleagues. It became apparent that this man of iron will, despite his strength and guile, could never conquer the world. How would he establish Christ's empire if even an unworthy subaltern could defy him simply by taking refuge behind a throne? The Chief in Rome who thought he was serving the Saviour was not even serving the Pope!

Paul had, without reservation, indicated what he thought of the Portuguese Inquisition. The Inquisition had absolutely no bearing upon Christian belief, but on the other hand was typical of the spite which the older Christians felt for the converted Jews. Pope Paul had even denounced the King to the Portuguese ambassador as being more concerned with the Jews' money than with their spiritual welfare. John, according to this statement of the highest Christian authority, was certainly not a very Christian ruler. How did the "janissaries of the Holy Father" react to this sinner against Christ and His representative on earth? Did they rally around their indignant master? The leader of His Holiness' spiritual guards assured the unchristian king that the "most unworthy Society of Jesus" belonged more to his majesty than to itself. He, the General, would not only acquiesce to anyone John requested, but would himself gladly undertake the journey, despite feebleness and old age, if the king wished. Instead of rigorously judging John, the diplomat in Rome forbade his men to take sides, and mediated uncritically between Pope and King. His fidelity to power was stronger than his fidelity to Jesus and he would have had to capitulate if John had decided to keep Rodriguez. The man of iron will at Rome who was magnificently determined to enforce his concept on all humanity, and who on behalf of this concept clashed with the gods of the German pastors, the Indian pearl fishers, and the Japanese bonzes, would not raise a finger (and in this respect again he resembled his great adversary Luther) against the divine order of kings. Not by any means because he was a courtier. He wanted worldly power neither for himself nor for his men. He wanted a world revolution, the Christianization of mankind along with the careful preservation of all privilege.

Two years earlier, on the occasion of a visit to Rome by the Portuguese subaltern, Loyola was forced to realize "that dearest brother Simon could be very obstinate"—as was strictly forbidden—that Rodriguez had made himself the head of a local clique, that the garrison of Portugal showed separatist tendencies. He had tightened the reins. To the Portuguese province, the man in Rome was still a dim figure in the background. His will was as yet only an incomprehensible legend. For two years now he had tenaciously and effectively fought for the endangered cause. There certainly would have been no need for this special delegate, Miguel Torres, if Father Jacob Miron, Rodriguez's intended successor, had not bungled his ticklish task. Miron, "a child of the light," pure and simple, was completely unaware of any difficulty. He did not even discuss matters with John, but baldly, thoughtlessly, announced his appointment as Provincial and forthwith banished his refractory predecessor. Rodriguez, however, did not permit himself to be packed off to Valencia. He negotiated with the King. He feigned illness. He participated in a jubilee indulgence at the college of Coimbra where Miron had made himself decidedly unpopular. Rodriguez had been a good-natured, agreeable principal. Miron, on the other hand, was a niggling kill-joy who even refused to become the King's father confessor because of the special honors connected with the position. The deposed subaltern gave new impetus to the dissatisfied elements. The world empire of the Company next to the Church of Mary was on the verge of collapse.

The King, however, had no special interest in the man who had fallen into disfavor. The insubordinate official, deposed for reasons of discipline, finally took his leave. Miguel inexorably assumed his functions as the General's strong arm. The garrison personnel was thoroughly sifted and more than half its members dismissed. The delegate knew that his Chief never hesitated to draw blood, that he preferred mediocrity to genius which could not be subordinated.

Meanwhile, in his Spanish exile, Simon Rodriguez brooded bitterly over the change in his worldly position. He had, he was sure, got in wrong with the touchy old man in Rome. How much better off the ancient monks had been! They had lived in deserts and sequestered cloisters, barred from all temptation. The General spared his men nothing. He drove them out into the world. He compelled them to live at court. He required them spontaneously to assume any role. And now Simon Rodriguez had taken his role too seriously. Secluded on a mountain top or behind high walls, he might have remained a holy man. The seraglio of Lisbon had been too much for him. Now it was too late. The soldier was no longer ready to go wherever he was commanded. The nomad, whose law was mobility, had taken root. The stoic had turned sybarite. Simon longed for Lisbon; he had lost the freedom which comes from being able to renounce everything. He was willing to give up much, his post, his brotherhood, his

311

reward in heaven, itself, if only his little earthly paradise would not be taken from him.

Perhaps John would help him against Íñigo. Gomez and other malcontents were working for Simon. They circulated a petition asking the reinstatement of the old Provincial. The General was far away. There would be no difficulty in slandering him at court. When these intrigues failed, the lax subaltern turned, whining and injured, to his master. The weak son informed the austere father that he had stumbled because of the weight of his tasks. Only one thing could save him now: return to Portugal, even without office. Rodriguez could not complain to the greedy spider in Rome who had drawn them all into his web, of how he had suffered under the inexorable necessity of yielding to another man's will. He inveighed instead at the unknown persons who had denounced him, who had come between him and his good friend Íñigo. The exile requested a re-examination of "the improper reports" which had caused his demotion. Was he prepared to abide by the decision which his master in Rome would hand down after due consideration? The soldier who had betrayed his obligations could not even wait for an answer to his demands. He deserted exile at his own risk and returned to the life he loved.

What were the reactions of the war lord in Rome? Thirty years had passed since the peacock of the garrison at Pampeluna had drawn his dagger on the harmless muleteers who refused to make way as he walked up the narrow street. The sixty-year-old General was no longer moved by his passions. The man had developed into a world power; now he was motivated only by the interests of his domain.

Brother Íñigo was neither disappointed nor vindictive because his authority had been defied. He entered the Rodriguez case without sentiment. Benignly and ceremoniously, as though the traitor had never endangered the empire, the General permitted him to return to Portugal without office. The rehabilitation of the great god, obedience, was of greater importance than the settling of personal accounts. In a circular to the superiors of the order he enjoined the immediate dismissal of any recalcitrants. The General had suddenly come out of retirement, no longer the dim star of Rome. He still remained invisible but his reflections could be discerned everywhere. The pupils at Coimbra received the proclamation of their chief without seeing his eyes or hearing his voice. His constant absence lent the messages a greater magic and impersonality. They didn't seem to issue from a human being at all. Just as he himself remained invisible, so the motives for this solemn proclamation remained unrevealed. The mentor in Rome did not discuss the case which had moved them all so profoundly. He made no mention of the great disappointment he had suffered, or of the purge to which they had all been subjected. He did not berate the college in which the rebellion had broken out, nor did he justify the expulsion of one of its highest functionaries. To the uninitiate, there was nothing about the letter indicative of the severest crisis in the history of the young order. But every student understood exactly the sentence, "We may even be pleased that other orders outdo us in fasting, vigil, and various austerities; but, dearest brothers, I wish urgently to know that in this society those who have consecrated themselves to God the Lord, are exceptionally distinguished in pure and complete obedience, which includes veritable renunciation of our own wills and the denial of our own judgments." The author of the message and its recipient had the same incident in mind. But what did the youngsters know of their master's rigorous law! Their brains still echoed with phrases suggestive of laxity, "Law of Mercy," "Spirit of Love." "A difference of opinion between subordinates and superiors is out of the question among Christians," they murmured, "because the Law of Mercy distinguishes neither between superior nor subordinate. Any other interpretation would profane the freedom of a true Christian."

The man in Rome offered them a freedom which cut deep. They were to rise from the depths of servile submissiveness and scale the dizzy heights. They were to desire of their own accord whatever was commanded. Compulsory obedience produced sullenness and stupidity. The father wanted open-hearted, eager sons. The students must, with their entire heart and being, will what their superior willed. The Lord God's recruits must have gone faint when this feat was described to them. Going naked through the streets, self-castigation, blind and stupid obedience to the commands of the chief, were all child's play, compared to the sublime and sustained violation of self which was now demanded of them. And even so they had not yet reached the peak.

The General now imposed an exercise which even the most pliable and co-operative students found disheartening. They were not only voluntarily to identify their will with the will of their Chief, but they were also spontaneously to think with his mind. Of course the youngsters were accustomed to yielding to the judgments of their superiors, and mediating only within certain limitations. But that scarcely accorded with the intentions of the father in Rome, that was not obedience enough. "Your General, students of Coimbra, is no tyrant, training beasts with a leash. He does not permit the Society of Jesus to resort to jail and handcuffs. Men who have to be chained do not belong in his Company." When visitors to the house in Rome asked where the student's brig was, he significantly pointed to the street. "Nor, students of Coimbra, is your General a Pied Piper who woos poor dupes into trotting along behind him." He was much more powerful and dangerous. Slaves might one day break their bonds. Victims of illusion might become disillusioned. But the General required every individual to bring his free will and all his personal sagacity and endowments, to being ruled. He did not want his students to relinquish their own will and mind. His was not the narrow egotism of the military officer who is satisfied as long as the will and mind of his subordinates do not affect his company's morale. He made greater demands than any tyrant, any general, any demagogue; he wanted the free, candid, sincere, aggressive yes men.

He was now teaching this transcendent obedience to young men who had just learned how vulnerable a superior could be. Dangerous questions must have occurred to the students, "What if we followed the will and mind of a superior who lacked understanding and was illwilled, dear General? Have you not dismissed those who modeled themselves after Simon Rodriguez whom you appointed and retained in office thirteen years?"

The Chief had already answered these questions before they were asked. "We must never consider the person we obey. We must see in him, Christ our Lord in whose name obedience is due." The imperialist could not rule his empire without the strictest obedience. Absolute obedience is not only the cement of every hierarchy, but a necessary factor, as well, in the administrative routine of any planned economy. The wise administrator in Rome, with a masterly insight into human nature, planted this obedience in the deepest pit of being, in the "free" will of those who were required to obey. Follow instructions implicitly! The Jesuit, when receiving the command of a superior, must not stop to finish a word though his pen is in hand; must not continue celebrating mass when his General calls. "Like a corpse which may be turned this way and that," or "the staff of a senile man which may be leaned upon in whatever way it is held," or "a little wax pellet which may be pressed and pulled into any shape," or "a little crucifix which may be dangled however the notion takes one"; thus the dictator in Rome expected his lively and sensitive recruits to react. And what if he who pressed the wax pellets and dangled the little crucifixes this way and that, were a Rodriguez? Then the creator of the system would step in and take matters in hand, himself.

Rodriguez, however, was no mere nonentity who could quietly and without much ado, be put out of the way. He was a first ranking personage in the Order. The Chief invited him to a conference in a letter which did not seem in any way directed to a deserter, "In order to comprehend correctly what is essential to the greater tranquillity and spiritual comfort of those brothers who have remained loyal in the Portuguese territories, and also to discuss with you other matters of importance to the Society which can be settled only in person, I have resolved in our Lord to ask you to submit to the physical hardships of coming to Rome." To be sure the same mail contained a second letter, a private postscript to the public document. Officially, anybody to whom Rodriguez showed the letter from Rome could be deceived into believing that the ruler and his ex-subaltern were on the friendliest terms; privately, however, the loving father advised the erring son to deliver himself trustingly to the cold arms of justice.

Simon Rodriguez had no liking for the party court. He did not attend it. He did not even answer. Loyola waited in vain, with growing uneasiness. He begged his old comrade to accept the course which had been charted for him. Íñigo in fear of a final rift almost became tender: "Simon, my son! Trust in me! Your soul and mine will be comforted in our Lord by your coming." Rodriguez was in a strategic position. He had nothing to lose but his rank. The powerful General, on the other hand, had his spiritual principles at stake. The only thing that mattered to Rodriguez was a little strip of land. The General, much less free, was possessed by a dream which every passing day could endanger. The man of iron discarded his stiff armor to win the weak brother. He transformed himself from the prime force, the god of his Society, into the nameless pilgrim. There was a time, before he had ever possessed any commanding authority, when Simon merely at Íñigo's word, had traveled to Portugal in the midst of fever. Would this pathetic reminiscence touch the comrade who had changed his ways?

The General waited. "It is now the twelfth of July," his last letter ended, as though the passing days might goad on his negligent subordinate. The Provincial still put in no appearance. He did not even reply. On July 26, Ignatius Loyola wrote the order of expulsion. The writ of excommunication lay on his desk for ten days. He must have considered and reconsidered it in many frames of mind. On the twelfth day, the order which expelled the old comrade of Paris from the ranks of the troops of Christ was sent out.

Simon Rodriguez came to Rome. Ignatius of Loyola received him lovingly. The subordinate had, after all, turned back into the course indicated for him. His superior was greatly gratified at the restoration of harmony. He wished "to bury the past in the deepest pit of oblivion." But that was not Rodriguez's intention. He cared nothing about the divine hierarchy. He wanted only to return to his Portugal. Arbitrarily, he demanded his case examined. He even appealed to the Pope, "at the prompting of the devil." After three months of investigation four arbitrators passed judgment. Rodriguez was exiled from the province of Portugal for life; he was to "retreat" two years and fulfill prescribed penances.

Rodriguez yielded. The father remitted all of the obedient child's punishments except banishment from the land of his longing. The manager did even more for his representative, he protected his authority. Rodriguez's prestige had suffered most on the scene of his long-standing operations. A letter from the Roman central office was sent to the College of Coimbra to the effect that the General daily derived more satisfaction from association with Brother Simon; the Provincial had been called away only because Provincials, according to the laws of the Company, must remain only three years in the same locality; Rodriguez himself wished relief from the burdens of office. Was Loyola unaware of the guilt of his fellow warrior? During the trial, the Cardinal Infante of Portugal had declared that the accused had never tried to alienate the students from the Chief of the house. The General had answered with frigid courtesy that this testimony sufficed to destroy other reliable

319

testimony which proved the contrary. Loyola knew the traitor for what he was. Yet as company commander, he protected him for finally yielding in obedience. Not because of sentiment, but because of party spirit! It was dangerous, the old officer thought, to publicize mistakes. Silence was preferable, even if the Society's authority were to an extent discredited.

The Final Ordeal

No ONE was more embarrassed by Paul's successor than portrait painters. There was nothing attractive about the coarse, peasantlike face. The nose was curved and exaggerated, the eyes were piercing and the lips gave the whole face a pinched expression. Julius III seemed never intended for the words of the prophet Isaiah, "The key of the house of David will I lay upon his shoulder, so he shall open and none shall shut, and he shall shut and none shall open." Julius did not even try to play the part for which he was so miscast. A heavy eater, fond of dishes flavored with garlic, he spiced his indigestible meals, as well, with witticisms equally hard to swallow. A fancier of cardplaying, comedies, and court fools, he was scarcely a source of joy to even the more robust of his contemporaries. Although he had medals struck in praise of *hilaritas publica,* his geniality was merely a fleeting interval between violent anger and cowardly apathy. His gayety was nothing more than an escape from the darker side.

The man in the house next door to the Church of Mary, had committed himself twenty years before to "yes" every Pope as long as he lived. The greater the discrepancy between his concept of the highest spiritual office and the gentleman holding office at the time, the more

321

oppressive became the burden which the former Paris student had undertaken. He bore his onerous obligation in noble silence. He accepted the consequences of his life's mistake as valiantly as a hero. Julius was weak and ready to be very friendly to strong-willed Ignatius. The Pope wanted to make the Duke of Gandia a cardinal. The General, who used all his power to guard his men from distinctions, convinced his master that the Duke was much better off in his undistinguished state. The glutted weakling Julius then complained that God had not permitted him to be a poor idealist, albeit he definitely preferred the role of a simple Jesuit warrior to papal dignity. "You men have no desires, no worries other than serving God; we are involved in many things which distract the mind." Among these distractions, for example, there was the Vigna di Papa Giulio whose banquet halls, painted by the hand of the Zucchieri, were covered with Bacchic processions, wanton bodies, and decorative garlands. Julius had no time to tramp sore-footed over dusty roads. God had burdened him with the task of being rowed upstream along the Tiber in a magnificent barge, surrounded by richly liveried flunkeys and fanned by ostrich plumes. God had further required him, after a short sail, to be lifted into a litter of gold and velvet and in the midst of quips and laughter to be carried to his villa. There it was further necessary for him to take a refreshing bath among marble nymphs and creeping vines, and then subsequently at the table, heartily to devour his favorite giant onions from Gaeta.

It was with such matters that Julius was "involved" while he enviously observed his "free" Jesuit guard. Free, that is, to renounce all worldly joys in order to increase the wealth and power of Pope and princes.

Loyola's opinion of this visible representative of the invisible God remained hidden from the world. The Pope, whoever he was, was above criticism. The Pope, Paul or Julius, was always the master; Ignatius always the servant. The faithful servant exacted stern atonement from his men for any expression which could have been interpreted as a stricture on the holy government. An attack on the Holy Father was an attack on the guiding star of existence. To others, a bad man might compromise a good idea. To the Platonist, Loyola, a good idea justified even the worst man. "We must," the master taught, "be more inclined to praise than to censure the actions, commands, and instructions of our superiors. Though at times they are or seem to be unworthy of praise, criticism of them, nevertheless, in public preaching or in conversation, and in the presence of ordinary people would do more harm than good. It would result only in stirring up people's feelings against their spiritual or temporal superiors." His loyalty to the Pope was only the crown of his loyalty to all earthly powers. He did not discriminate between *de facto* power and divine power—a significant precursor of Hegel. He tried always, and vainly, to render power spiritual; he never tried to render the spirit powerful.

Yet the discrepancy between the Pope to whom he

had pledged himself on the Montmartre and the Pope, whom he had to serve, was in no way veiled to him. The General knew precisely what kind of man he who sat on the chair of Peter was not. "Any Pope would have to do only three things to reform the world," he confided to his intimates. "Reform his own character, reform his house, and reform the Roman court and the city of Rome." He left the equalization of reality and ideas to his God. And God seemed to justify his unalterable trust. The King of Portugal at the death of Julius proposed the General for Pope. But that was not Loyola's idea of success. He forbade his men even to mention the undesired candidacy. He did not want to become Pope. He merely wanted as Pope somebody to whom he could inaudibly acquiesce. And what he longed for was granted.

Toward the end of his life, a man who incorporated perfectly the image which the General had dreamed of for so many years was chosen for the chair of Peter. Slender, wasted Marcellus, whose pale earnest face was impressively framed by a black beard, was the ideal shepherd the six students had in mind when they took the oath on Montmartre. The thorns and prickles of the papal throne hurt Marcellus. The tiara weighed so heavily upon him that his shoulders drooped. He had come into office in order to take upon himself the responsibility for all earthly woe. Luxury was the source of the worst evil. No dweller in the Vatican could therefore have more than one servant. Barley was no longer distributed, hay was given to very few. The communal kitchen was discontinued; the usual supplies of salt and oil, vinegar, barley, and wood were curtailed. As cardinal, Marcellus had kept a simple table. Election to the papacy changed nothing in his household. Gold service was never touched. Copper was substituted for the silver kitchen utensils. In answer to his nephews who asked whether they should move into the Vatican, he replied, "What connection have you with the apostolic palace? Do you think it is your heritage?" And then as his nephews were further misguided into affecting purple boots and silk cloaks, he rebuked them sternly. Was this Marcellus the precursor of Paradise?

Spiritual Marcellus' reform of the world began with a plan for subjecting sodomites to the Inquisition, and banishing prostitutes and Jews to a quarter on the other side of the Tiber. Marcellus was merely a ruler appropriate to the General who had been waiting for him twenty years. "You create the warriors," the Chief encouraged the old Guard Officer in his first audience, "we shall put them to good use." After twenty years, Íñigo had arrived. Marcellus II died on the twenty-second day of his pontificate. No good fairy spared the old warrior who had already survived so many disappointments, the fate of surviving the consummation of his dreams as well.

If a dramatist had conceived the life of Loyola he could not have chosen a more bitterly effective final act to follow the beautiful brief idyl of Marcellus. The time was Ascension Day, May 23, 1555. The General was seated on a window ledge; before him sat Father Gonzalez, secretary of the Roman office to whom the Chief had been dictating his memoirs. The successor to Marcellus II was about to be selected. Bells rang out, loud cries announcing the name of the new Pope carried into the main cell of the chapter house. The General's face became rigid and deadly white. His body quivered as though it had just been struck an invisible blow. He rushed out of the room without a word. In the Chapel he gained possession of himself. When, after a short while, he returned, he was as serene as if the election had turned out exactly as he had expected. In Rome there was grumbling. Nothing good was anticipated of the sullen, arbitrary, ill-tempered old crow, Caraffa. The General made every effort to win the prejudiced over to his old-time mortal enemy. Two days after the election he reported on the event to the brothers. He praised the extraordinary virtues of their new supreme head. He prescribed prayers of thanks for the election which was a special act of divine Providence. He eased their doubts. Of his own doubts the world knew nothing. Perhaps the eighty-year-old Caraffa would play havoc with the work of his old adversary Loyola.

Cardinal Caraffa became Pope Paul IV to the annoyance of all parties concerned. There is an Italian proverb to the effect that only evil blows in from the Bay of Naples. Neapolitan priests had the reputation of serving Satan. For centuries cardinals who hailed from

Naples had all votes against them in the papal elections. Caraffa was a classic illustration of the bad reputation of his birthplace, although the antipathy for him was not entirely due to his place of origin. His fanatic austerity was feared. Even serious-minded men took offense at his harshness. Nor was there any love lost between him and the emperor. One of Charles' envoys extraordinary had declared to his face that he might as well give up any hope of the tiara. Caraffa had answered that the emperor could not prevent the election if God willed it, and that in any case the person elected was obligated only to God. He was even disliked by the French, Charles' opponents. Who actually wanted him? "This election has come about," a chronicler affirmed, "not because reason and wisdom have so willed it, but in order to make the miraculous nature of the conclave manifest to all; so that we may all be certain that it is God who creates the Pope."

Yet might not this man, a terror to all his contemporaries, be the General's salvation? Orthodox Caraffa had the stuff to restore the papacy to its old prestige. Caraffa believed, "The world would rise and fall with the orders." He proclaimed that if such measures as the burning of infected houses and clothing were to be taken in combating the plague, similar measures were necessary in extirpating spiritual disease. Surely this Caraffa was Loyola's man! Under the influence of the new ruler, the governor of Rome issued a draconian edict. The refrain ran: galleys, hanging, strangling, con-

fiscation, banishment. Idle promenading in the churches
was strictly forbidden. Women must no longer trail
gallants behind them through the houses of God. Even
carnival masquerade, most sacred right of the Romans,
was infringed. To the gallows for those who were found
armed in the mobs. Into the buildings of the Inquisition,
which the none too affluent Cardinal Caraffa had built
with his own means and equipped with bars and strong
locks, stocks and chains, all blasphemers, violators of
virgins, and procurers were now hustled. Death was the
penalty for sodomy and polygamy. The regulations,
which the master of the dread court noted down, began
with the sentence: "In matters of belief one must not
delay an instant, but proceed with the utmost severity
upon the slightest suspicion." Was not this holy Draco,
who would rather punish a hundred innocent men than
let a guilty one escape, Loyola's man?

Caraffa took care of the Jews in right Christian fashion
too. When Leo X on his coronation ride through the
city had been approached by the Israelites, who, according to ancient custom, submitted their privileges for
confirmation, his answer had been *"Concedo non probo."*
Caraffa made no concessions. Roman Jews and the
Jews in other Papal States were segregated in a quarter
or street with only one entrance and one exit. They were
permitted no more than one synagogue to a locality.
They were compelled to sell their landed property to
the Christians. They were to be identifiable by yellow
headgear. They were not to employ Christian servants.

The list of prohibitions for the Hebrew pariahs was long and loving. Let them not sell pledged chattels until eighteen months after the day on which the debt falls due! Let them not deal in grain! Let them not minister to the Christians medically! Let them not permit poor Christians to address them as "sir." Talmuds were confiscated and burned in great quantities. The Ghetto in Bologna soon gained the name of Inferno. Surely this ruthless octogenarian who deemed it more important to fortify Rome than enhance it with paintings was a man after the Pampeluna and Manresa victor's own heart!

Caraffa hated Loyola although he was akin to him in both zeal and aim. It dated back to Venice. The petty, anonymous Paris student had dared to attack the proud and magnificent head of the Theatin order, in a humble letter: "When a personage like yourself, of superior family, of high rank, enjoys a more finely appointed household than others, certainly no one can reasonably complain. Yet, would it not be well worth considering, in this respect, too, the example of such blessed saints, as Francis or Dominic? How did they appear to their comrades at the time they founded their orders and bequeathed to their sons the rules and examples for the conduct of life?" This thrust, nearly twenty years old, still rankled. The insignificant, nameless carper had become the great competitor whose society quickly outstripped the order founded by Caraffa. The "tyrant of the order" was certainly no more congenial to Caraffa than the critic in Venice had been. For twenty years the influential prince of the church had not overlooked an opportunity to express his antipathy for the upstart. Occasions to cross swords had not been lacking. There was the story, for instance, of Ottavio Cesari, who two years ago in Sicily had entered the Society of Jesus. His father had consented to the step only after the boy had already become a member of the order. Later, when Ottavio was transferred to Rome, his parents followed him there and decided to take their son back. The father suddenly claimed that he did not approve the step his son had taken. The mother ran from door to door, weeping and wailing to gain sympathy. Cardinal Caraffa, to whom the decision of the case was entrusted, ordered Ottavio Cesari's return. The Pope, however, after an audience with the General, countermanded the unfavorable verdict. The vengeful Neapolitan certainly could not forget the insult which had attracted such wide attention. One name was conspicuously absent from the list of cardinals' subscriptions to Loyola's Collegium Germanicum. That name had now become Pope Paul IV.

The disagreeable Spaniard, it was true, was a native of a country which the Italian patriot Caraffa hated above all others. Who had introduced discord into Italy? The Spaniards! Who had brought shame to Caraffa's home town, Naples, and to his papacy? The Spaniards! Who had secretly abetted the German Protestants in order to destroy the power of the Papal States? The Catholic Spaniards! Once these lowliest people of the earth had served Italy as cooks, bakers, and stableboys.

Now Spaniards were the lords of Italy. For hours after dinner the Neapolitan sat over his Mangiaguerra, the black, thick, volcanic wine of Naples, roaring like a cataract with hatred for these heretics, these accursed of God, spawn of Jews and Moors, dregs of the earth. "You will grind serpents underfoot; you will stride over lions and tigers," the raging Italian would then soothingly say to himself. Yet he could not be comforted.

The tall, vigorous octogenarian who had never in his life known illness, was still all brawn. His movements were quick and elastic. Vehement, intolerant of contradiction, he dominated any conversation, impatiently interrupting interlocutors who forced his attention. Paul IV was no shepherd who pastured his flock. He was a hard master whose servants felt the whip. Princes, too, were his servants. Once when he was to celebrate mass and the young emperor notified him of a delay, the proud priest answered, "I do not wait in holy vestments." Now the powerless sovereign informed his diplomatic corps that their emperors and kings belonged at the feet of the Pope from whom they would receive instruction like schoolboys. The sickly little Basque, on the other hand, hampered at every step by his dragging right foot, always ailing, sustained only by his quiet, tenacious will, knew no sudden fits of temper. He never became violent, unless it was for some deliberate pedagogical purpose. He always permitted his interlocutor to say his fill and listened gladly. He was courteous even when he was inexorable. It was his precept that the garment must be cut out of whatever was available. The fire-spitting crater at the peak of the mountain range which was the Church, was the very antithesis of such conceptions.

Caraffa was influenced by sudden impressions. Loyola offered them all the resistance of a soul at anchor. Caraffa was impetuous and given to sudden transitions. Impatient by nature, embittered by long waiting, he was inclined to go to extremes, to give and withdraw confidence impulsively. He had no principles which could weather the rages of his own temper. Soon, this chief defender of the Roman Church was to call upon the Protestants and Turks to help him against the Catholic Spaniards. Loyola, on the other hand, never came to even the most trivial decision without long preparation. He never reacted enthusiastically or belligerently, as his nature might have demanded, but always followed the dictates of his beliefs. He sublimated his personality so completely that during his lifetime he was more a code than an individual.

Caraffa bound himself to no rules. He obeyed the promptings of the moment. He slept in the daytime, if so disposed, and studied at night. Loyola lived by rules, only. His day was strictly organized. He even permitted his Society to define and supervise the routine of its dictator. Caraffa loved to talk and talked volubly; language poured from him like a torrent, blunt and violent words were accompanied by similar gestures, sometimes culminating in acts of violence. The Florentine ambassador called him a man of steel. The stones which he struck

sprayed sparks. The sparks burst into conflagration when
somebody did not do what was wanted. Loyola worked
through system, not conflagration. He was a letter writer,
not an orator; a lawgiver not a tyrant. He was no chau-
vinist, no believer in race. Pierre and Francisco traveled
by their own homes without even halting for a moment.
Íñigo himself overcame a native antipathy to the Hebrews
to the point of wishing that he himself might have been
born a Jew, and thus related to Jesus Christ and the
Virgin on the mortal side. Caraffa and Loyola were as
divergent as it is possible for two men to be when they
are following the same direction. Yet Loyola submitted
to his great opponent without contradiction, without complaint. Don Quixote mistook a barber's basin for a helmet. Loyola was a realist. He knew a barber's basin for
what it really was. Yet he wore it as a helmet because
he preferred to.

Now, at the end of his life, his loyalty was to be put
to the most exacting and ridiculous test. The warrior,
weary to death, must begin the battle all over again.
Paul IV wanted not only to revise the rules of the Society,
but also to revoke all the privileges which his predecessors had granted. He wanted to deprive the order of all
character, limit the General's tenure of office, divert the
Society's energies from conquest and apply them to cult.
Perhaps Paul IV had forgotten the wrath of Cardinal
Caraffa! He received Father Bobadilla cordially with
embrace and kiss. (Was this reception a gambit? Bobadilla was the *enfant terrible* of the Imperium Jesu.) He

insisted Lainez remain in Rome, arranged a room for him in the Vatican, and offered to elevate him to cardinal rank. (Was this strategy? Loyola believed that the acceptance of honor could effectively destroy his Society. He would oppose elevations in rank even though the whole world pleaded with him on bended knees.)

The temperamental Caraffa soon lapsed into open hate. While the conflict between Rome and Spain was brewing, the rumor spread that the Jesuits had concealed weapons to bring to the assistance of their countrymen. Paul IV instigated house searches in the camp of his most devoted bodyguard. The governor, accompanied by bailiffs, would refrain from executing the writ if the General pledged his word that he was innocent of the charges. The General thanked them politely for trusting him and insisted that a thorough search be made. He personally showed the officers through the house, and then escorted them out, as if taking leave of visitors who had come to pay their respects.

For he obeyed without reasoning. The Pope's nephew Carlo Caraffa was a subject of common gossip: The young man after a life of army debauchery had become *persona gratissima* to the austere Paul, who, however, knew that his nephew had waded in blood to his elbows. Loyola never, even in his most intimate letters, took advantage of the scandal in the household of his proud enemy to avenge his indignities and humiliations. He forbade Father Ribadaneira, who was on his way to Flanders, to mention the Pope's unjust behavior. When asked how the various papal reprimands were to be justified, the Chief answered, "Say nothing about that—speak of Pope Marcellus, of his love for the Society."

Paul had broken with the Colonnas who favored the emperor. He excommunicated them and issued the edict: if Ascanio Colonna or his son should come into the church of the Jesuits in Naples, services are to be suspended at once and not resumed until after the excommunicated ones have left. Although Loyola was on good terms with the Colonnas, he instructed his rector in Naples: "We must not neglect our duty of obedience in any way—much as we should like to include all in our love." So helpless that phrase, "much as we should like!"

Above the Christian law of love hovered the non-Christian law of blind obedience. At the end of a pure life the General proved once again that he, a holy man, had in all innocence and with praiseworthy fervor served Satan, the strict god of all possible gods, the god who permits masters to rise and flourish. Loyola's star had been, not the rebel of Jerusalem, the martyr of Golgotha, but the best ally of those who own the earth. If it is heroic to remain indiscriminately true to a symbol, Loyola was a hero. As a hero he served the forever unheroic: force. As a sacred chief, he led a sacred bureaucracy into battle for the sacrilegious.

In July, 1556 he came down with a severe colic. Songs of the good faith, sung by the brothers, eased the pains. But the wasting of his strength was not to be counteracted

335

by even the mightiest will. He abandoned the direction of Company affairs and went to the country house which he had built for the Society near the Baths of Caracalla. The sojourn in the open air did him no good. The summer heat aggravated his condition. After three miserable days he returned to the chapter house. According to the rule of the house those confined to bed were under the command of the resident physician. The obedient General had not even struggled against the physician's order to eat fowl on Good Friday. He was no longer Chief now, merely an invalid inmate of the house. Merely someone who did not complain, who did not make himself conspicuous by his impatience. Among the sixty inhabitants of the house, there were many who seemed to Doctor Alessandro Petroni in much greater danger than Brother Ignatius. Nobody paid very much attention to him. "This is the last letter I shall write you," he had already replied in May to his patroness, Doña Leonore de Mascarenas, who had asked him to pray for her pupil Philip, the Spanish King. "Soon I shall be a suppliant before the Lord, in Heaven." Now in July, those about him still had no presentiment of his approaching death.

The doctors ordered the ailing patient to put out of mind whatever was troubling him. The patient, who was not ill-prepared for such a cure, considered the worst contingencies. He asked himself, "How long will I really be unhappy if the Society collapses?"—"A quarter of an hour spent in thought with God would restore my peace of mind even if the Society dissolves like salt in water." He was so insulated that not even the disintegration of the structure on which he had built his life could daunt him. Every intellectual work is, from its very beginning, an indirect means of arriving at internal peace. Loyola had put twelve provinces and a fighting army between himself and the restlessness of the days at Pampeluna. If he had any fear of the old gulf widening, his will could bridge it. This readiness to begin again at the beginning in the face of death was the most important proof of his own strength. Such consistency of will left no room for skepticism. He was not a brooder who time and again questioned the meaning and worth of his ideal. He did not probe the ground on which he stood. He built ever upwards—until the whole structure crumbled. And he continued building until the last day. As papal legates his men had penetrated Ireland, Poland, Egypt, Japan. As theologians they had distinguished themselves at the Council of Trent. As preachers they had gained recognition at the universities of Louvain and Salamanca, at the courts of Valladolid, Brussels, and Vienna. He never asked, either in good fortune or adversity, where the road led. Like the blessed Xavier who swept through one country after another, Loyola, the archimperialist, planned and organized one province after another.

On his deathbed, he certainly did not think about Christ's will which he unquestioningly carried out. He thought, instead, of Ethiopia. A new hope beckoned. The Negus of Abyssinia had appealed to the King of Portugal. A man had appeared before Claudius Atanaf Sagad claiming to be, by grace of the Pope, Patriarch of Ethiopia. This adventurer—a cleric, Bermudiz—had arrived in Africa fifteen years before with a Portuguese group and impersonated the holy legate. Claudius Atanaf Sagad had no quarrel with the Roman ruler, but a great real of resentment against the worthless Bermudiz. The General sent out a band of thirteen priests to annex the half-Jewish, half-Greek-Catholic country. A pious general order had gone in advance of the group, an expression of thanks to God for having inspired the African with the will to preserve the Faith in a land "which was so remote and surrounded by so many heathen nations hostile to the name of Christian." And as if the first concern of the Paris student were also to be the last concern of the dying General, the matter which engaged his loneliest hour involved his defense, against the jealous claims of the Franciscans, of a concession to work in the Holy Land. He never doubted where the road led. He never despaired.

Never! We find no instance of the kind of lassitude experienced by those low in spirit. Difficulties were frequent enough along his way, yet they did not undermine his will. Loyola pursued his path, with equanimity. He was impervious to the deadliest elements in any combat: the vindictiveness of defeat, the arrogance of victory. The Cardinal Archbishop John Siliceo, without warning, had issued, to be read from all pulpits, a decree which forbade the Jesuits to celebrate mass, to give the

338

sacrament, to hear confession, and to preach. This order was contrary to all the privileges of the Society, the Governor's command, the wish of the crown prince, Philip, and even the will of the Pope! "We can dispense with the Pope here," the Spanish Cardinal had rudely informed the papal squires. Was the General inspired to aggressive action by such injustice, and with such powers on his side? Did he not boldly fight off a man who demanded the impossible of a Society which boasted such members as Bolanco and Lainez, a Society which had just received the first Japanese Jesuits into Rome, and which was establishing colleges to educate Indians? He mollified his men: "The Archbishop is old, the Society young. Naturally it will live longer than he." Finally, after the Archbishop had been defeated, victorious Loyola wrote, "Although it is novel for me to write Your Eminence, no one should find it novel to experience and show gratitude for benefits received." He wrote these words not out of cowardice, not out of irony, not even out of magnanimity. What was the reason for them, then?

He never increased his difficulties by introducing his own sensitive nature into the struggle. He never fought for the joy of fighting, and never out of anger for an enemy. He never fought out of braggadocio and never for hatred. He circumvented obstacles as unobtrusively as possible. He conquered not by aggression, but by evasion. The Parlement de Paris struck a bitter blow when it condemned the Society of Jesus. The French locked the Company out with a hundred objections. The Chief of the highly respected Company, attacked on all sides, merely smiled; a reply would only prolong the quarrel. "One must neither write nor commit any act from which bitterness may arise." He respected the authority of the Paris theologians and did not permit himself to be misled into a counterattack. To what end? Truth might, indeed, "be combated but not suppressed." He applied "a different, less dangerous, and milder balm to this wound" which "the foremost of all universities, not only in this kingdom but in the world" had inflicted. He had been using this formula for twenty years with the greatest success. A mountain of endorsements from the Dominican Inquisitor of Ferrara, the Bishop of Modena, the archepiscopal vicar-general of Florence, from the universities of Valladolid, Lisbon, Coimbra, and Louvain, covered the strictures of the Paris university. The King of Portugal, in reference to the matter, wrote two letters to the Pope. The Rector and thirty-two professors of the University of Ferrara appealed to the theological faculty of Paris. Loyola defended himself only with certificates of good character. He did not wish to avenge himself, but merely to convert an adversary to friendliness. He succeeded by an approach which deprived the adversary of his best weapons.

He declined conflicts which could not be settled by gentle means.

Such an unfeasible conflict embittered his last days on earth. What would Loyola have answered if anyone had pointed out this war-between-the-mighty which was rending his heaven? The anti-Spaniard Caraffa had clashed so fiercely with the Emperor in April that he spoke of deposing Charles. While Loyola tossed in the fever of his final illness, the advocate and procurator of the apostolic chamber laid before the consistory, July 27, a juristic opinion which was vicious special pleading. It was notorious, said the Vatican prosecuting attorney, that in the Kingdom of Naples, and with the knowledge of Charles V or Philip II, a conspiracy had been formed against the Holy See. The rulers of Naples had taken oath of allegiance to the Popes Julius III and Paul IV, consequently they were perjurers. It was further known that the Emperor and the Spanish king had furnished the excommunicated Collonas with money and troops; the Emperor and king thereby incurred excommunication and the loss of all their offices and honors. Did it occur to the dying Loyola that subjects could not obey blindly when their commanders were not in agreement with each other?

On his deathbed, the error of his life loomed before him, mighty and importunate. Did he realize now that the ruling conditions established by his God waxed and waned according to quite unholy laws? The lawgiver decreed: "Every difference of opinion, which creates discord and endangers harmonious agreement, must, as nearly as possible, be avoided." And what if it could not be avoided because the dissension was fundamental? Then the sophistry began. The fruits of great errors are always libraries. Loyola, faced by conflicting duties to both Charles and Paul, philosophized: "(1) Those who go to war at the command of their master commit no sin, since they bear no responsibility. (2) Those who volunteer for service and do not consider whether or not the war is just, commit a mortal sin because they expose themselves to the dangers of homicide and robbery. (3) If one knows that the war is just, or arrives at such a conviction after weighing other possibilities, one commits no sin by participating in the war." The Sermon on the Mount is not as complex.

Three days after his Emperor had been attacked by his Pope, Loyola summoned his secretary. Polanco was sent to the Vatican to report to His Holiness that no hope of temporal life remained to Ignatius of Loyola who asked His Holiness' benediction. Polanco had seen his General weak and suffering before, and although it was his habit to carry out every command at once, he now paid little heed to his Chief's request. "The doctors see no danger in your illness," he answered. "I hope that God will keep your reverence active among us for many years." To evade carrying out his order the secretary then asked: "Does your reverence really feel so bad?"

"So bad," replied the patient sufferer who had been an imperious General, "that I am almost ready to give up the ghost." The General had never asked anything for himself before. Now his first and last wish met with hesitation. Again Polanco asked, a second time, as though death could be postponed with questions, whether the next day would be soon enough to go to the Vatican. "I would rather it were today than tomorrow, the sooner the better—but do whatever seems best to you. I put myself completely in your hands." The General, for fifteen long years, had considered the most inconsequential details important enough to justify issuing an order. The dying man renounced all power now as he asked for the last, the most pressing aid. What question was there of the salvation of his soul! The organization was concerned. His trivial personal woe was scarcely involved. Polanco consulted the doctor. The General's pulse did not seem so bad, but his condition could not be definitely decided until the next day. Ignatius, who had long before come to a final decision about his condition, respected the opinion of the house physician, Doctor Torres, and forewent the last consolation. It was even possible to die without the help of the Church. Without obedience, however, no world empire could flourish. The ascetic Íñigo had fulfilled his highest aims. In the most comfortless hours, he eschewed the Comforter because his work required it.

Why did Loyola's adjutant shirk going to the Vatican? All correspondence was required to be in the hands of the courier of Spanish, Genoese, and Indian mail, by Thursday evening. The Chief's death agony could disrupt the whole week's program. God would bestow upon the Order, another living Loyola for the deceased one (to vary the Chief's obituary on his best friend) but if the letters were not dispatched at the right time any number of troublesome difficulties would arise. Therefore Polanco, true disciple of his master, adhered to his schedule, and the General, for the last and final time, adapted himself to the discipline of the house. At eight o'clock he had dinner with Father Madrid and Polanco according to long-standing habit. The evening was as uneventful as any other.

But later that night Ignatius could not sleep and spoke aloud to himself. Subsequently, he sank into a silence so profound, that it was noticed by those in the house. Toward morning Madrid sent in haste for the father confessor, who was not to be found. Polanco hurried to the Vatican as though to make up lost time. Friday, August 1, 1556, at six in the morning, a man named Íñigo, after burning his journals, departed this life, without extreme unction, without the Pope's blessing, without a parting word to his brothers, without a memorable deathbed text, without naming a successor. "In a quite commonplace fashion!" which astonished the brothers. That was the last miracle of Ignatius of Loyola. A few months earlier, Tullia d'Aragona had died. She had been inscribed on the list of Roman courtesans and had to take the yellow veil. She, at the end, commended her soul to Almighty God, to the Virgin Mary, and the whole heavenly court. A few months after the death of Ignatius, Pietro Aretino died, at the age of sixty-four, of apoplexy, sitting in an armchair. He had never attained the eminence of cardinal, although he had inveighed with great moral indignation against the indecency of Michelangelo's *Last Judgment*. Legend has it that the old reprobate died laughing at a dirty story. In truth, "the fifth gospelist," as he liked to call himself, died after confessing and repenting his sins. Christ's dearest servant, however, left the earth without a word. Perhaps he could more readily forego the other world than the harlot and the rake.

His men kissed his hands and feet. Pieces were torn out of his clothing. Painters, now that he could no longer prevent them, did his portrait. Doctor Realdo Colombo cut the body open and found the stomach empty and shriveled. Three little stones were secreted in the liver. They served, for lack of more impressive phenomena, as objects of great edification. These petrifactions, according to holy medicine, had been produced by continence. The father confessor, Diego d'Eguia, could not conceive how Ignatius could ever have lived with such a liver, had God not compensated the organic defect. The corpse was not thrown to the birds and dogs to be devoured as the dead man had commanded. It was carefully embalmed. On the next day, after vespers, the coffin was lowered into the ground near his church; a great stone covered the grave. The memorial of his Company was as unsentimental and worldly as something the dead man might have composed himself: "Now that our father has exchanged earthly for heavenly life, we expect greater and more fruitful assistance from him, since he is so much closer the source of spiritual grace and all good."

They did not mourn. They did not miss him. They

expected more service. It was not that a father was dead. The Chief of the house had been transferred by an even mightier Chief to heaven, where he would find an even more influential protector than Pope Marcellus, the King of Portugal, and the Duke of Gandia. Naturally, in the Company and in the colleges the loss of his "amiable presence" was felt. "At the same time this feeling was not one of grief." Why should there be grief? God had wished him to remain on earth until the time, "when the work of this most insignificant Society had achieved progress because of his example, his intelligence, his prestige and his prayers"; "now, however, since it had taken root," he was no longer necessary on earth. Loyola had taught them: the individual is nothing; the Company is all; the Christian departs without consolation; the mail goes through on time.

Index

A B C, the Spiritual, 103
Abyssinia, 253
Agostino, Fra, 227-230
Africa, 279, 303-304
Alberto, Jacopo, 71-72, 84-86, 98
Albertus Magnus, 109, 129
Alcalá, 103, 107, 109-110, 112, 122,
 127, 136, 143, 150, 169, 191, 194,
 234, 254, 257
Alexander VI, 179
Alexandria, 211
Alonso, Prince, 4
Alvarez, Captain, 280, 298, 300
Amadis, 22, 30-31, 35-36, 38-39, 41-
 43, 49-50, 54-56, 93, 126
Amador, 141-144, 153, 271
Aman, 302
America, 45, 244, 304
America, Central, 41
Anabaptists, 172
Angelo, Fra, 93, 95-96, 100
Anjiro, 280-282
Apostolic See, the, 9, 264
Aquinas, Thomas, 146, 157, 209,
 218
Arabia, 279
Aragon, 151
Aragona, Ludovico d', 221
Aragona, Tullia d', 221-223, 344
Aretino, Pietro, 201, 203-207, 209,
 212, 215-216, 222, 263, 344
Arevalo, 112, 155
Aristotle, 152, 218
Armada, 16
Arsenius, Saint, 259
Arteaga, 104, 109
Arthur, Prince of Wales, 8

Asia, 273, 304
Augustine, Saint, 241
Azador, Jacob, 210
Azpeitia, 46, 54, 191, 194, 199
Aztecs, 41-42, 45-46

Barbaran, Fray, 252
Barbarossa, Cheireddin, 183, 185,
 225
Barbarossa, Harudj, 183
Barcelona, 43, 55-57, 63-64, 73, 97,
 102-103, 108-109, 135-136, 150,
 182, 191, 254
Battista, Gian, 225
Benavente, Anna de, 107
Benedict, Saint, 243
Benedictines, 243, 256
Bermudiz, 338
Bethlehem, 91
Bobadilla, Nicholas, Alfonso, 170,
 174, 248, 266, 333
Bolanco, 339
Bontempelli, the firm of, 69
Borgia, Francis, Duke of Gandia,
 268
Broët, 217, 240, 248, 263
Buddha, 285, 299
Bungo, 293, 295, 298
Bungo, Prince of, 294
Burgos, 7, 15
Burgos, the Bishop of, 14
Burgundy, 156

Cáceres, 104, 109
Caiaphas, 89
Callisto, 104, 106, 109, 125-126
Calvin, John, 135, 162, 172

347

INDEX

Cano, Melchior, 267

Canton, 273, 298, 300

Capitol, the, 117, 238, 250

Caraffa, Cardinal, 326-335, 341-342

Cardinals, College of, 228

Carthage, 185

Carthage, Council of, 113

Castile, 3, 46

Castro, Juan de, 141, 143, 149

Catalina, Infanta (Catherine of Aragon), 8

Catherine, of Aragon, 8

Cellini, Benvenuto, 190

Cesari, Ottavio, 330

Charles V, Emperor, 23-28, 31, 46, 116, 119, 121, 150, 155-156, 177, 179, 183-190, 196, 202, 216, 225, 231-232, 240, 267, 327, 341-342

Charlotte, Princess, 28

Chigi, Agostino, 202

China, 253, 294, 300-303

China, Emperor of, 300

Cifuentes, Count of, 18

Cistercians, the, 256

Clement, VII, Pope, 116-117, 120-121, 177-178, 180-182, 202-203

Cochin-China, 272

Codure, Jean, 248

Collona, 341

Colombo, Doctor Realdo, 345

Columbus, Christopher, 10, 42, 152, 157

Company, of Jesus, 234, 250-256, 259, 265, 267-268, 270, 279, 284-285, 290, 292, 294, 303, 311, 315, 319, 336, 340, 345, 346

Constantinople, 184, 188, 211, 240

Contarini, Antonio, 70

Contarini, Gasparo, 215, 233

Contarini, Girolamo, 99

Corpus Christi, 69, 186

Cortes, 13

Cortez, Hernan, 41-42, 56, 157

Crete, 99

Crimea, the, 211

Criminale, Antonia, Father, 293

Cuellar, Don Juan Velásquez de, 11, 20, 23, 37

Cyprus, 71-72, 77, 79, 81, 83-84, 93, 99, 211

Dog Street, 138-139

Dominic, Saint, 38-40, 123, 126, 329

Dominicans, 21, 75, 123, 196, 256

Don Quixote, 63, 333

Doria, Andrea, 102, 183

Duns Scotus, 129

Eguia, Diego d', 345

Egypt, 255, 337

Eleanor, Queen, 156

England, 67, 118, 253

Erasmus, 120, 125-126, 132, 136-137, 158, 160, 172

Este, Ippolito d', 215

Estienne, Robert, 159, 160

Estrada, Antonia, 97

Ethiopia, 337

Europe, 41, 45

Famagusta, 77

Farnese, Alessandro, 177, 180, 182

Farnese, Constanze, 247

Ferdinand of Aragon, 12-13, 16-19, 23-24, 27, 44-45, 52

Fermet, Jean, 157

Ferrara, the Duke of, 65

Figueroa, Rodriguez, 104, 108-110

Fisher, John, 181

Flanders, 45, 67

Flor, Maria de la, 105-108

Fonseca, Archbishop, 122, 124

France, 27, 29, 45, 67, 82, 118, 128, 151, 156, 178, 252

Francis I, King of France, 25-26, 28, 131, 134, 155-156, 159-160, 163, 172, 177, 179, 184, 186-188, 190, 231-232

INDEX

Francis of Assisi, Saint, 38-39, 61, 93, 269-270, 329
Franciscans, the, 85, 88, 96-97, 162, 256, 338
Frias, Vicente, 126

Galaor, Brother, 22, 49
Gama, Vasco da, 303
Gandia, Duke of, 267, 322, 346
Genoa, 100, 102
Germaine, Queen, See Germana
Germana, Queen, 19-23, 30, 35, 37-38, 50, 257
Germany, 68, 178, 252, 262, 264
Giberti, Cardinal, 203
Gomez, Rector of Goa, 294, 312
Gonzalez, Father, 326
Gouvea, Jacques, 144-145
Gregory I the Great, Pope, 164
Gritti, Andrea, 67, 202
Guadalquivir, 4, 45
Guidici, the, 206
Gundemar, Bishop of Manresa, 51-52

Hagen, Philipps, 87, 99
Hapsburgs, the, 23-24, 27
Harun al Rashid, Caliph, 86
Helen, Empress, 90
Henry VIII, 17, 26, 157, 164, 181
Hernandez, Francisca, 107
Herrera, Francisco de, 29
Holy Land, the, 74, 84, 100, 188, 191, 199, 219, 224, 240
Holy See, the, 114, 341
Holy Sepulcher, the, 56, 67, 71, 80, 87, 90, 91, 96
Humanists, 104, 157-158, 172, 178

Incas, 45
India, 45, 240, 244, 253, 276, 278, 291, 295, 303
Inigists, the, 231
Inquisition, the, 123, 125, 325, 328

Inquisitor, the, 125, 143
Ireland, 252, 263, 337
Isabella, Princess, 4-5
Isabella, Queen, 3-10, 12-14, 18-21, 27, 45-46, 52, 113, 117
Italy, 45, 178

Jaffa, 71-72, 84-85, 97
James of Compostela, Saint, 99
Janissaries, 96
Japan, 271-273, 275-276, 279, 284, 294-295, 297-298, 301, 337
Japan, Emperor of, 271, 291
Jerusalem, 40, 48, 56, 70, 77, 82, 84-85, 90, 93, 95-97, 114, 136, 155, 168, 171, 264, 289, 301, 335
Jesuits, 307, 334, 338-339
Jews, 44, 90, 104, 128, 250, 252, 299, 304, 308-309, 325, 328, 331
John III, King of Portugal, 303, 306, 308-312, 324, 340, 346
Juana, Infanta, 3, 5-9, 13-19, 21, 23, 27
Juanico, 104
Judica, 206
Julius II, Pope, 179
Julius III, Pope, 321-324, 341

Kagoshima, 281-283, 286, 288, 292, 294

Lainez, Diego, 169, 174, 192, 218, 227, 233, 248-249, 301, 334, 339
Last Supper, the, 88
Latin Quarter, the, 130, 138, 148, 151
Latus, King, 38
Le Fèvre, Pierre, 147-150, 164-169, 171, 217, 227, 233, 248, 255, 266, 301, 307, 333
Le Jay, Claude, 217, 248
Leo X, Pope, 178-179, 181, 184, 202, 328
Leonor, 107-108
Leto, Pomponio, 180

INDEX

Lisbon, 303-305, 307, 311
Lisbon, University of, 340
Llanivar, Miguel, 228-230
Lombard, Peter, 109
London, 117
Louise, Princess, 28
Louvain, University of, 340
Loyola, Martin y, 34, 192, 255
Ludolf of Saxony, 36-37, 48
Luke, Saint, 52
Luther, Martin, 117, 158, 164, 170, 172, 195, 209, 309
Lutherans, 172, 228, 244
Lutherism, 247

Machiavelli, 270
Madera, 146
Madrid, 344
Magellan, 42, 157
Malacca, 271, 276, 294
Malaga, Bishop of, 15
Malayan Archipelago, 277
Manresa, 57, 62-63, 75, 100, 124, 145, 155, 164, 191, 246, 256, 261, 267, 329
Manuel, 271-272
Marcellus II, Pope, 324-326, 335, 346
Marfisa, 203
Margaret of Hapsburg, 237
Marguerite, Queen of Navarre, 160-161, 163
Maria, Doña, 20-21
Martha Foundation, the, 252
Mascareñas, Leonor de, 122, 336
Matthew, Saint, 89
Medici, Alessandro de', 237
Medici, Lorenzo de', 180
Mendoza, Francisco de, 126
Mexia, Alonzo, 103-104, 107
Mexico, 41, 240
Miako, 289-291, 297
Michael, Saint, 51
Michelangelo, 185, 344

Miraflores, 12
Miron, Jacob, Father, 310
Modena, Bishop of, 340
Mohammed, 279
Mohammed, the law of, 117
Mohammedans, 52, 104, 299
Moluccas, the, 276, 279, 303
Montaigu, Collège, 131-134, 136-137, 139-142, 157, 191
Monte Cassino, 243, 260
Montezuma, Emperor, 42
Montserrat, 50-52, 54, 56-57, 64, 75, 136, 183
Moors, 304, 331
Morocco, 3
Mount Calvary, 89, 96
Mount Zion, 85, 88, 94-95

Najera, Duke of, 18, 25, 37, 49
Naples, 185
Navarre, 25, 28-29, 44, 150-151, 153
Navarrete, 49
Negroes, 304
Negrona, the, 77-78, 80, 83-84, 99
New World, the, 27, 44, 152
Nola, Roberto de, 19
Numalio, Cristoforo, 120

Occident, the, 67, 241, 278
Onfroy, Father, 268-270
Oriana, 22, 43
Orient, the, 67, 211
Oviedo, Andrès de, 268

Padua, 74
Palestine, 48, 93, 96
Palmio, Benedetto, 260
Pampeluna, 29-30, 32, 34, 40, 44, 49-50, 93, 151, 153-154, 196-198, 246, 264, 276, 312, 329, 337
Paris, 117, 137, 143, 150-151, 164, 182, 197, 228-229, 231, 234, 266, 289, 301, 318, 329
Paris, Parlement de, 131, 162, 339

INDEX

Paris, University of, 129, 157, 159
Pascual, Inez, 57, 75
Paul III, Pope, 177-181, 184, 186-190, 216, 225, 228-229, 231-235, 237, 240-241, 247, 300, 308, 319, 321, 326
Pavia, 155
Peking, 273, 300
Pena, Juan de, 146
Peralta, Doctor Pedro de, 141, 143
Persia, 279, 303
Peru, 183
Peter, Saint, 36, 52
Petroni, Alessandro, Doctor, 336
Philip I, 6-8, 12-17, 19, 23
Philip II, 341
Philip, Infante, 122
Pia, 38
Polanco, Juan de, 262-264, 342-344
Poland, 337
Polo, Marco, 273-274
Portugal, 244, 253, 301, 303-306, 310, 312, 318-319
Protestants, 158, 178

Quetzalcoatl, 42
Quixote, Don, 48

Rabelais, François, 132, 137, 155, 160
Ramleh, 86-87, 98
Reichstag, at Worms, 31
Rialto, the, 66
Ribadaneira, Father, 334
Rodriguez, Simon, 169, 220, 224-225, 240, 248, 255, 305-307, 309-312, 316-319
Rome, 56, 73, 116-117, 119, 125, 171, 177, 185, 187, 224, 227, 229-230, 232, 237-240, 244, 252-255, 257, 263, 266-267, 276, 280, 289, 296, 300-302, 305, 307-318, 326-327, 330, 334, 339
Roser, Isabela, 75, 137, 255, 257
Russia, 66

Sagad, Claudius, Atanaf, 338
Sainte-Barbe, Collège, 139-142, 144-145, 147-148, 150, 157, 161, 164, 169, 191, 218, 228, 299
Salamanca, 4, 122, 126, 128, 136, 143, 150, 194, 234, 267
Salmeron, Alfonso, 169, 174, 192, 247, 263
Sanchez, Alfonso, 75
Santa Maria della Strada, 250, 257, 263-264, 270, 275
Santander, 4
Saracen, the 84, 86-88, 90, 96
Saragossa, the Archbishop of, 18
Satsuma, 288
Scarpi, Bartolomeo, 200
Schnudi, Abbas, 259
Scotland, 263
Senate, the, 65
Siam, 300
Siliceo, Cardinal, 338
Singapore, 271
Societas Jesu, 154, 268, 303, 309, 315, 317-318, 320, 330, 332-333, 336, 339
Soliman, Sultan, 81-83, 91, 94, 183-184, 190, 201
Sorbonne, the, 133, 146, 148, 158, 160, 218, 284, 297, 308
Soto, Pedro de, 109, 123-125
Spain, 27-29, 45, 66-67, 128, 174, 211, 213, 229, 231, 253, 304, 334
Standonck, Jean, 136
Syphilus, 152
Syria, 211, 255
Switzerland, 67

Tanegashima, 274-275
Tempête, Pierre, 132
Terracina, Bishop of, 120
Theatin, order the, 329
Theodosia, Fra, 249
Thomas à Kempis, 109, 254
Titian, 68, 205

INDEX

Toledo, 7-8
Toledo, Archbishop of, 4, 103, 113, 115
Torquemada, 124
Torres, Miguel, Doctor, 307, 310-311, 343
Turks, 71, 86

Vado, Luisa del, 108
Vado, Maria del, 108-110
Valencia, 16
Valladolid, 7, 122, 170, 254
Valladolid, University of, 340
Vecellio, 68
Venice, 43, 56, 65, 67-68, 70, 72-74, 76-77, 79, 82, 97, 100, 117, 191, 199, 204, 207, 209, 211-214, 216, 221, 223, 225, 228-229, 231, 234, 240, 244, 252, 289, 329
Vinci, Leonardo da, 160

Worms, the Reichstag at, 31

Xanones, Father, 53, 60
Xavier, Francisco, 147, 150-154, 158, 161, 169, 192, 197-198, 220, 228, 248, 253, 255, 262, 271, 275-276, 278-280, 283-285, 287-291, 293-302, 305, 333, 337
Ximenes, Cardinal, 7, 11, 13, 23, 107, 109; 112-115, 122

Zaffetta, Angela, 200-201, 212, 215, 222

ABOUT THE AUTHOR

LUDWIG MARCUSE *belongs to the distinguished company of German exiles and has been making his home in the south of France since shortly after Hitler took power. In the days of the Weimar Republic he lectured at Königsberg, Frankfort, Danzig, and Berlin in various institutions of higher learning. He had taken his doctorate in Berlin in 1917,* summa cum laude, *with a thesis on Nietzsche; his lectures dealt with philosophy, ancient and modern, German idealism, and contemporary politics and culture. He was just beginning to establish himself as a writer, but it was not until he left Germany that he completed his first full length book,* Ignatius Loyola, *which is translated under the title* Soldier of the Church. *Since then he has also written a life of Richard Wagner.*